Tropic Suns

Tropic Suns

SEADOGS ABOARD AN ENGLISH GALLEON

JAMES SEAY DEAN

The History Press

'Let sea-discoverers to new worlds have gone,
Let maps to others, worlds on worlds have showne ...
Where can we finde two better hemispheares
Without sharpe North, without declining West?'

John Donne, 'The Good Morrow', 1633

First published 2014

The History Press
The Mill, Brimscombe Port
Stroud, Gloucestershire, GL5 2QG
www.thehistorypress.co.uk

© James Seay Dean, 2014

The right of James Seay Dean to be identified as the Author
of this work has been asserted in accordance with the
Copyright, Designs and Patents Act 1988.

British Library Cataloguing in Publication Data.
A catalogue record for this book is available from the British Library.

ISBN 978 0 7524 5097 1

Typesetting and origination by The History Press
Printed in Great Britain

Contents

Preface

This is a seafarer's book that draws from hundreds of sixteenth-century and early seventeenth-century ocean voyages. It was written to convey the realities of everyday life aboard the galleons sailing between England and the West Indies. From jack tar to captain, what was life like aboard an Elizabethan ship? How did the men survive tropical heat, storms, bad water, rotten food, disease, poor navigation, shifting cargoes and enemy fire? With a whiff of oakum, salt spray and gunpowder, and in the words of Hawkyns, Drake, Ralegh and the ordinary seaman aboard, what was it like to live on a galleon or pinnace in the American Tropics?

These are matters deeply familiar to a man who has sailed the Atlantic and West Indies for many years as crew, mate, navigator, sailing master, captain, owner and lecturer, on vessels ranging from small sloops and cutters to brigantines and four-masted barquentines. The author is as comfortable on deck as at a desk, as practised at going aloft as negotiating the upper floors of library archives. To an emeritus professor of Elizabethan studies, the details of these lives at sea have been a particular fascination for many decades.

The structure of *Tropic Suns* follows the sequence that a common sailor bound across the ocean would have observed: first the state of his ship, his food and water, then his weather, the climate and best time of year to sail, the tools and skills of getting from here to there and back again, the way the ship is run at sea, various measures for recognising and treating illnesses and, at last, being paid once the long trick is done.

Tropic Suns: Seadogs Aboard an English Galleon complements *Tropics Bound: Elizabeth's Seadogs on the Spanish Main* (Stroud: The History Press, 2010), which narrates the voyages undertaken in the name of gospel and gold between 1516 and 1618, a century before events at Plymouth Rock. *Tropic Suns* was initially intended to be part of *Tropics Bound*, but here it sails on its own as a companion volume, not as technical ballast but as the on board lore of another ship alongside. Read together, the two books encompass the Elizabethan mariners' remarkable accomplishments.

The span of both begins with the same first English voyage to the West Indies in 1516, but where *Tropics Bound* ends with some finality at Ralegh's beheading in

1618, the terminus for *Tropic Suns* is the decade of the 1640s. That decade was one of major transitions, including the end of a century of Dutch, English and Irish efforts to plant settlements in South America. In England, it covered the start of a civil war over divine versus popular rights, then the death of a king and installation of a commonwealth. The 1640s were also the cauldron of a new empirical fusion of theory and practice in medicine, astronomy, physics, magnetism, optics, mathematics and navigation.

Elizabethan and Jacobean maritime history has been the focus of many of this author's many articles and three of five books. The sources were researched incrementally during the years the author worked toward his doctorate from the Shakespeare Institute of the University of Birmingham, England and during research fellowships in the USA at Wisconsin, Illinois, Chicago, Vanderbilt, Brown and Williams universities. In England, this interest in the maritime history of the period was reinforced during fellowships at Exeter University, at the University of East Anglia, in Norwich, and at Harris Manchester College, Oxford. The approach has been to present maritime history in the light of modern knowledge and science, scrutinizing the period both as a sailor and as an historian.

Tropics Bound and *Tropic Suns* honour the 400th anniversaries of the first permanent settlements in or off the coast of North America: St John's, Newfoundland (1583), Jamestown (1607), Bermuda (1609) and Plymouth (1620). Both books were written to celebrate the extraordinary drive and courage of early sailors who left the familiarity of their English estuaries for the dangers of the Cabo Verdes and the Caribbean, the Rivers Amazon and Orinoco and the Strait of Magellan.

Notices to Mariners

The prudent mariner, here the reader of *Tropic Suns*, will appreciate knowing the essential chart datum: its scope and terms. Following the practice of the Naval Records Society (but not that of the Hakluyt Society), the spellings of early texts have been modernised for the common reader's sake, though the syntax, vocabulary and punctuation of the originals have generally been kept. Notes and bibliography direct the reader to early sources. Only a very few manuscripts from the period have survived; certainly, no ships' logs or charts are known to exist. Even contemporaneous accounts of life aboard can be second hand, the tales generally having been reported and written in port, after the fact. The author is happy to clarify or expand any point for the interested reader and can be reached through a letter to the publisher. The aim is to present a readable book framed and ballasted by reliable research.

Times and Dates

At sea, time is traditionally measured from noon zenith to noon zenith, not as on land, where civil time begins the day at midnight. This book is mainly about English Tudor and Stuart sailors and uses the calendar they used, the Old Style (Julian) calendar and not the New Style (Gregorian) one, which puts the English about ten days behind the Continent. Exceptions are noted in the text. During this period the English observed both 1 January and 25 March as the start of the new year. In this work, 1 January is generally taken as the start.

Calculations

Latitude then, as now, was easy to measure, but not longitude. No accurate chronometer to calculate time from a prime meridian or any instrument to measure celestial angular distance was yet available. Minutes and seconds of latitude were then divided by sixty, not in tenths as today. A ship's tonnage originally meant her cargo capacity – that is, how many tuns or barrels she could carry. The measurement of tonnage differed for naval vessels and from country to country. An English ton, for instance, was smaller than a Spanish one.

Names

Obsolete, obscure or ambiguous sailing terms are explained contextually, in the glossary or by means of the index. Meanings and usage shift over time and place, as, for example, the spellings 'gage' and 'gauge', where the former on both sides of the Atlantic maintains 'gage' as in 'weather gage' to mean being upwind of other vessels. Naval ranks, whatever the country, are generally given the usual English way – e.g. admiral, vice-admiral, rear-admiral, captain, master, land general. People then often spelled surnames in a variety of ways. Hawkyns sometimes appeared as Hawkins. Ralegh was also written as Raleigh, Raley, and as the Spanish heard the full name of 'Walter Ralegh', Gualterral. As for Drake, he was El Draque the dragon and worse. Finally, place names and diacritical marks here follow present-day practice, though I have generally preferred Nueva España over New Spain or México. The northern coast of South America – the Spanish Main – sometimes also appears here as Tierra Firme.

Acknowledgements

No author can be expert on all the matters covered here. I wish to thank those with specific knowledge, the people who have helped with *Tropic Suns*, sequel to *Tropics Bound*. All of these authorities sail. For expertise on tropical disease and diet, I thank Robert Desowitz, world authority on malaria and tropical diseases, and Lyman Dwight Wooster, Johns Hopkins Medical School, for reviewing the chapter on tropical medicine. For clear expression on matters of food and drink, Ian Gordon, FRSC and master brewer. For climate and weather, meteorologist Alan Watts and geologist Brian Fagan. For cargoes and trade, historian Anthony Ryan, Liverpool. For ship design and construction, and maritime trade, the Bristolian shipwrights of Cabot's 1490s *Matthew* and Andrew Shaw, bosun/ shipwright of Maryland's *Dove*, replica of the 1630s original.

The technical chapters on architecture, ship handling and tactics required close review by seasoned mariners. For sailing tactics, strategy, and keeping argument on trajectory, then, I thank Bryan Barrett, Commander RN retired, expert in deep sea demolitions; Jerry Breast, Rear Admiral, USN retired, aircraft carrier commander and pilot,; and John Hoyt, naval architect and engineer, consultant at the USN Naval Surface Warfare Center and lecturer at the US Naval Academy. For sailing ship handling, I was for some years sailing master under the late Ulrich Prüsse, merchant navy captain, Hamburg, whose ticket read 'any tonnage, any ocean in the world'. Navigation I learned from Aubrey Smith, lecturer at the US Naval Academy, and from Robin Wilshaw, yacht captain, with whom we sailed transatlantic and elsewhere for over a dozen years under the red ensign. Other sources at the U.S. Naval Academy, Annapolis, and at the Royal Naval College, Dartmouth, have also helped.

To years of sea time in Atlantic and Caribbean waters, add hours spent in company with the irreplaceable staff of the Bodleian Library, the British Library, the National Maritime Museum, the library at Greenwich, the U.S. Naval Academy Library, the John Carter Brown Library, the Folger Shakespeare Library, the Library of Congress, and that of Harris Manchester College, Oxford, with special thanks to its principal, Rev. Dr Ralph Waller, and librarian Sue Killoran.

The eminent Canadian maritime and Commonwealth historian, Professor Barry Gough, has again weighed in with authority, friendship, kindness and a sharp read of draughts. Over the years, he and I have sailed the Great Lakes, the Pacific north-west and New England coasts together and have navigated the channels of historical method in both England and America. Canadian editor Camilla Turner has eased the line of the manuscript as it developed from my researches, as she did for *Tropics Bound*. Mary Gregory, emeritus fellow in economics at St Hilda's College, Oxford, besides logging over 200 miles at sea in the author's yacht, found time off watch and when not sailing Antarctica to offer up twenty-eight pages of insightful criticism of an early draft of *Tropic Suns*. The publishers and authors have done their best to ensure that quotations and all illustrations are clearly within the public domain. At The History Press, I thank editors Mark Beynon and Lauren Newby, and earlier editors there, Simon Hamlet and Abigail Wood, for seeing these efforts from conception to completion.

Journal and magazine editors have also contributed – at *The Northern Mariner/ Le Marin du Nord*, Roger Sarty and Paul Adamthwaite, and at *Sailing Magazine*, William Schanen, editor and publisher. Philip Webster, board member of the Chesapeake Bay Maritime Museum and the National Maritime Historical Society and its journal *Sea History*, supplied information on the exploration of the Chesapeake Bay by Captain John Smith's shallop. At the University of Exeter, the celebrated maritime historians Professor Michael Duffy and Nicholas Rodger have helped, the former with a research fellowship and the latter with insightful criticism. At the University of East Anglia, historian Dr James Casey, authority on Renaissance Spain, offered support. In America, the University of Wisconsin kindly provided several sabbaticals and fellowships to this book's end. As before, Dr Angélica Guimarães Lopes, Brazilian scholar, saw the start of the idea for *Tropics Bound* and *Tropic Suns*. Throughout years of research my sons Christopher and Alexander have been both my *Cruzeiro do Sul* and my Polaris, stars to my wandering bark. Besides love, these two have added their expertise in sailing and computers. I dedicate this book to them. Mary, my wife and first mate by land and sea, has helped bring both these volumes from hidebound idea to hardback reality.

As a navigator, I hope that others will check my calculations and bring any errors to my attention via the publisher. For as the Hanse mariners and Dutch cartographers observed, *navigare necesse est, vivire non necesse est*. Such navigations as these naturally require regular course correction.

J.S.D., from Soundings on the Chesapeake Bay
May 2014

Introduction

Tropic Suns is based on accounts of hundreds of ocean voyages undertaken during the Elizabethan and early Jacobean periods. The words of English captains, pilots, gunners and common seamen speak of icy decks and parched planking, chapped hands, black powder burns, with only rancid beer and soured wine to slake a thirst.

This how-to book ranges as far south in the Atlantic as the frigid waters of the Strait of Magellan, and as far north as Newfoundland, though most of the voyages described here were to the warmer latitudes between the Tropics of Cancer and Capricorn, 23.5° N to 23.5° S. In their scope, the chapters treat England's quest for trade and colonies in the waters from Florida to Tierra del Fuego. Their perspective is not from court or courtroom or counting houses but from rolling and pitching decks. It was in the early voyages to the Caribbean that English mariners learned naval tactics that helped them win the Armada battles in 1588 and the later battles with the Dutch and French in the next century.

What went into a transoceanic voyage in those early days? First, the sailor must have a seaworthy ship to venture not just along coasts but across oceans. The design of ships was changing. Sir John Hawkyns, as Treasurer of the Navy, ordered ships after 1570 to become more weatherly, which was done by cutting down forecastles and sterncastles to reduce windage and changing the aspect ratio of length to beam from 2:1 to 3:1 and even to 4:1. Such race-built (razed, or cut-down) galleons were soon adopted by most European mariners. Sailing the New World rigorously tested Old World shipbuilding methods. The designs of Northern European hulks and carracks joined with Portuguese *caravelas* and *naus* (Sp. *naos*), and combined square sails with lateen rigs to develop pelagic vessels that could sail both arctic and tropical waters. Such changes are apparent in the oldest surviving English scale drawings, attributed to master shipwright Matthew Baker, in *Fragments of Ancient Shipwrightry, c.1586*. And for ships' gunnery, English foundries produced superior bronze cannon and smaller truck carriages that allowed for quicker and safer firing than iron cannon mounted on the larger field carriages used by the Spanish.

A sailor's attention might go next to victuals, stores and cargoes. Before any long voyage, any prudent captain would attend closely to provisioning and to the drying, salting or pickling of food, aiming to provide a diet that would delay the onset of scurvy or, better, that would keep his crew alive and working. A ship's stores also included all that would be needed for self-sufficiency: items such as extra cordage, sails, iron, a full chest of tools, even knocked-down pinnaces to be assembled once in the Americas. At times they might need to build a ship from keel up on some distant strand. Castaways on the beaches of Bermuda, and the river-travelling English and Cimarróns in dire circumstances in the jungles of Panamá, salvaged their ship's tools first, prizing them to build a shallop or pinnace.

Setting out from port and off soundings, what climate and weather would these early seamen face southbound from England for the islands of the Canarias or the Cabo Verdes and then westward for the West Indies? Following the example of Matthew Maury's *Wind and Current Chart of the North Atlantic* (1847, with supplements), this book pricks out the start of a tropical pilot atlas, a rutter, of sixteenth- and early seventeenth-century tropical climate, weather, winds and ocean currents for the North Atlantic, the West Indies and the South Atlantic, based on the weather reported in journals for some 150 years. Entries allow us to track the period's major storms, their location, force and direction. Though the Little Ice Age affected some parts of the world during those centuries, weather in the tropics then was essentially weather in the tropics now, so that modern climatology, oceanography and meteorology can with some adjustment be applied to the earlier period.

We must next know how the mariner navigated offshore. How did he traverse the Doldrums, especially when sailing to the South Atlantic, or how set a course for the West Indies, run along the South American coast and up the rivers Amazon and Orinoco, and later turn north and east to return safely toward England? Because the English at first lagged in skill behind the Portuguese, Italians and Spanish, they would often kidnap an Iberian pilot to guide them across oceans. Over time, they came to overtake and surpass their predecessors in navigation.

Tropic Suns traces this growing English mastery of the new transatlantic navigation. Since the first half of the sixteenth century Portuguese and Spanish pilots had led the way in producing books on navigation. It was only in 1574 that mathematician, artillery soldier and mariner William Bourne published *A Regiment for the Sea,* the first practical book in English on navigation. Captain and pilot Sir John Davis, experienced in sailing the tropics and both arctics, devised his back-staff in 1594, an instrument that eliminated parallax error and the problem of direct glare from the sun that occurs when using an astrolabe or the familiar cross-staff. He then followed his invention in 1595 by publishing *Seaman's Secrets.* Captain John Smith, that soldier of fortune and governor of Jamestown, though no true sailor, published in 1626 *An Accidence or the Pathway to Experience Necessary for All Young Seamen,* a word-book and collection of forthright and useful advice for all those who were called to or fancied the sea. He followed it with *A Sea Grammar,* 1627, taken largely from a popular early manuscript by the pirate, admiral and lawyer Sir Henry Mainwaring, who years later published his work as *The Seaman's Dictionary*. Mainwaring's was the most practical and authoritative English book to that date on the way of a ship from truck to keel.

Present maritime science can help clarify sixteenth- and early seventeenth-century navigation, then at best an imprecise science. The Elizabethan navigator had some tools: an astrolabe, a cross-staff, a lead line, compass and chip-log for dead reckoning (with which by calculating time, speed and distance, the one unknown is deduced from the two knowns). At the time, he could accurately determine only latitude, since determining longitude accurately requires either calculating angular distance between celestial bodies or telling time highly accurately, both beyond the ken of the Elizabethans. As for charts, especially those covering the American Tropics, the best were usually Spanish or Portuguese, and closely guarded.

How did the English mariner, from captain to cabin-boy, deckhand to gunner, face the formidable naval firepower power of Imperial Spain? Outgunned and outmanned, it was rarely an even match. The sixteenth century saw the end of some long-standing traditions of naval warfare, though the Spanish would maintain them longer than the English. One was the galley, a warship as old as the Greek triremes. Powered by sail and oar, these warships with their battering rams had stopped the Persian advance at the Battle of Salamis in 480 BC. Two thousand years later, in 1571 at the Battle of Lepanto, Christian galleys closed and rammed, grappled, and boarded the Turkish galleys, decisively defeating the Moorish threat. That victory turned out to be the last glorious contest of such warships. Within ten years galleys were seen to be as archaic as the mounted knights on Bosworth Field in 1485 in full armour – another swan song.

Yet habit dies hard. Throughout the sixteenth century, Spanish officials in the West Indies still pleaded for Seville to send galleys to protect their plantations and ports against French and English corsairs. Port captains, though, pointed out that galleys were expensive to maintain and, except in calm waters, were largely useless in open Caribbean wind and wave. Galleys were certainly no contest against the newer technology of the heavily armed pinnace, a quick, nimble vessel also fitted with sails and oars and of relatively shallow draught but, unlike the galley, sturdy and with fine sea-keeping qualities.

Tactics too had changed. No longer were ships thought of principally as ferries to carry marines for boarding an enemy ship but as manoeuvrable floating gun platforms. Another innovation was amphibious warfare, employed early on along the shorelines of the Caribbean. Marines were landed at night on beaches away from a port, then marched to a port's rear gates and attacked, while from sea naval broadsides pounded the city in a surprise sea–land operation. The powerful new English bronze naval cannon had such a powerful recoil that ships had to be redesigned, and the new weapon changed tactics and ships. Cannon had long been used as pursuit weapons by galleys. In galleons a few were kept as chase guns, but the real firepower now lay in concentrating battery fire in broadsides, close in if Spanish and longer range if English. Though boarding enemy ships with harquebus, pistol and sabre still continued, English ships took the lead in using long-range naval artillery as the primary weapon.

New tactics called for prescribed formations – gaining the windward gage, then crossing the T – to concentrate firepower and present the least target to the enemy. Such techniques were first tried and tested by the English in the West Indies, where decades of sea battles had tempered the steel of the weaker English against more powerful Spanish ships. Those lessons were carried back to European waters and later were to become regular naval practice.

And what of disease? Going to sea, particularly to tropical waters, was at best a desperate measure taken only in the face of starvation, or of no work in the fields and markets, or the plague. Once at sea, sailors were more likely to die from disease than from harquebus or cannon fire. We cannot examine the bones of Sir John Hawkyns and Sir Francis Drake, committed long ago to the waters off San Juan and Nombre de Dios, but early journals by captains and chaplains describe tropical diseases graphically, including how these leaders died. Though epidemiology has in some cases changed, the deadly ailments facing Elizabethan seadogs are still present today. The immune systems of North European sailors, more than the African or even the Mediterranean, were susceptible to malaria (then called the ague), yellow fever, amoebic or bacillary dysentery (called the bloody flux) and a variety of parasitic diseases. These contagions were often enough contracted off the African coast, particularly in the Cabo Verde islands, where mariners had to land for water and from where they would catch the northeasterly Trade Winds for a transatlantic crossing. Catch the winds they did, but as well, they often caught yellow fever, malaria, dysentery and other ills.

Water and food went off quickly in the tropics, and foul water and food poisoning caused many deaths. Fresh water at sea was a constant concern whether sailing in torrid or frigid climates. Sir John Hawkyns' son, sea captain Sir Richard Hawkyns, was particularly mindful of his men's health. As early as 1593, he distilled seawater mid-ocean to fill his ship's freshwater casks.

Sir Thomas Cavendish during his 1586–88 circumnavigation was the first Englishman to issue lemons and limes to prevent scurvy, a practice known to the Spanish captains since at least the 1540s. Later, in February 1601, after a disastrous first voyage that lost many to scurvy, master mariner Sir James Lancaster set off for the Spice Islands and, following Cavendish's example, dosed his crew with lemon juice to prevent scurvy. It worked.[1] Only much later, in 1753, did Dr James Lind tie scurvy to ascorbic acid deficiency. Still later – 1794 – the Royal Navy first ordered a test of limes to prevent scurvy aboard naval vessels.

Documents record the first attempts to identify cures, whether by oranges, limes, lemons, cabbage, cinchona bark, spoonwort or new-found remedies. One of the most spectacular New World simples was the wonder drug from Trinidad and elsewhere in the tropics: sotweed. This was the tobacco so loved by Sir Walter Ralegh, so detested by King James I. The English sailors contracted new diseases in the Americas, but their ship's pharmacy grew richer with newly discovered local cures for both known and new diseases.

Commerce? From merchant adventurers to the boatswain's mate, the aim was profit. A voyage normally followed the triangular trade route from Europe to Africa to America and back to Europe, mostly carrying finished items in exchange for raw materials such as hides, tropical woods, cochineal and tobacco. In some cases the West Indies sent finished products back to Europe, but it was not just a matter of dyes and cloth. In a letter from La Havana to the Casa de Contratación in Seville, the governor writes in 1591 that he has already built two of eight frigates ordered constructed for Spain. The keels of the other six, he writes, would be laid when the Crown sent more money, supplies and labour. Still other ships, intended to augment another Armada against England, were also ordered from Cuba.

Profit and national interest? Sir Walter Ralegh wrote in 1614 that 'whosoever commands the sea commands the trade; whosoever commands the trade of the world commands the riches of the world, and consequently the world itself'.[2] As for profitable cargoes, the English hulls took out hardware and cotton and linen fabrics, and though the preferred payment was in gold bullion and silver, such cargoes came only to the lucky few. The American tropics were enemy waters for the English, thanks to the Spanish embargo on foreign trade. It is little wonder that merchant ships mounted cannon. In the fifteenth century the Portuguese had learned this lesson the hard way, when attacked by pirates in the Indian Ocean. The English, whether naval men or pirates, traded goods and broadsides with the Spanish in the West Indies to one end: profit.

The age is embodied in the stories of three famous West Country seafaring families. The Hawkynses, the Drakes and the Raleghs sum up the period's gains in trade, warfare and colonisation. Each family had different ways of meeting the challenges of a sea voyage, whether for plunder or policy. The Hawkynses since the 1530s had been merchant mariners primarily out for trade, and though they preferred gold, they traded goods for slaves and in payment received woods, spices and hides. With little modification, their armed merchantmen were to serve the Crown when Spain's threat to England finally materialised in 1588. Since the 1560s, firebrand Drake had sought revenge in Spanish blood and Spanish gold, raiding homeland and overseas colonies. Piracy was a way to profit, and, coincidentally, to national power. Piracy could thus serve national policy. Ralegh, like his fellow courtier Sir George Clifford, Earl of Cumberland, went to sea to repair his fortunes (and his reputation at Court), but in planting colonies, his own interest was also England's. He despised picory or thievery, which on a larger scale became piracy and marauding, but it was these activities that funded his grand enterprises: Virginia in the 1580s and Guiana in the '90s.

The seadogs were tough sailors who waded ashore onto tropic strands in the Americas, their salt-caked bodies riddled by malaria, dehydrated by the bloody flux, or sweating and feverous from tertian and quartan agues. Such are the realities they endured, and it is they who flesh out this story of Maritime England's coming of age.

At the start of the sixteenth century England was a marginal seapower deep in the shadow of Spain and France. But a century of battles for free trade in the West Indies hardened England to face in her home waters the Dutch and French navies over issues of trade, politics or religion for the next three centuries. On ship and shore the Tudor and early Jacobean seafarers' painstaking advances in naval arts and sciences prepared the way in a later age for Britannia to rule the waves.

Notes

1 Giles Milton, *Nathaniel's Nutmeg* (London: Sceptre, 1999), 79, provides a vivid account of Lancaster's voyage.
2 *History of the World*, written whilst in the Tower.

'Ships Are But Boards'

'Ships are but boards, sailors but men.'
William Shakespeare, The Merchant of Venice, *1596–97*

One day toward the end of January 1556 the English merchant Robert Tomson, passenger in a fleet of eight Spanish ships, was anticipating a landfall within hours at Nueva España's San Juan de Ulúa. The ship was 15 leagues (45 nautical miles) from port. He had left England some years before, moved to Spain, and had set out for the New World to pursue his fortune through trade. Tomson expected to step ashore before dinner on Mexican soil and to make his way to lodgings in nearby Vera Cruz. But from out of nowhere – it was a full three months beyond the hurricane season in the Gulf of Mexico – came a deadly storm, a Norther typical in those waters. The storm battered the fleet for ten days. One 500-ton hulk was cast away. As for Tomson's ship, he writes that in its 'boisterous winds, fogs and rain our ship being old and weak was so tossed, that she opened at the stern a fathom under water, and the best remedy we had was to stop it with beds and pilobiers,[1] and for fear of sinking we threw and lightened into the sea all the goods we had or could come by'.[2] The captain cut away the mainmast and threw all but one cannon overboard. Tomson was fortunate to live to tell the tale of steep waves and archaic design.

Ships in the sixteenth century were indeed boards, vulnerable especially in the tropics, where wind, wave and sun challenged traditional European designs and construction. In the 1520s English shipwrights were building hulks, cogs and carracks largely designed for coastal sailing but not suitable for transoceanic voyaging. The next seventy-five years were to see radical changes in design and practice in English shipyards. This chapter examines how the English first followed Portuguese and then Spanish examples, then over the decades caught up with and surpassed these great maritime nations in both design and construction. It considers first the carracks, *caravelas*, galleons and their refinement as race-built galleons. Second, it turns to the techniques of construction. The old tradition of building with green wood proved troublesome, especially in the tropics. As ships

were built from a series of ratios, shipwrights wasted much wood. New powerful cannon required stronger and more stable ships. The race-built galleon was
such a ship. Its design could support the more powerful armament, and such
vessels were fast and manoeuvrable. From 1570 on, most of the Navy was built
or rebuilt the new way. By the 1590s English race-built galleons were copied
by the rest of Europe. Related to design was the measurement of a ship's tonnage. Third, the chapter considers lessons learned from oceanic voyaging, during
which the English saw new designs or on occasion fashioned a vessel from local
raw materials. New vessels include the Dutch *vlieboot*, the Moorish *gallizebra*, the
Brazilian *jangada*, Panamanian and Argentinian rafts and Chilean bladder boats.
In the Americas, local shipwrights built Cuban frigates for use in Europe, and
English shipwrights built a Panamanian pinnace, and a Bermudian bark.

Portuguese *Caravelas*

A generation before the English sailed off soundings into the Atlantic, the
Portuguese and Spanish were Europe's uncontested maritime nations. The venerable Portuguese *nau* (a generic name for a large ship) was beamy, short-keeled,
with a deep-draught and a large hold for cargo. *Naus* could carry much cargo,
but they were not weatherly vessels. The early Portuguese navigators favoured the
smaller but more seaworthy *caravela redonda*, relatively narrow in beam, with its
hermaphrodite rig of square and fore and aft sails on as many as four masts. Here
was a design that sailed well and was seaworthy, though smaller. In 1498 a *caravela*
took the Portuguese navigator Vasco da Gama around Africa to India's pepper
and cinnamon. It was a *caravela* that Pedro Álvares Cabral commanded when he
discovered Brazil in 1500. The Portuguese were to write the first manuals on
ship construction. About 1565 Fernando de Oliveira published his *Livro da fábrica
das naus*. The Spanish were quick to follow. In 1575 Juan Escalante de Mendoza
brought out *Itinerario de navigación de los mares y tierras occidentales*, a work that
considers, among other matters, the proportions of ocean-going vessels, then the
usual way to build a ship.

Tudor Carracks and Galleases

England, on the periphery of power, lagged behind the Continent in maritime
construction. Shortly after Henry VIII became king in 1509, one of his first acts
was to build his navy, a late medieval navy, where size, not efficiency, mattered.
The old ways are figured in Henry VIII's great ship, the carrack *Henry Grace à Dieu*
(colloquially, the *Great Harry*), and her contemporary, the carrack *Mary Rose*.[3] To
challenge the Scottish great ship, *Michael*, built in 1511, Henry VIII the next year
ordered the *Great Harry* built at the Woolwich yard. Henry's *Harry* was the greatest of them all: four-masted, 1,000–1,500 tons, 165ft in length, with a four-deck
forecastle and a two-deck sterncastle, ordnance of forty-three cannon of which
twenty or twenty-one were the new bronze (colloquially called brass), and some

200 smaller ordnance. Her crew numbered between 700 and 1,000 men. Besides her size and the latest bronze cannon, she was the first English warship to have gunports cut into her hull. When launched, she was the grandest vessel afloat in European waters. But like the carrack *Mary Rose*, the *Harry* also proved top-heavy, and her rolling made for wildly inaccurate gunfire. In 1536 she was sent back to the shipyard for refitting. Shipwrights there anticipated Hawkyns' race-built design by over thirty years by reducing the *Harry*'s top hamper, cutting down her tonnage to 1,000 tons, and improving her sail plan. In this refit, to make her easier to sail and to balance her centre of effort, her two masts forward carried the main, topsail and topgallants and the two aft carried five lateen sails. She became more responsive, faster, and was a more stable platform for firing her cannon. It is this refitted *Harry* that is shown in the Anthony Roll, 1546.[4]

Like the Portuguese *naus*, though, even rebuilt carracks were slow and sailed poorly. Their capacious design, however, had long worked for the Hanse merchants trading in Scandinavia. Their high freeboard had proved a bulwark against attackers and against the steep cold waves of the North Sea. Their deep holds could carry many tuns of profitable cargo. One example was the 700-ton, 70-gun *Jesus of Lubeck*, 1544. She was one of five carrack traders built originally as merchantmen, 400 to 700 tons. Henry VIII bought her in 1544–45 in Hamburg from the Hanseatic League, and armed her as a warship to augment his navy. The refitted *Jesus* as shown in the Anthony Roll[5] was in 1546 an impressive ship of great bulk, tonnage and substantial firepower. Of her four masts the fore and mainmasts carried a course and topsail, and on the mizzen and bonadventure mizzen a single lateen sail each. In battle she carried 300 men. Like most vessels of the time the *Jesus* had been built of green wood, as had Cabot's caravel, the *Matthew*, in the 1490s. Her unseasoned timber soon rotted. Her high forecastle and poop and full-cut sails made her poor in going to weather but good for defence from boarders.

Her high freeboard and broad beam allowed her to carry some heavy ordnance (seventy cannon in all) at a reasonable distance above the waterline, with smaller guns on the upper decks. Her stern's flat transom was high, with a centre-hung rudder mounted outboard on the transom, usual for the time. The stern was armed with eight cannon of somewhat smaller bore than her main cannon. Two were positioned close to the waterline, on either side of the rudder. Despite these modifications, she was built to be a Baltic trader, not a warship, and the hull suffered from the pounding recoil of heavy artillery. Spanish galleons, with more closely spaced ribs, could take the stresses better. The *Jesus*' cannon out-muscled her timbers.

Besides carracks, Harry had galleasses. Any captain wants a ship that can manoeuvre in any direction, independent of the wind. The galleass seemed the answer. The galleass, variously called galleys, galleasses or barks, was powered by as many as sixty oars, and had three masts that supported a full sail plan. She was sleek, with a length-to-beam ratio of 3:1 (2:1 was then normal). The vessel was armed with light cannon. She promised to be more versatile than the huge carrack. If there were wind, sail; if calm, row. Underwater, the galleass had the sleek lines of the galley, with a full keel and relatively deep draught, and a pronounced tumblehome that added stability. Such was Henry's *Great Galley*, launched in 1515 just a year after the *Great Harry* slid down the ways in 1514. This huge clinker-built vessel of 800 tons had four masts, 120 oars and 97 cannon. But Henry's massive *Great Galley* (really a galleass) unfortunately proved leak. Furthermore, 800 tons were simply too much to row. In 1544, she was sent back to the yards to be rebuilt as a great ship of 500 tons, without the oars.

In 1545, the war with France proved the uselessness of the large oared galleas-ses. Both the galleass and the carrack were dying breeds. Even as they came down the ways at the Chatham yard, smaller and faster vessels had for a half century proved their worth in Europe. Yet though Henry's feet were firmly planted on a medieval deck, in some ways he was farseeing. He had always insisted on a fine turn of speed from his horses, women and ships. Thus when his galleasses proved too heavy and too slow he ordered them all back to the shipyards. There they lost their oars and some tonnage. By 1549 they had all been rebuilt as ships.[6]

Galleons

When the northern carrack met the southern *caravela*, the result was a three-masted ship with both square sails and a mizzen lateen sail, and a stern-mounted rudder. Size had met speed. The hermaphrodite plan sailed better than the plan of the bulky northern European ships and on the open sea could go to weather or reach well in following seas. This new vessel was the galleon, so successful a design that from the fifteenth to eighteenth centuries, the galleon was the princi-pal merchant and naval vessel of the English and European fleets. Like all ships of the time, the design was generic so that a single ship could serve as a cargo vessel or warship. Galleons had a pronounced tumblehome that brought the upper gun deck closer to the vessel's centre line, improving stability and making for accurate gunnery. Longer and narrower than carracks, they sailed better than the earlier design. So successful was the galleon as a design, that one, the *Lion*, was rebuilt three times over her extraordinarily long lifespan of 141 years, from 1557 to 1698.[7]

The galleon's hull was similar to that of the *caravela redonda*, but she was more stoutly built to withstand heavy seas and to carry heavy ordnance. She was fully rigged like her predecessor. Galleons of this period had three or more masts, of which the fore and main masts were rigged with squares, and lateen-rigged on the after masts. She had a beak, a high forecastle and sterncastle and one or two gun decks. In both merchant and naval use she was armed. It was this sort of vessel that Sir John Hawkyns in the 1570s typically modified as the race-built galleon.

Hawkyns' Race-Built Galleons

Storms and battle encountered in Hawkyns' third trading voyage in 1567–68 to the Caribbean convinced him that a new ship design was needed. D. W. Waters argues cogently that from the disaster at the small port of San Juan de Ulúa in

1568, Hawkyns understood that the Elizabethan navy's 'narrow seas' now had to mean 'oceanic', and that 'battle by boarding' had to give way to 'battle by bombardment'. In that one battle Hawkyns recognised the need for a different design and for new tactics.[8]

By the 1560s the old carrack *Jesus of Lubeck* had been well past her useful life and was headed for the breakers when she became Elizabeth's major stake in Hawkyns' second voyage, 1564–65, and then the third, 1567–68. For that third voyage the queen valued her condemned vessel not worth the repair costs of £4,000, and Hawkyns had to spend a considerable sum to make the 24-year-old ship seaworthy. Overhauled, the *Jesus* sailed as Hawkyns' admiral (flagship). Though archaic in design, she still had a cavernous capacity for cargo and the potential for substantial profit. She was leak and unseaworthy, but Hawkyns had to keep her, as she was the queen's impressive royal vessel, part of her stake in the enterprise. Elizabeth's other contribution was the *Minion*, 300–600 tons, much younger, purchased in 1558. But within six years of her launching she was likewise condemned as unseaworthy and deemed not worth repairing. Like the *Jesus*, she too was overvalued by the queen. On the West Indian run, Spanish ships rarely undertook more than four voyages out and back before being retired.[9] In the sixteenth century it was rare that a ship would last fifteen years. Five to ten years was the average life before she went to the breakers, and for Spanish ships even less. Shipwrights knew that within fifteen years even a very well-built vessel would surely need to be completely rebuilt. Keep in mind that the tea clippers of the nineteenth century were built to last only a couple of years. By any standard, then, both of Elizabeth's ships were long past their prime.

On the return leg during that third voyage the *Jesus* suffered serious damage in a hurricane. In the Gulf's steep waves, we read, the planking of her transom opened the seams enough for fish to swim through the gap, so large a man's wrist could reach in. Hawkyns had to head for the Spanish port of San Juan de Ulúa, where he was attacked by the Spanish. Hawkyns lost the battle, all his valuable cargo, the old carrack and her new bronze cannon, and other vessels. On escaping and once back in England, he knew his course – to design and build the race-built galleon. The term 'race-built' comes from the French '*razer*', to cut or scrape away, as to cut away a highly charged superstructure.[10]

Two years later, in 1570, Hawkyns joined in partnership with the Deptford shipwright Richard Chapman to build this new kind of vessel. The result was a race-built galleon less than half the size of the carrack *Jesus of Lubeck* but stronger and faster. The race-built galleon *Foresight*, keel 78ft, 295 tons, 28/36 guns, had a length-to-beam ratio of 3:1, not the usual 2:1. Below the waterline her hull shape was modelled on that of the galleass. Locating her gundeck on a stepped deck above the cargo deck relatively higher above the waterline gave increased freeboard and kept the heavier cannon drier and increased their range. To offset the higher centre of gravity caused by the placement of the heavy ordnance, Chapman increased the draught, which not only improved stability but also decreased leeway. He decked over the galleon's waist to add a battery of lighter ordnance of shorter 9lb demi-culverins. He cut down the fore and stern castles to reduce windage and to improve windward performance. Her bows were angled to break the seas and to keep the lower forecastle drier. Her lengthened bowsprit, supported and strengthened by the beakhead, along with a forward-raked foremast, allowed this new-styled galleon to carry a square spritsail forward, thus balancing the helm better and making the ship drier.

So successful was the *Foresight* that in the same year two other vessels were rebuilt to Hawkyns' new fashion. Both were older galleasses (oars had given way to gun decks): the *Bull*, 1546, 160 tons BM (Builder's Measurement), six demi-culverins, eight sakers and lesser ordnance (by 1585), reclassified as a ship from 1549; and the *Tiger*, pictured in the Anthony Roll, 1546, 160 BM tons (increased after rebuilding in 1570 to 200 tons, armed with six demi-culverins and ten sakers and lesser ordnance (by 1585). Over the next few years, the bulk of the navy's existing fleet was modified, and newly commissioned vessels were constructed from keel up to the new design. Hawkyns reduced the top hamper of the older galleons, increased the length-to-beam ratio so that the ships appeared to float 'low in the water' like galleasses, and recut their sails to make them flatter, thus allowing the vessel to sail closer to the wind. The improved ships could then sail within six or seven points of the wind (each point 11° 15', a 'point' being one of the 32 points of the compass card), about what a nineteenth-century ship of the line or a modern schooner can do. These changes made them faster, stronger and more seaworthy. By 1588 when the English fleet met the Spanish in the English Channel, sixteen of the twenty-one front-line ships had been either modified or built afresh as race-built vessels.

In November 1577 the queen had stipulated that on the death of Benjamin Gonson, Treasurer of the Navy and Hawkyns' father-in-law, Hawkyns would be given the post as Treasurer. Hawkyns took up the job in early 1578, within a few months of Gonson's death. Besides the ongoing ship modifications, Hawkyns promptly authorised funds for speeding repairs and shipbuilding by ordering dry-docks with moveable floodgates. Before, the gate had been a massive earthen berm, built up shovelful by shovelful and pumped dry once the ship was inside. Once the work had been completed, the berm was breached so the dock filled with water, a lengthy process. The new floodgates allowed for faster ship maintenance and repair of the twenty-four ships and other vessels of the Royal Navy.[11]

Shipbuilding, Old and New

Significantly, it was not in Spain or England but in Cuidad México, Nueva España, that the first detailed book on ship design and construction was published. This was Mexican naval architect Diego García de Palacio's *Instrucción náutica para navegar*, 1587. With this work, the New World came into its own in ship design and shipbuilding. In just two generations Mexico had rivalled and then surpassed the mother country, Spain. García de Palacio provides the proportions for the hull and the rigging and considers methods of construction, sailmaking and more. He extends the length-to-beam ratio, sets the hold's depth at half the beam and, to gain stability and reduce windage, razes the fore– and aftercastles following the recent English practice of race-built design. So advanced was Spanish-American shipbuilding (timber and labour there were cheap as well) that Seville ordered the Mexican and Cuban colonials to build frigates for the attacks planned on England. Even later, in 1617, the Spanish king contracted with La Havana, Cuba's port on the Gulf of Mexico, to build four galleons. On the Pacific side of Mexico, ports such as Guayaquil were kept busy filling royal shipbuilding contracts.[12] Shipbuilding had moved to the New World.

The experience of more than 100 years of sailing the West Indies had made for better design. A Spanish ordinance in 1607 specified that vessels sailing in the *carrera de las Indias*, the convoy system that had long transported New World treasure to Spain, have a keel-to-beam ratio of 2.59 to 1. By 1613 that ratio was increased to an average of 2.55–2.71 to 1. In contrast, the Swedish *Vasa*, 1628, had a lean ratio of 5.1 to 1 and a depth-to-beam ratio of 0.41 to 1. Though impressive, the royal warship *Vasa* quickly proved herself unstable and she capsized while still in Stockholm harbour on her maiden voyage, thanks to insufficient ballast, shallow keel and a high superstructure and thus a high centre of gravity. By 1618 the maximum tonnage for Spanish ships of the *flota* was limited to 624 *toneladas* (after 1590, the measure was 1.42m³ per *tonel macho*). Such a vessel was large enough to carry a profitable cargo and ordnance when serving as a warship and yet small enough to sail over the shallow bar at a Spanish port such as Sanlucar, navigate the shoal waters of the Gulf off San Juan de Ulúa, or cross the bars (often less than 3 fathoms deep) at the mouths of the Amazon and Orinoco rivers. The shoal waters of the West Indies archipelagoes meant that deeper-draught vessels, not just carracks but the larger race-built galleons drawing 16ft or more, could not navigate among the islands. Returning from the West Indies in the summer of 1586, Drake wanted to anchor within Albermarle Sound behind the Outer Banks of North Carolina near Nags Head, but his deep-draught vessels had to remain offshore. Vulnerable, his fleet was hit by a severe June storm, changing American history by way of the Roanoke colony.

Over the objections of merchants and shipbuilders that such smaller vessels were unseaworthy and unprofitable, increased trade won out over bulk. Whereas in the sixteenth century a significant number of Spanish and a few English ships were between about 700 and 1,000 tons, early seventeenth-century trade in Tropical America could be undertaken only in medium-sized vessels. The Duke of Medina Sidonia noted in 1610 that these vessels were between 300 and 500 *toneladas*, half the size of the old carracks 100 years earlier.[13] The Americas were also building such mid-sized vessels, race-built in design and of moderate draught. The smaller ships fit the waters they sailed.

Shipbuilding

Construction techniques in the period were both old and new. The old European practice of using green wood in building ships was severely tested in the tropics. As the unseasoned wood dried out under hot sun, seams in deck and hull planking soon opened. Like planking, the wooden staves and hoops of water casks would split, leaving a ship without drinking water. In large Atlantic swells or the steep waves of the Gulf of Mexico, rolling and pitching was increased by the excess weight and higher centre of gravity caused by heavy cannon and highly charged superstructures of fore- and sterncastles. This opened the hull planking, especially the flat transoms but also the deck planking of the old carracks. Their highly charged superstructures further reduced their ability to go to weather, as Admiral Pedro Sarmiento de Gamboa and others discovered in the stormy Strait of Magellan in the 1580s.

The seaworthy and responsive smaller *caravelas* and pinnaces had already proved their worth in the Portuguese explorations. These ships' boats, pinnaces and shallops had been used to explore and trade along the coast of the Indian Ocean, whatever the winds or depths. They now proved equally suitable in the Caribbean's Golfo de Paria, near Trinidad, and up the Amazon and Orinoco rivers, as well as farther north in the shoal waters guarding the barrier islands off North Carolina, and later in the shallow Chesapeake Bay.

Despite new conditions, construction of hulls generally maintained the traditional ways, sometimes with good reason, sometimes without. In Bilbao and Vizcaya, major centres of shipbuilding in northern Spain, for centuries the shipwright would go to the forests and cut during winter, when trees had no leaves and there was little sap. Most woods were cut during a waning moon, when it was thought the sap had gone down to the roots and any lumber would hence be straighter. Knees were cut from where tree trunks branched in limbs. From a tree's tough roots came trunnels (tree nails). The shipwright at this time did not work from plans or half-models but from ratios. His basis was the swimming line (waterline), 'a horizontal line around the ship, from the point where the third and fourth futtocks of the ship's main frame joined just below the widest beam dimension'.[14] The swimming line further marked the limit for safe loading, a Plimsoll line of sorts. From that line the height of the decks and other vertical measurements were taken.

Traditional Mediterranean-framed vessels were built beginning with the keel, to which was scarfed the stempost and, at the stern, the sternpost. Oak was used for the keel, keelson, ribs and lighter-weight pine for the superstructure. After laying the keel, the shipwright fashioned the stem and stern, then used the main frame (the largest frame) to shape the others in a system called whole moulding. Depth was figured to be between a half and a third of the beam length. Critical to building the frames was the ratio of the length of the lower deck beam to the flat length of that frame's floor timber. The *Treatise on Shipbuilding*, c. 1620, cautions: 'If the proportion between the flat floor and the beam was exceeded to get more buoyancy, the ship became tender-sided or crank and needed furring or girdling to restore the proportion'.[15] Newer galleons had five identical frames forward or aft of the main frame. The result was a pronounced rise of the bottom at the bows and stern, offset at the stern by deadwood that directed the flow of water past the rudder and gave it bite.

The keelson strengthened the keel and helped secure the ribs. The ribs, starting with the largest first, were added next, according to the proportions of length-to-beam ratio. Once in place, the ribs were joined laterally from stem to stern. Futtocks (corner braces) joined the floor timbers to the main frame's lower deck beam, onto the top timber line.[16] After the hull's internal joinery was in place, the hull and deck were planked in the new carvel style (butt-joined) and caulked, rather than employing the lapstraked (overlapped) planking of the old northern European way. The seams were payed with oakum or hemp, then tarred. To protect against the teredo worm, tarred cloth and lead sheeting were added below the waterline and sealed with a tar-grease mixed into the tar.

Masts were white pine, with the foremast shorter than the mainmast. Their length required scarfing a number of pieces together. Masts were tapered at their tops, and their bases were cut to fit into the mast-step on top of the keelson, then shimmed with wedges at deck level to keep the mast secure. Masts were supported by shrouds and stays of hemp line. Like the hull, the yards too were a matter of proportion, fullest in the middle and tapered at their ends. The location of the masts on the axis of the vessel was proportionate to the hull, and a function of the centre of the vessel's gravity and resistance. Sails were rectangular, trapezoidal and triangular, and sewn as vertical strips of canvas. Later, these full sails were cut flatter to aid in going to weather.

As for the masts and rigging, a frequent problem at sea was that they cracked or broke, called 'springing'. It is mentioned in many journals, both English and Spanish. Pitching and rolling caused wear on the hemp rigging. When heeled, the weather shrouds would stretch and stiffen, leaving the lee side so slack that masts would bend at least a foot to leeward. As the hull flexed, masts and spars often broke. The long spar of a Mediterranean lateen sail was particularly vulnerable on the open ocean.[17] And, as is true with most aftermost sails, the lateen sail on the mizzen mast of sixteenth-century vessels, nearly useless when running, helped to balance the ship when going to windward.

Ship design was affected as well by armament. Heavy, powerful cannon raised the centre of gravity and strained the vessel's framing from the recoil. Henry VIII's Master Shipwright, James Baker (father of the more famous Matthew Baker, Royal Master Shipwright), thus first located the gun deck for such cannon between the cargo deck (the main deck) and the upper deck, but later in the 1530s he added guns to the main deck as well. It was Baker who first changed from round to square gun ports, as they could be sealed shut better in heavy weather. His cannon were mounted on trucks with small wheels that could easily be run inboard, to shift weight closer to the centre line of the ship and to reduce heeling moment. The resulting vessel was at once watertight and more stable.[18]

Culverins

Since the early sixteenth century, guns had improved, thanks to better refining, casting and design. One such example is the full-length bronze culverin, a beautiful piece of work, but at 14ft, too long and too heavy for the sleek new race-built galleons. Nine-foot demi-culverins were a good compromise. Yet the tendency for longer and heavier guns continued, and so after about 1600, that is, after Hawkyns' death in 1595, race-built galleons grew beamier, recalling pre-1570 vessels.[19] Hawkyns' race-built ships, though nimble, pitched badly because of reduced buoyancy fore in the bows and aft at the stern. They were affected too by their relatively short keels and they also hogged (curved down).[20] Captain Sir Richard Hawkyns, son of John Hawkyns, reported that his *Revenge*, 464 BM tons, though relatively stiffly built with heavy bulkheads to provide extra hull strength, was notoriously difficult to handle. In her brief 14-year life she ran aground six times and once when she beached, turned keel up. Thrice she sprang planks, making for leaks that could sink her. The bulk of Hawkyns' merchant fleet, however, was made up of much better designed and built vessels.

Spanish galleons, in contrast to English ones, were built more stiffly, their frames more closely spaced – good for strength when firing cannon, but too stiff in the North Atlantic's steeper waves found in higher latitudes, where the ship needed to be able to work a bit in heavy seas. The high hamper of their fore and sterncastles increased heeling moment. The Spanish ships would spew their caulking, spring their hull planking, and in straining the longitudinal axis of the ship, proved leak.

There were other new ship designs, but as pinnaces and other vessels are significant more for their use than for any innovations in construction, they are considered later in the chapter on the tactics of fighting ships.[21]

Tonnage

Another factor affecting design was a vessel's cargo capacity. Ships were rated by armament and tonnage. What is a ton, a tun or butt? Warships and merchant ships measure tonnage differently. Peter Kemp defines a 'ton' as 'a measure of capacity at sea', deriving from a 'tun', a large cask equivalent to two pipes, or four hogsheads, or 252 old wine gallons. Thus tonnage originally was the number of tuns of wine a vessel could carry in her hold. It measured cargo capacity.[22] Sir Julian S. Corbett notes the three ways the English calculated tonnage during this early period: first, by cask, where two butts (four hogsheads) equals one ton; next, in feet, where 40ft of timber equals a ton; third, by weight, where 20 hundredweight equals a ton.[23] Rather than counting the number of barrels a vessel could carry, shipwrights had a simpler way. The basic method of calculating tonnage, according to F.C. Prideaux Naish, 'was to multiply the length of the keel by the beam, and the result by the depth'.[24] This 'Solid Number' was divided by 94 or 100 to give the vessel's burden in tons. 'To this burden in tons was added ⅓ or ¼, and the total of these two amounts was called the ship's tons and tonnage'. Thus: kl x b x d = SN / 94 or 100.

For example, the tonnage and dimensions of the *Pelican* (*Golden Hinde*), Drake's vessel that completed the circumnavigation of 1577–80, was, depending on the values used, reckoned at 100, 120 or 150 tons. Mathew Baker, Royal Master Shipwright, standardised tonnage in 1582 and cites two bases of measurement, the burden given in 'merchant's goods', and 'dead weight of ton and tonnage'.[26]

Why these newer ways? First, the old way to measure a vessel's capacity 'to carry pipes of oil or Bordeaux wine', as Baker writes, was outdated in a new age of warships that carried butts of gunpowder, not tuns of wine. Merchant ships were carrying different cargoes and sailing under the bounty system whereby the Crown would contract merchant vessels for naval use. As of the mid-sixteenth century, ships' length-to-beam ratio had increased, freeboard had been lowered, and beam shortened. The new narrower ships took more space to stow tuns of cargo. It was a case of round pegs fitting into the oblong hole or hold of a ship. Design thus affected tonnage. After 1570, when the hulls changed still more, the formula had to change again. Where Baker's Formula had originally been keel length times breadth times depth divided by 94 or 97, or kl x b x d / 94 or 97 = Tons Burden, Builder's Measurement, (BM; capacity), the new hulls were now measured using a divisor of 100, reflecting the narrower and lower hulls.[25]

In 1592, William Borough, the brilliant mathematician and Controller of the Navy from 1589 to 1598, saw to further changes in design and set forth in a paper the three orders of ships and their rules of proportion. 'Order 1: The shortest, broadest and deepest Order. Used by Merchant Ships for most profit = To have a length by the keel double the breadth amidships and the depth in the hold half that Breadth. Order 2: The best proportion for merchandise, likewise very serviceable for purposes = Length of Keel 2 to 2.25 of the beam. Depth of hold 11/24 of that beam. Order 3: The largest order of galleons or ships of war. Made for the most advantage of sailing = Length of keel three times the beam. Depth of hold 2/5 of beam.'[26]

Borough explains the proportion between the 'Solid Number' and the ship's burden:

> When a ship or any other vessel is filled with merchandise, that is to say, forced by weight down in the water to the breadth in the midships or to the place commonly appointed for the lading-mark, she may then be compared to a solid or massy body, as a cube or globe. A similar cube or globe may be weighed by comparing their measured contents with one whose weight is known; and so the tonnage of a ship may be compared with one whose capacity is known.

The Report of 1626 speaks of 'Mr. Baker's old way' that was 'established in Queen Elizabeth's time and never questioned all King James his time.'[27]

Using that rule, the burden of a ship is the Solid Number divided by 100. The dead weight of ton and tonnage is derived from the burden by adding one-third. Other countries used other methods and values. The Spanish *tonelada*, for example, contained 53.44 cubic ft, versus the English ton of 60 cubic ft, making it a smaller ton.

Money, a common measure of value, is also related to tonnage. In the 1620s Charles I, facing an uncooperative Parliament, was finding that hiring merchant ships to fight against France was expensive. A resistant Parliament asked whether the king was paying merchant ship owners excessive bounty by calculating too much tonnage. Such bounty came down to whether the measurements were taken from the outside or inside the hull. On warrant from the Duke of Buckingham, the Lord High Admiral, and the Navy commissioners, a committee met in 1626–28 to revise 'Mr Baker's Old Way' of 1582 of measuring tonnage. The committee measured and measured, and on 26 May 1628 presented 'Mr. Baker's New Style'. The order went out that ships built or rebuilt after 1603 would be measured according to 'the length of the keel, leaving out the false post, the greatest breadth within the plank, the depth from that breadth to the upper edge of the keel, multiplying these and dividing by 100'.[28]

By the 1620s, ships' bottoms had grown fatter and their ends more buoyant than in Baker's time. Measuring BM from inside the hull and adding a half factor of the smaller BM to itself resulted in a smaller dead weight. It all came down to money. Under the new measurement merchant vessels could now be requisitioned more cheaply. The Parliamentary Formula issued in 1652 calculated the Builder's Measurement, giving this new datum point for the vessel's main dimensions and the dead weight figure.[29] Simpson's Rule, which naval architects now use to determine the volume and centroid of a ship, was still 100 years in the future. But tonnage was not just a question of money. For over fifty years Hawkyns' fine-lined race-built galleons had sacrificed buoyancy and strength at bow and stern for speed and manoeuvrability. Since then, warships were made to carry increasingly more powerful ordnance, especially the great weight and recoil of the heavy bow and stern-chaser culverins, and they needed the stability and buoyancy that greater beam provided. If a merchantman, then the greater beam meant greater cargo capacity. Ultimately, seaworthiness won out over thrift.

The Establishment

When Henry died in 1547 he left his young son Edward VI a Royal Navy of fifty-seven vessels, a sizeable fleet. On Edward's death in 1553 and on the accession of Mary I, the Royal Navy or Establishment had shrunk to thirty-nine vessels. During her five-year reign Mary built only three galleons, all between 550 and 600 tons. By the time she died in 1558, the navy had shrunk to just twenty-seven vessels. That number included ten galleons and four great ships. This was about half the navy that had been left by Henry VIII eleven years earlier. As a change of monarchy generally brought with it the condemning or selling off of older ships, twelve vessels went off Establishment on Elizabeth's accession in 1558.[30] But she also ordered things set right. Her shipwrights completed rebuilding six of Henry VIII's eleven galleasses as galleons with half- and quarterdecks at the stern, and forward, a single-decked forecastle.

Lessons from the Caribbean

Oceanic sailing, especially to the tropic latitudes of the West Indies (and in both Arctics), required new standards of seaworthiness. There were the long passages out and back, and once in the Caribbean, the ships had to be responsive to sailing in shoal, hot tropical waters with generally lighter winds. The Spanish usually outnumbered the English in tonnage, cannon and men, and the English counted heavily on their one advantage, superior gunnery. An English captain wisely preferred to batter with cannon over committing waves of marines with pikes, muskets and sabres. Artillery made the difference that changed English naval tactics.

The distance to and from the American tropics further affected the size of a trading or naval enterprise. Most commercial and privateering voyages set out with a ship or two, though sometimes as a squadron of three or four ships sailing both commercially and as privateers (a later seventeenth-century term, used here for convenience). Captains were issued letters of reprisal for private wrongs suffered by the English from the Spanish or others. If the captain were important, he was issued a letter patent by the queen. Whatever the paper, gain was the object.[31] Pirates operated without any license, usually alone, with small, fast vessels. Over the period, only a few large fleets voyaged overseas. Four went to the West Indies, three under the authority of the Crown: Drake's armada in 1585–86, Hawkyns' and Drake's joint command in 1595–96, Cumberland's in 1599, and one smaller, privately financed voyage, Ralegh's in 1617–18. Why so few large fleets? To sail such a distance from home waters into the great power of Spanish naval might in the West Indies was an expensive gamble that Elizabeth was reluctant to make. To allow a large fleet to sail for the Americas would leave England largely defenceless. Under James, such a voyage was contrary to peace with Spain. Moreover, commanding great numbers of ships without adequate communications, over a matter of months, and over wide oceans, was difficult.

Once across the Atlantic, whether a single ship or a fleet, a captain needed seaworthy tenders. The West Indies' predominantly light winds and shoal waters called for the right vessels. From centuries of Mediterranean experience, at first it seemed that fast manoeuvrable shallow-draught galleys, with both oar and sail, would be the best craft for the Caribbean. But galleys could navigate only in calm waters and were outgunned by frigates, *caravelas* and pinnaces. Pinnaces were the better vessel. They were often transported to the Indies knocked down and stowed in the hold, then assembled on site. Rowed and sailed, seaworthy and stealthy, pinnaces allowed for another English Caribbean innovation: commando-style raids on unsuspecting ports, most often in the dead of night with shortened sail and muffled oar as marines landed unopposed a few leagues from town for a surprise attack. From offshore, ships would fire on coastal ports, and provide covering fire for the marines coming from behind to catch the local hidalgo still in his nightshirt. This tactic was classic Drake, tested and perfected in the 1570s. It was tried in Europe, with some success and notable failure by both the English and the Spanish.

Brazilian Hamacas and Jangadas

Once in Africa and the Americas, the sailor found new hardwoods (pernambuco, jacarandá and others), different cuts and weights of sails (lighter weights for most Pacific winds), *hamacas* (hammocks, Brazil beds) and different boats such as the African and Caribe dugout canoes and the Brazilian coastal sailing raft, the *jangada*. This last consisted of tree trunks lashed together, a bench to keep the sailor above the raft surface awash in ocean swells, a loose-footed lateen sail, and a sweep for a rudder. The mariner soon adopted these new inventions to his own use.

Author John Sparke, in his account of Hawkyns' second slaving voyage, 1564-65, describes canoes he saw off Sierra Leone:

> In this island of Sambula we found about 50 boats called almadyes, or canoas, which are made of one piece of wood, digged out like a trough but of a good proportion, being about 8 yards long, and one in breadth, having a beakhead and a stern very proportionably made, and on the outside artificially carved, and painted red and blue: they are able to carry threescore and upward. In these canoas they row standing upright, with an oar somewhat longer then a man, the end whereof is made about the breadth and length of a man's hand, of the largest sort. They row very swift, and in some of them four rowers and one to steer make as much way, as a pair of oars in the Thames of London.[32]

Panamanian Biscuit-Sack Sails and a Pinnace

Drake's Caribbean voyage of 1572–73 shows Drake's ingenuity. No sooner were his two ships anchored off Panamá on the Acla coast at Port Pheasant, July 1572, than he ordered a fort built and his prefabricated pinnaces, transported across the ocean in pieces, constructed on site: 'As soon as we had moored our ships, our captain commanded his pinnaces to be brought ashore, for the carpenters to set up.' It took just a week to construct three pinnaces and to load and arm them before setting out to surprise the treasure mule trains in Panamá. But the English botched the job, failed to get the booty, and worse, the Spanish had discovered the English pinnaces hidden in the bush.

How to escape? Writes Drake:

> let us therefore make a raft with the trees that are here in readiness, as offering themselves being brought down the river, happily this last storm, and put our selves to sea. I will be one. Who will be the other? ... The raft was fitted and fast bound, a sail of a biscuit sack prepared; an oar was shaped out of a young tree to serve instead of a rudder, to direct their course before the wind. At his departure he comforted the company by promising that if it pleased God he should put his foot in safety aboard his frigate, he would, God willing, by one means or other get them all aboard, in despite of all the Spaniards in the Indies.

Drake's author continues:

In this manner putting off to the sea, he sailed some three leagues, sitting up to the waist continually in water and at every surge of the wave to the armpits, for the space of six hours, upon this raft. What with the parching of the sun and what with the beating of the salt water, they had all of them their skins much fretted away.[33]

Drake's *jangada*, built in haste on a Panamanian beach, carried Drake and his crew to safety.

An Elizabethan shipwright had to learn to be able to work anywhere: on beaches, in the mountains, in the jungle. Such was the case in 1575 for another Plymouth man and friend of Drake, Captain John Oxnam, and his crew. Oxnam sailed to Panamá in 1575 with his own ship, determined to sail the Pacific and have gold. He hid his ship, took supplies and weapons and marched into the San Blas Mountains. There he felled cedar, milled the timber, and built a pocket war-ship deep in the jungle. According to Sir Richard Hawkyns, Oxnam 'went with the Negroes about twelve leagues into the main land, to a river that goeth to the South Sea, and there he cut wood and made a pinnace, which was five and forty foot by the keel. And having made this pinnace, he went into the South Sea.' The vessel, fitted with twenty (or twenty-four) oars and sails, drew less than half a foot of water – just a handspan – we are told. She was armed with two small fast-loading cannon. Oxnam's was the first English warship on the Pacific coast, he was the first Englishman to sail the Pacific, and he was the first to seize Pacific treasures, the largest haul anywhere of gold, silver and jewels to that date taken by an Englishman. His Pacific coastal navigation, of course followed the earlier examples of Balboa and others. Magellan's ships had navigated the Pacific in 1521, and since 1565 a regular Spanish transpacific trade route had connected Manila and Acapulco.[34]

Argentinian Driftwood Raft, Chilean Bladders

Drake's circumnavigation, 1577–80, took his fleet into the Strait of Magellan. Once through, a storm separated the ships. Drake now commanded only his flag-ship, the *Pelican*, and a tiny 7-ton pinnace. The pinnace too was soon lost, but two survivors were eventually cast up on an island offshore from the mainland, too far to swim. The men built a raft by tying wood to a 10ft driftwood plank using withes, and they fashioned poles as oars. A flood tide helped carry them to the mainland, 3 leagues away, to safety. Relieved, one of the two soon died from a sur-feit of water and food. The other sailor, Peter Carder, after many misfortunes set foot on English soil a full nine years after sailing from England with Drake. The queen gave him audience and was reported to be much taken by his adventures.[35]

In 1586, just a week before Drake returned to England from his 1585–86 voyage to the West Indies, a resourceful Thomas Cavendish set out with three ships from Plymouth on his own circumnavigation, 1586–1588, following Magellan and Drake. It was a well-prepared enterprise provisioned for two years. Once across the

Atlantic, Cavendish turned south for the Strait of Magellan. On 1 November on an island off the South American mainland he set up a forge, and, writes the author, 'had our cask on shore: our coopers made hoops, and so we remained there until the 23. day of the same month: in which time we fitted our things, built our pinnace, and filled our fresh water'. On any voyage, coopers, blacksmiths and carpenters were among a ship's most valuable men. On 17 December, in the afternoon, Cavendish dropped anchor at Port Desire and notes that 'this harbour is a very good place to trim ships in, and to bring them on ground, and grave them in: for there ebbeth and floweth much water: therefore we graved and trimmed all our ships there'. Graving, scraping and recaulking the bottom were essential maintenance on a long voyage, especially in tropical waters. Careful captains, like Cavendish and Drake, graved their hulls every few months. Cavendish passed through the Strait of Magellan, and on 1 March, once in the South Sea, like Drake almost ten years before him, was soon hit by a storm from the north. The *Hugh Gallant* was separated from the rest of the fleet, so leak that the author writes that we 'looked every hour to sink, our bark was so leak, and our selves so delivered and weakened with freeing it of water, that we slept not in three days and three nights'.[36]

Like other European sailors, Cavendish's eye was open to new and strange watercraft. Near Antofagasta, Chile, Cavendish discovers early inflatables. The Indian 'canoas or boats are marvellous artificially made of two skins like unto bladders, and are blown full at one end with quills: They have two of these bladders blown full, which are sown together and made fast with a sinew of some wild beast; which when they are in the water swell, so that they are as tight as may be. They go to sea in these boats, and catch very much fish with them.'.

North of Guayaquil he careened his fleet again. 'We had hauled on ground our admiral,[37] and had made her clean, burnt her keel, pitched and tarred her, and had hauled her on float again. And in the mean while continually kept watch and ward in the great house both night and day' for the Spanish. Early in 1588 he had reached the Orient, and the island of Guana (not the one in the Caribbean Virgins), where he comments on the native canoes:

> As artificially made as any that ever we had seen: considering they were made and contrived without any edge-tool. They are not above half a yard in breadth and in length some seven or eight yards, and their heads and sterns are both alike, they are made out with rafts of canes and reeds on the starboard side, with mast and sail: their sail is made of mats of sedges, square or triangle wise: and they sail as well right against the wind, as before the wind.

Along the islands of Manila he notes:

> another Balsa or canoa of a great bigness which they which were in her, did set along as we do usually set a barge with long staves or poles, which was builded up with great canes, and below hard by the water made to row with oars; wherein were about 5 or 6 Indians and one Spaniard.[38]

The Twelve Apostles

In late summer 1588 the English had just escaped the threat of the Spanish Armada. It was in part luck, in part through using the new tactic of long-range bombardment by race-built galleons. Spanish hulls were broad-bottomed with short keels, carvel-planked, 4in thick, strong, with oak ribs of over a foot thick. The powerful English demi-culverins, while firing three shots to every one from the Spanish cannon, still could not penetrate the strong Spanish hulls. Though the victory went to the English, it was at the time rightly viewed by both sides as inconclusive. Spain soon built the Twelve Apostles, massive race-built galleons of over 1,500 tons burden, intended to carry the day in a subsequent attack on England.[39] The design of the Apostles was good, but they were poorly built. By 1597, when the English took two of them in Ferrol, they were so 'leak' that the prizes could not be sailed home to England.

Cuban Frigates

In Cuba, the Spanish colonists in 1590 had been ordered by the Crown to build five frigates for the treasure *flota,* and another eighteen frigates (as a servant wrote in 1590) for an attack on England planned for 1592. One Spaniard in the Caribbean writes: 'They are very strong ships, and will draw but very little water, whereby they may enter amongst the shoals on the banks of Flanders: they are builded the higher because here is great store of timber and excellent good and incorruptible.'[40] Such was the power of the Spanish navy in both the Caribbean and in the home waters of the Azores, that when Lord Thomas Howard sailed to the Azores to interdict the Spanish treasure *flota* in 1591, he was met by a formidable Spanish fleet of fifty-three ships, including sixteen new galleons, mostly the new twelve Apostles.

From the Caribbean, the local advice was to adapt in the face of the English attacks. So wrote the governor of La Havana in 1592 to the Casa de Contratación in Seville. Take back the two galleys on station at Cabo San António, Juan de Texeda writes, in exchange for the four frigates he is building. Galleys he finds useless against the English. Two of the frigates ordered by the Crown were now ready, but he says he will need additional shipwrights, money and tools for the other six on order. He had hired carpenters but has no money to pay them, nor do they have tools. The warehouse has only forty-five cases of nails, eight barrels of tar and a little iron left. But once built, these fine Cuban frigates, boasts the governor, can certainly clear Cuba of the English.[41]

Brazilian Pinnace, Bermudan Bark

Cavendish's next voyage for the South Sea set out in 1591 with three ships and two barks. At sea he had earlier built a replacement for a ship's boat. Ashore at Santos he built a pinnace. Before transiting the Strait of Magellan, he anchored at Port Desire in March 1592 and built replacements for the longboat and light-horseman lost in storms on the transatlantic passage.

After sailing with James Lancaster in the *Edward Bonaventure*, author Henry May later found himself aboard a French ship. When the pilot miscalculated, the ship was lost on the shoals off the Bermuda Isles in December 1593. Before she sank May and others saved the carpenter's tools, some fastenings, rigging and other essentials. Ashore, they felled trees, milled timber and built an 18-ton bark, using trunnels and a few iron nails and some tackling from the shrouds salvaged from the wreck. The castaways mixed lime with tortoise oil for pitch, then plastered this mortar into the seams of the hull's planking with sticks. May and the French sailors left the island on 11 May 1594, and nine days later, on 20 May, sucessfully reached land near Cape Breton.[42]

Moorish *Avisos* and *Gallizebras*

By 1592 the Spanish were protecting their West Indian seaports by building stronger fortifications and garrisoning them with seasoned soldiers. To further protect these seaports the Spanish in La Havana designed a new and faster design of dispatch boat. These were the *avisos*, built on Arab lines, for quick communication (one made the Seville–La Havana crossing in a record twenty-eight days). Another vessel drawn from Moorish lines was the *gallizebra* (called frigates by northern European sailors). These small fast vessels were built locally in La Havana – another example of Spanish America leading Spain in ship design and construction, here taking Arab designs. The naval architect for these vessels was Pedro Menendez Marques, son of Admiral Don Pedro Menendez de Avelis. He gave his *gallizebras* long keels, a length-to-beam ratio of 3:1, freeboard low to the water. They were fully masted, powered with auxilliary oars and armed with twenty guns. Their lines recall the earlier English galleasses of the 1540s. These were so fast and bristled with such firepower that they could carry royal bullion unescorted by galleons and still beat off attacks by pirates. So fast were they that no *gallizebra* was ever taken by an English vessel during this period, not even by a pinnace.

Cuban Sails

The Spanish commander Don Sebastián de Arencibia wrote to the Crown from La Havana in May 1595 in great frustration. He had been patrolling the coast from Cabo San António to La Havana to clear it of corsairs in preparation for the yearly arrival of the treasure *flota* from New Spain. But 'the hulk I had for vice-admiral was such a laggard that with her in my company I could not possibly execute my orders and return to Havana by the specified date'. Off Pan de Cabañas in a dead calm he had met an enemy ship of 300 tons. This was Michael Geare's vessel. The Spaniard closed:

His flagship and mine were not 300 paces apart, but because he was a good sailer he broke out three in addition to his regular sails, whereas my flagship had not even its usual number and those it had were old. I tried to get new sails, but they were not to be procured in this city, for Don Francisco Coloma carried off everything when he went. So the enemy flagship got away from me.

Such backbiting amongst Colonial officials was not uncommon.[43]

Caribbean Teredos

Whenever possible, the English followed the Spanish practice of sheathing hulls against the tropical teredo worm. In the warm waters of the Caribbean worms could riddle a hull in short order. In September–October 1594 the merchantman *Rose Lion* was fitted out for privateering in Plymouth by her captain, Thomas West, to sail for four leading London merchants. Depositions mention using lead sheathing on the hull against the teredo worm. A Dutchman testified that the ship had called at Seville, where she was 'new trimmed and sheathed in lead', common practice before sailing to the West Indies. We learn that 'such ships as go from Seville to St Domingo are commonly sheathed in lead to avoid the danger of worms which otherwise would hazard such ships and their ladings greatly'.[44]

Mediterranean Galleys, Dutch *Vlieboots*

In 1602 fast Dutch *flieboots* or *vlieboots* (flat-bottomed three-masted flyboats, with both squares and fore-and-aft sails) controlled the shoal waters off the coast of the River Vlie. They challenged the Mediterranean galleys commanded by the Genoese Frederico Spinola, stationed in Flanders at Gravelines, Dunkirk and Lluys. The galleys, though fast and manoeuvrable, had little cargo area or deck space available for powder and shot. The Dutch *vlieboots* handily trumped them.

Decline of the Establishment

For a time after Hawkyns' death in 1595 until about 1600, the shipwrights and yards at Chatham and Portsmouth maintained Hawkyns' standards. But in those five years no new galleons were built, though three of the royal fleet's largest vessels – the *Triumph*, 760 tons, the *Elizabeth Jonas*, 684 tons, and the *White Bear*, 732 tons – were rebuilt according to Hawkyns' hull lines. Steep decline came when a new faction came into power with the accession of James I in March 1603. Robert Kerr, the king's favourite, and the Norfolk faction consisting of Sir Robert Mansel, Treasurer of the Navy Board, Sir John Trevor, Surveyor of the Board, and Vice Admiral, Sir William Monson, Keeper of the Armoury at Greenwich, oversaw the Navy's slipping standards during the years 1603 to 1618. In the shipyards, the corruption swept out by Hawkyns in the 1570s had settled back in. Costs under Mansel's rule rose to £16 a ton for new and rebuilt ships. Under the corrupt regime, to rebuild twelve vessels cost £60,000. After Mansel left in 1618, the cost soon dropped to £8 a ton, half the cost.[1]

In the last twenty-five years of Elizabeth's reign, the navy had nearly doubled in size. But of the thirty-two vessels within Elizabeth's Establishment in 1603, twelve of the galleons were to be condemned, scrapped or sold by 1618. The Royal Navy was by then reduced to twenty vessels in all: seventeen galleons, one pinnace, one ketch and one discovery vessel. It was a far smaller navy than that left by Henry VIII in 1547. The Treaty of London signed by England and Spain in 1604 brought peace for a time. Though Spain acknowledged the Church of England, it was at the cost of the Royal Navy and free trade in the New World. The Spanish, without question, had won the war. Early in his reign James further abolished letters of reprisal and letters of marque, so that privateers, the reserve muscle for the Navy, no longer had any legal basis for operating.

In 1616 Ralegh, once out of the Tower, engaged shipwright Phineas Pett at Deptford to build him a new ship, the *Destiny*. She was his pride, as his former *Ark Ralegh* (later the queen's *Ark Royal*) in the 1580s had been. At 440 tons, armed with thirty-six cannon, she was to be admiral of a powerful fleet of six, totalling nearly 1,400 tons and mounting about 140 cannon. To that fleet came other vessels, so that when Ralegh's fleet finally sailed for Guiana in 1617 from Cork, it had grown to thirteen vessels, a formidable squadron that, if light in tonnage, was heavy in firepower. After the fleets of Hawkyns, Drake and Cumberland in the '80s and '90s, Ralegh's was the fourth largest English naval presence to sail the Caribbean in 100 years. It is little wonder the Spanish ambassador Conde Gondomar was gravely concerned.

Once Ralegh reached the mouth of the River Orinoco in 1617 the draught of the *Destiny*, a deep 17ft, proved troublesome. Ralegh's memory of Caribbean sailing after more than twenty years had grown faint. He had forgotten that Caribbean waters and river mouths were especially shallow. Only with the help of 'one Janson of Flushing', a merchant mariner living at the Orinoco for some years, could he cross the bar at high water. At 3 fathoms of water, Ralegh could enter with only one foot to spare. Once anchored, Ralegh ordered the smith to set up his forge ashore to repair the casks and instructed the ships' carpenters to knock together barges brought for river travel upstream. It was to be the last bit of English naval construction in the American Tropics for many years. It was also to be Ralegh's final voyage. The *Destiny*, built by Phineas Pett, the age's finest shipwright, was a superb piece of shipbuilding – but totally unsuitable for the Caribbean. Ralegh was still navigating in the golden years of deep-draught race-built galleons better suited to the open ocean. 'Ships are but boards, sailors but men.'

Notes

1 See C.S. Knighton and David Loades (eds), *Elizabethan Naval Administration* (Farnham, Surrey: Ashgate for Navy Records Society, 2013), passim.

1 Pilobiers, possibly pillows or other bedding.

2 Richard Hakluyt (ed.), *Principal Navigations Voyages Traffiques & Discoveries … 1598–1600*, rpt. 12 vols, Extra Ser. 1–12, Hakluyt Society (Glasgow: James MacLehose and Sons,

1903–05). Facs. rpt. of 1903–05 edn (New York: Augustus M. Kelley Publishers, 1969), 9:338–58. *Principal Navigations Voyages Traffiques & Discoveries 1598–1600*. Abbr. *PN*.

3 See David Childs, *The Warship Mary Rose: The Life and Times of King Henry VIII's Flagship* (London: Chatham Publishing, 2007), 26–41, on design and construction.

4 The Anthony Roll (Pepys 2991 and BL Add. MS 22047) was drawn by Anthony Anthony [sic], an English civil servant and amateur artist of Flemish origin. First a beer exporter, he became the supplier of beer to the Navy, then Overseer of the Ordnance Office, and Master Surveyor of Ordnance for the Tower and elsewhere. His fifty-eight pictures of ships, in colour, represent the only known extensive depictions of the Tudor Navy.

5 Anthony Roll, 1546, Pepysian MSS., Magdalene College, Cambridge.

6 Arthur Nelson, *The Tudor Navy: The Ships, Men and Organisation 1485–1603* (London: Conway Maritime Press, 2001), 54–5. Much of this chapter draws on Nelson, just as Nelson drew on the earlier and the still standard work, Sir Julian S. Corbett, *Drake and the Tudor Navy: With a History of the Rise of England as a Maritime Power*, 2 vols. (London: Longmans, Green, and Co. (1898), rpt. London: Temple Smith, 1988). Several books by the naval architect Colin Mudie, consultant for the modern reconstruction in 1997 of John Cabot's caravel, *Matthew*, 1497, provided valuable details: *Sailing Ships, Designs and Re-creations of Great Sailing Ships from Ancient Greece to the Present Day* (London: Adlard Coles Nautical, 2000), and with Rosemary Mudie, *The History of the Sailing Ship* (New York: Arco Publishing, 1975), and *The Sailing Ship, a Voyage through the Ages* (London: Marshall Cavendish, 1984).

7 Nelson, 81.

8 D.W. Waters, 'The Elizabethan Navy and the Armada Campaign,' *Mariner's Mirror*, vol. 35 (1949), 95; and I.A.A Thompson, 'Spanish Armada Guns,' *Mariner's Mirror*, vol. 61 (1975), 355–71.

9 Phillips, 23.

10 Angus Konstam in *The Spanish Armada: The Great Enterprise against England 1588* (Botley: Osprey Publishing Ltd, 2009), 116–19, argues otherwise, that race-built galleons began in Spain and came to England via Queen Mary.

11 Egyptian drydocks date from at least 200 BC. The oldest surviving European drydock was built by Henry VII in 1495 at Portsmouth; it now contains Nelson's *Victory*. Nelson, 100–5.

12 Phillips, 249, note 4, 252, note 60.

13 Carla Rahn Phillips, *Six Galleons for the King of Spain: Imperial Defense in the Early Seventeenth Century* (Baltimore: Johns Hopkins University Press, 1986), 28–32, and Appendix B, 228.

14 Nelson, 79.

15 Quoted in Nelson, 89.

16 Nelson, 89.

17 *PN*, 10:9–74.

18 Nelson, 36–7; Phillips, 51–7, 72–3.

19 See Chapter 5, 'The Way of a Fighting Ship', for a fuller treatment of artillery development.

20 When the top of a long wave supports the centre of the keel, and without adequate structural support, the ends of a ship sag.

21 See Chapter 5, 'The Way of a Fighting Ship'.

22 Peter Kemp (ed.), *The Oxford Companion to Ships & the Sea* (London: Oxford University Press, 1976). Gross tonnage is figured at one ton equalling 100ft^3. Various tonnages have been calculated, based on cubic capacity divided by 100 (Builder's Measurement, BM). Displacement, the actual weight in tons of the ship herself, is the measure of water displaced when afloat. Deadweight tonnage, DWT, is the sum of cargo, fuel, water,

ballast, provisions, passegers, and crew, shown at the Plimsoll Line. Gross tonnage, GT, is the moulded volume of all the enclosed spaces within a ship. Net tonnage, NT, is limited to the volume of a vessel's cargo spaces. GT and NT are measured using Simpson's rule. Merchant vessels generally give their gross or deadweight tonnage; warships, displacement tonnage.

23 Julian S. Corbett, *Drake and the Tudor Navy*, vol. 2, Appendix C, 421.

24 F.C. Prideaux Naish, 'The Mystery of the Tonnage and Dimensions of the Pelican–Golden Hind, *Mariner's Mirror*, 34 (January 1948), 42–5.

25 Nelson, 88.

26 Quoted in Nelson, 100.

27 Quoted in Nelson, 95.

28 Quoted in Nelson, 94.

29 Nelson, 79.

30 Nelson, 81–6.

31 Kenneth R. Andrews (ed.), *English Privateering Voyages to the West Indies 1588–1595*, Ser. 2, No. III, Hakluyt Society (Cambridge University Press, 1959) 7. Abbr. EP.

32 *PN*, 10:17.

33 Irene A. Wright (ed.), *Documents Concerning English Voyages to the Spanish Main 1569–1580 I: Spanish Documents Selected from the Archives of the Indies at Seville … English Accounts 'Sir Francis Drake Revived'; and Others, Reprinted*, Ser. 2, No 71 (London: Hakluyt Society, 1932), 245–326. *Documents Concerning English Voyages to the Spanish Main 1569–1580.* Abbr. *DE.*

34 Sir Richard Hawkyns' account reprinted in *DE*, 327–39; Portuguese Lopez Vaz in PN, 10:75–81; also *PN*, 11:227–90.

35 Samuel Purchas (ed.), *Hakluytus Posthumus or Purchas his Pilgrimes, Contayning a History of the World in Sea Voyages and Lande Travells by Englishmen and Others, by Samuel Purchas … 1625*, rpt. 20 vols, Hakluyt Society, Extra Ser., Nos 12–33, Hakluyt Society (Glasgow: James MacLehose & Sons, 1905–07), 16:136–146. *Hakluytus Posthumus, or Purchas His Pilgrimes* 162. Abbr. *PP.*

36 *PN*, 11:301–2.

37 The commanding ship.

38 *PN*, 11:290-347.

39 Nelson, 168–79.

40 *PN*, 10:160–3.

41 Irene A. Wright, ed, *Further English Voyages to Spanish America 1583–1594*, Ser. 2, No. 99 (London: Hakluyt Society, 1951, issued for 1949), 266–7. *Further English voyages to Spanish America 1583–1594.* Abbr. *FE.*

42 *PN*, 10:194–203.

43 Kenneth R. Andrews, ed., *English Privateering Voyages to the West Indies 1588–1595*, Hakluyt Society, Ser. 2, No. III. (Cambridge: Cambridge University Press, 1959, 287–336. EP.

44 Quoted in *EP*, 359–67.

2

'Remainder Biscuit'

'His brain, which is as dry as the remainder biscuit after a voyage.'
William Shakespeare, As You Like It, 1599

What could the seaman expect in the way of victuals and drink? The cost of food and drink rose dramatically in the sixteenth century, making provisioning more expensive. What foods would last during a voyage, and how could they be preserved? At sea or on station, what to resupply, and where? Does a ship's captain give famished colonists his own men's food?

❦

Life aboard was tough, and bread and water were vital to the success of any voyage. Those aboard knew by training and instinct the nautical proverb: 'One hand for yourself and one for the ship.' They fed themselves as best they could and likewise worked the ship. Captain John Smith, soldier of fortune, celebrated governor of Virginia and explorer of the Chesapeake Bay, wrote in 1620 that seamen 'are so over-charged with the labour, bruises and overstraining themselves they fall sick of one disease or other, for there is no dallying nor excuses with storms, gusts, overgrown seas and lee shores, and when their victual is putrified it endangers all. Men of all other professions in lightning, thunder, storms and tempests with rain and snow may shelter themselves in dry houses by good fires, but those are the chief times seamen must stand to their tackling, and attend with all diligence their greatest labour upon the decks.'[1]

The ordinary seaman's lot, writes Luke Foxe, was 'a hard cabin, cold and salt meat, broken sleeps, mouldy bread, dead beer, wet clothes, want of fire'. On the 1587 expedition for Cádiz, food was the bone of contention when mutiny broke out on one of the queen's major ships, the *Golden Lion*, 500 tons. Aboard were 300 sailors, 30 gunners and 100 soldiers. In a letter to the captain, her men wrote: 'What is a piece of beef of half a pound among four men to dinner, or half a dry stockfish for four days in the week, and nothing else to help withal: yea, we have help – a little beverage worse than pump water. We were pressed by her Majesty's press to have her allowance, and not to be thus dealt withal you make no men of us, but beasts.'[2]

It is no wonder that before jewels, pearls or gold, victuals were often the major object of a raid. What maritime historian Kenneth Andrews observes for the privateer was true generally for any mariner: 'The seaman's life aboard a privateer was nasty, brutish and short. His diet at the beginning of a voyage might consist of bread or biscuit, oatmeal or peasemeal, salted beef or pork, fish, butter, cheese and beer, but even then gave no defence against scurvy.' In any case, the ship was not long at sea before the food would go bad and the beer sour. Despite captured casks of wine and baskets of tropical fruits, Andrews writes, 'crews sometimes simply starved to death'.[3]

Provisioning for the Tropics

Provisioning before departure and provisioning en route were separate considerations. The first was generally done with some forethought, the latter often in the desperation of the moment. Nathaniel Boteler, the early seventeenth-century governor of Bermuda and later of the tiny island of Providence in the Gulf of Mexico, was a 'gentleman captain' with some small sea experience. He wrote six entertaining Platonic dialogues on maritime matters. In the third, Boteler's fictitious admiral speaks to a captain about the scam of provisioning with bad food: 'The which was a foul coosenage and desperate abuse and might indeed (as you said) have occasioned a general ruin, as certainly it did a general wrong.' Such foul coosenage, such nasty scam was especially serious if the ship were bound for the tropics. It was:

> very ill dealing; and that not only in the provisions of flesh (which perhaps might be in part excused by the unreasonableness of the time that they were of necessity to be made in, being in the prime heat of a summer when flesh in these parts will not well take salt), but in the rottenness of the cheese, in the frowsiness [musty stench] and foul condition of the butter, and in the badness of the salted fish ... And for the beer, it was not only for the most part very undrinkable (whether by bad brewing, or the ill-seasoning of the cask, I cannot say), but a great deal thereof absolutely lost by a new device of petty saving in not affording some iron bound cask for the lower tier of hogsheads.

Boteler writes that in sailing from England to the Bay of Biscay and port of La Rochelle as captain, one ship in his fleet lost seventeen tons of beer 'by the only want of a few iron hoops; so that we were all of us put to the drinking of stinking infectious water'. Boteler had heard that some captains could distill sea water to make it potable, as indeed Sir Richard Hawkyns had done by 1593. 'I could wish that all ships that are designed abroad to long voyages over large seas should be furnished with the utensils proper to this purpose.'[4]

Victualling at Port

What did Elizabethan and Jacobean sailors eat and drink? Stores for a tropical voyage typically included fruits, fish, meat and grains. Inventories list tobacco, sheep, hens, calves, swine, pork, flitches (sides) of bacon, beeves (plural of beef); goats and young kids, poultry, mutton, mullet, dried stockfish, salted or dried hake; mussels, wild beasts, penguins, alligators, seals, powdered and dried turtles, train oil (usually from whale blubber); guinea wheat, flour, butts of meal, maize, pompions (squash), potato roots, colesworths, onions, oil, garlic; coconuts, lemons, figs, dates, oranges, melons, piones, pistachios, almonds, jars of honey and loaves of sugar, rice, cassava, baked biscuits – and mouldy bread.

Other lists include poor john (hake), butter, meal, grees (coarse oatmeal), pease (most often split yellow peas), flitches of bacon, cheese, sweet meats (sweets); penguins, oranges and lemons, wheat flower; currents, prunes, cinnamon, ginger, pepper, cloves, green ginger, Holland cheese, old cheese, wine vinegar, juice of lemon, white biscuit, oatmeal; gammons of bacon, dried neats' tongues, legs of mutton minched (minced) and stewed, dried suet or butter, marmalade, suckets (candied fruits), almonds, comfits (sugared dried nuts, spices, nuts and seeds); pylchers in hogsheads (pilchards, herrings), New land fish (Newfoundland cod) and Lyngs cod (from Aberdeen). To these foodstuffs the steward added spices and sugar, not so much to add flavour but to perserve them.

Captain John Smith writes that the ideal captain, besides furnishing his men with 'bedding, linen, arms and apparel', would include additional victuals and spices to sweeten the voyage: 'Fine wheat flower, close and well packed; rice, currands [currants], sugar, prunes, cinnamon, ginger, pepper, cloves, green ginger; oil, butter, Holland cheese or old cheese; wine vinegar, Canary sack [sherry], *Aqua vitae*, the best wines, the best waters, the juice of lemons for the scurvy.' To entertain strangers there was 'marmalade, suckets [fruit preserves], almonds, comfits [confiture, preserves] and such like'.[5] Smith then declares: 'Some it may be will say I would have men rather to feast than fight; but I say, the want of those necessaries occasions the loss of more men than in any English fleet hath been slain since '88.'[6]

Drake calculated for his West Indies 1585–86 cruise that 100 men needed twelve hogsheads of beef and pork, three thousand 'New land Fyshe', thirty hogsheads of pilchers, ten burdens of ling cod (Aberdeen cod), 'Bysket in hundredths – 10,000 wayght', 22½ barrels of meal, two barrels of oatmeal, fifteen hogsheads of pease. Then, various wines (for the officers): six pipes of Canary, one tun of French; and thirty tuns of beer (for the crew). 'Besides bacon, butter, cheese, honey, oil, vinegar, rye', he says, 'whereof there is provided a good quantity, but the particular proportions for each ship is not yet set down at the time of the writing here of'. Such measure was presently aboard, he adds, less what had already been consumed. 'Written at Plymmouth the last of August 1585.' With God's grace, within a week Drake hoped to depart from Plymmouth.[7]

Provisioning for a large fleet of twenty-seven vessels was no small undertaking. Hawkyns and Drake's fleet for the West Indies voyage of 1595–96 embodied some

2,500 men and 6,000 tons of shipping. (In the Armada year, 1588, the rate had been one man for every two tons of ship.) Hawkyns and Drake's victualling was economical. Hawkyns spent more on fitting out and provisioning, than Drake did, but then the tonnage of Hawkyns' fleet was much greater than Drake's.

Kenneth Andrews provides fourteen pages of stores and their cost for the fleet. Excerpts of entries include: wheat, malt, rye, barley, pease, £4,650 1s 11d; beer, 1,339 tuns, 1 puncheon, 1 kilderkin, £2,985 9s 9d; wines, Canary, Muscatel, Gascony and Spanish, £942 3s 4d; beef, £131 17s 10d; stockfish, Iceland and Holland ling cod, dry Newland fish (Newfoundland cod), buckhorn (whiting), corfish (salt cod), tunny, North Sea cod, sturgeon, skatefish, herring, £1,600 9s 4d. Staples and other foods are listed: oatmeal, 53 qrs. 3 bls; £122 17s 0d, butter, £219 17s 4d; cheese, £104 5s 11d; and porks (250 pigs, salted) £338 10s 0d.

Andrews lists still more food and spices: cuskoes or 'Negro's meat' (couscous), £45 14s 0d; oil, £266 2s 3d; vinegar, £64 15s 0d; mustard seed, £28 19s 3d; garlic, raisins, 11 barrels, £13 19s 1d. The manifest continues: pipes of Canary wine, barrels of herring, dry fats, 'lasting victuals' of some sort for sea service, and four barrels of a 'certain victual in the form of hollow pipes', called 'by the name of *Macaroni* among the Italians' which had been supplied by Hugh Platt, who was 'recommended by Count Maurice of Nassau to the Earl of Essex, £18'.[8]

Purveyors of Coosenage

The cost of food was a general problem for the Elizabethans. England in 1585 experienced extensive malnutrition, made worse for the poor and unemployed by bad harvests. The next year, 1586, brought a spike in inflation that had been steadily rising since the 1530s. One example was maize or corn, because a shortage that year drove its price high, and provisioning a ship cost considerably more in those two years. Edward Baeshe, Surveyor General of the Queen's Victuals for the Sea, calculated that in 1586 victualling four ships for three months at sea would cost on average £2,623, whereas in 1565 it would have cost £2,100. Beef that had cost a 1d for 3lb in 1532, and a 1d for 1lb in 1565, now cost in the 1580s over 2½d per pound. The rate for victualling the queen's ships was 14s per man per month. Privateers allocated less per man, counting on adding to stores from prizes taken. As for the quality of the food, despite victualling at a shilling less, 13s per man per month, merchant sailors (including privateers) ate somewhat better than the navy.

If a ship's burden were 350 tons, the value of victuals was £683 and the total investment £3,425. If she were 200 tons, victuals £390, total £1,789; if 100 tons, victuals £195, total £693; if 50 tons, victuals £117, total £360; if 30 tons, victuals £78, total £222. Larger ships required a proportionally larger investment, as they were generally at sea for a longer time. About half the fitting-out expenses went for victuals, and even more if soldiers were carried or if the voyage went beyond the usual six months. Andrews has determined that for the years 1588–95, a 300-ton privateer required a total outlay of about £3,000 to prepare for an ocean voyage, of which £1,000 for expendable provisions was thought reasonable.[9]

A common coosenage during the age was for the supplier to give food short measure and sell poor quality. As food in London was expensive, it was better to provision in the West Country, where it was cheaper and where its freshness allowed for it to be preserved longer. The West Country was better too because sailing from there was better than departing from London and beating westward out of the Channel. Whatever the port of departure, a captain tried to get to sea as quickly as possible before a voracious crew, aboard but still at dock, ate through the perishables.

Then there was timing. To keep ahead of the queen's stay of sailing (an order to remain in port, the intention being to defend home waters), Drake more than once set sail before being fully provisioned. Clearing Plymouth, he would plan to complete his provisioning in the Canaries or Cabo Verdes. He left only partially provisioned in 1585 bound for the West Indies in order to avoid such a stay. Whether early on or later during any voyage, landfalls were needed to replenish wood, food and water.

Butts and Bungs

As the Brazilian song goes, '*cachaça não é agua, não*' – *cachaça* is not water, but firewater, made from sugarcane. What of the contents of the barrels, the water, wine, beer, spirits and their containers? In the heat of the tropics, the wooden staves and hoops of the water butts typically dried and shrank, and the contents leaked out. Next to the ship's carpenter and blacksmith, the cooper was indispensible. No water, no staying at sea.

The seaman's drink often went bad because of chemistry. Water, a bacterial soup, soon grows foul when stowed below in oak casks. Casks that seeped water after a week of swelling were defective and hastened things. After just two days, bacteria in the water begins to grow. With water so chancy, alcohol was the answer. Beer and wine lasted longer. Casks full of wine have free SO_2 (sulphur) in the wine that protects both the wine and the cask. An empty cask loses that protection, and every two months it must be rinsed with water, dried, and citric acid added or a stick of glowing sulphur lit so its fumes can maintain the staves. The cask must then be thoroughly cleaned or the citric or sulphurous residue will produce hydrogen sulfide. Barrels must be treated in this way every four to six weeks to prevent acetobacter (vinegar bacteria), wild yeasts, and lactic acid bacteria from spoiling the wine and destroying the barrel.

Ashore, wine barrels are normally stored in cool cellars ($12.8°C/55°F$) and do not mould. Humidity aboard ship, especially in the tropics, soon produces mould in the barrel. Any mould must be thoroughly cleaned out. One critical place where mould starts is on the wooden bung, as it is moist and exposed to air. Wine stored in casks is, like water, chemically active. Alive, it continues to age in the butt. If ashore, such wine at a certain stage would be bottled, slowing the process. But at sea, especially in hot, humid conditions, wine in casks ages more quickly. To keep wine fresh, the casks must remain full, but this is impossible when the cask is drawn from daily.

As for the ordinary seaman's beer, it too must be kept cool at no more than about 13°C. Above that temperature the bacteria rapidly become active. Beer brewed by the Elizabethans could last for about six weeks at best. If above 13°C it goes off in a few days, most certainly within a week, as was the case aboard English ships facing the Armada in 1588 when the beer went bad.

Water too was a perishable commodity. During the voyage, rainwater was collected in barrels, and occasionally fresh water was drawn from rivers such as the Amazon, which flowed far out into the sea. Along the littoral, in marshes or on sandy beaches, fresh water could be found by digging a pit in the sand. If raiding a port, sailors could refill casks from local wells or cisterns, first making sure that the Spaniards had not poisoned them. Seamen's journals frequently note places where a ship could get water, wine, beer, spirits and victuals. Some places were looted for their pipes of Spanish wines and hogsheads of cider, while others were known as being dry, such as the island of Dominica, the Dry Tortugas, or the Florida Keys: no water, much less wine. Cumberland, Chidley, Ralegh and many other captains report being dangerously low on water during their voyages.

Though the Canarias had little water, there was (thankfully) Canary wine (the last stop for good wines if sailing west from Europe). From the mainland the steward could find more potent drink, such as sack from Spain (sherry), port from Portugal and aqua vitae (a fortified wine such as brandy and distilled spirits such as aquavit). Sir Richard Hawkyns rued the day in 1594 that his gunner on the *Daintie* sought courage in a strong local Chilean wine before engaging a Spanish fleet in the Pacific. The gunner could not shoot straight, and the ship was seized.

When England took Jamaica from Spain in 1655, the Royal Navy changed from issuing French brandy to stiffen its traditional daily beer ration – nine and a half pints (4.5 litres) issued at midday – to rum (Sp. *ron*), readily available in the Caribbean. Half a pint of rum was issued twice a day,[10] along with the beer allowance, nine and a half pints. The high alcoholic content meant fewer casks to stow. The rum was taken neat or with lime juice in Brazilian fashion (a *caipirinha* but without sugar). Brazilian *fazendas* before the 1620s had been distilling molasses from sugar cane to make *cachaça* (a form of rum from which *caipirinhas* are made). About the same time rum ('kill devil') appeared in Barbados. As *aguardiente* it had long been drunk along the northern coast of South America and in Central America.[11]

Dried, Barbecued, Salted, Spiced, Pickled

Preserving food was vital. The methods were to dry it, barbecue it, salt it, spice it or pickle it in brine or vinegar. When Sir Richard Hawkyns was captured in 1594 by the Spanish off Perú, he and his captor Admiral Beltrán de Castro Ydelluca discussed the advantages of each method of preservation, most likely over a glass of Chilean Gran Reserva during a fine dinner. Only three years earlier, in 1591, Sir Thomas Cavendish had discovered to his dismay that penguins, though tasty and plentiful in the Strait of Magellan, must be eaten promptly. Even when preserved in salt, penguin meat rotted quickly under a hot tropic sun. As for beef, it would keep no more than a day unless it had first been cut into two sides like bacon, 'thicker than one's hand', had been rubbed with salt, left twelve hours, and dried in the sun for four days. Then it could be flayed, placed on a frame and scorched over a fire (Arawak *buccan*, a frame for smoking wild meat, Sp. *boucan*, hence 'buccaneer'). So wrote Juan Caballero de Bazán, owner of an *ingenio* (sugar plantation), to his secretary, Anton Catalán, from the port of Santo Domingo, on Hispaniola, December 1593.[12]

Water, wood, meats, fresh fruits and vegetables to ward off scurvy were the first matters a captain tended to on making landfall. Spoilage was the next concern. In the searing heat of hostile seas controlled by the Spanish, the English had no friendly bases for resupply of victuals and water once in the West Indies. One hand for the ship, one for the sailor to feed himself.

Reprovisioning at Sea

Sailing along a populated friendly coast, a captain could rely on finding a port within the next kenning or two for restocking or visiting the local fishmonger. Off soundings and ultramarine, it was a different matter. When England expanded from littoral to transoceanic sailing in the early sixteenth century, the general rule was to provision for six months if the destinations were Europe, Africa, the Azores or other nearby archipelagos. If to the West Indies, then the practice was to lay in food for eight to twelve months. If it were a circumnavigation such as Cavendish's, provisioning was for eighteen to twenty months. On any voyage, long or short, captains would expect to victual and water along the way by buying or raiding.

Journals of voyages to the American Tropics record where food could be had, and importantly too, where not. Victuals, particularly fruits and meats, were found in Africa along the Barbary Coast or at the Cabo Verde islands, and in Brazil at Bahia, Rio de Janeiro and São Vicente. In the higher latitudes, the Newfoundland Grand Banks provided cod and water. Penguins, though perishable, could be taken in great number within the Strait of Magellan at Penguin Island. Various Caribbean tropical foods could be found at Port Plenty, Toulon, Mona, Saona, Trinidad, Truxillo, the Caymans, Aguava, Dominica, Jamaica and La Margarita. But food at Spanish settlements could not be bought at any price because of Spain's prohibition against any trade with the English or other foreign nations.

At sea, crew caught sea birds, fish or turtles, and closer inshore, whelkes (shell-fish). On rivers, using sieve nets, they caught fish, and with pike or sword killed alligators (*lagarto* or *caimá*). When raiding a ship or port, taking such consumables as water, food and wood was the first concern, ahead of any treasure. The English sailor by necessity ate food wildly different from the common English fare, and washed it down with Canary wines or beers. Food and drink nourished the body; gold, silver and pearls did not. In revenge for savaging their country, Peruvian Indians once forced a hated Spaniard to drink hot molten gold to slake his thirst.

Puddles and Rain

Filling water casks on foreign beaches could be dangerous, as Sir John Hawkyns found out on his second slaving voyage, 1564–65. Near Taggarin on the coast of West Africa the crew had taken casks ashore, filled them 'with water, to season the same, thinking to have filled [them] with fresh water afterward'. It was then when 'Negroes set upon them in the boats, and hurt divers of them, and came to the casks, and cut off the hoops of twelve butts, which lost us 4 or 5 days' time'. At the end of January Hawkyns and his ships sailed from Sierra Leone for the West Indies. Watered and victualled, his ships full of slaves, Hawkyns was becalmed for eighteen days in the Doldrums, encountering contrary winds and tornadoes:

> which happened to us very ill, being but reasonably watered, for so great a company of Negroes, and ourselves, which pinched us all, and that which was worst, put us in such fear that many never thought to have reached to the Indies … but the Almighty God, who never suffereth his elect to perish, sent us the sixteenth of February, the ordinary breeze.

After forty-one days of contrary weather, Hawkyns at last made landfall at Dominica, an island of fierce Caribes. He writes that he quickly 'forsook the place for want of fresh water, for we could find none there but rain water, and such as fell from the hills, and remained as a puddle in the dale, whereof we filled for our Negroes'. Hawkyns relates that:

> not two months past, in the said island, a caravel being driven to water, was in the night set upon by the inhabitants, who cut their cable in the hawser, whereby they were driven ashore, and so taken by them, and eaten. The *Green Dragon* of Newhaven, whereof was captain one Bontemps, in March also, came to one of those islands, called Grenada, and being driven to water, could not do the same for the cannibals, who fought with him very desperately two days.[13]

Hawkyns sold his slaves along the Spanish Main and weighed anchor to return home. Set westward by currents and at sea longer than he expected, Hawkyns found himself among the offshore islands of the southern coast of Cuba, again short on water. At the island of Pinas he was relieved to find water, 'which although it were neither so toothsome as running water, by the means it is standing, and but the water of rain, and also being near the sea was brackish, yet did we not refuse it, but were more glad thereof, as the time then required, then we should have been another time with fine conduit water'. No sooner had most of the fleet got under way and set the foresail than a storm blew up. But one bark had not fully watered, and 'was fain for haste to cut the cable in the hawse, and loose both anchor and cable to save herself'. The south coast of Cuba was dangerous,[14] as Columbus had discovered earlier.

A Surfeit Kills

In Hawkyns' last of his three slaving voyages, 1567–68, Drake and Hawkyns and whatever crew could flee, escaped from the Spanish at San Juan de Ulúa in two ships, their water butts empty and larder bare. After fourteen days 'hunger enforced us to the land, for hides were thought very good meat, rats, cats, mice and dogs, none escaped that might be gotten, parrots and monkeys that were had in great price, were thought there very profitable if they served the turn one dinner'. They endured until they reached land on the Gulf coast at 2° 30' N but there in northern Mexico they 'found neither people, victual, nor haven of relief.'[15]

Half the crew voted to take their chances ashore; the rest, to sail on and seek water. They found water and fruits, but:

> some of our men drunk so much, that they had almost cast themselves away, for we could scarce get life of them for the space of two or three hours after. Other some were so cruelly swollen, what with the drinking in of the salt water, and what with the eating of the fruit which we found on land, having a stone in it much like an almond (which fruit is called capule) that they were all in very ill case, so that we were in a manner all of us both feeble, faint and weak.[16]

After a stormy Atlantic crossing Hawkyns and crew arrived later in 1568 at Pontevedra, Galicia, and were fed by hospitable Spanish. But a surfeit of meat after near-starvation quickly brought on sickness to many and death to some.

The best captains did their best to feed their crews. Cumberland resupplied frequently on his twelve voyages. Drake, in his circumnavigation of 1577–80, and on his West Indies voyage of 1585–86, sought landfalls for fresh food and drink. Yet, as said, short rations from incomplete provisioning were common to several of Drake's voyages. In Drake's 1577–80 circumnavigation the Portuguese writer Lopez Vaz takes pains to note that the choleric Drake had been 'determined to seek the Straits of Magellan, and to pass into the South Sea' by plundering provisions and other valuables as he went. At the Cabo Verdes, he writes, Drake 'took a Portugal ship laden with wine', as well as the Portuguese pilot.[17] It was generally known that if making for the Strait of Magellan, Bahia and São Vicente were good places to reprovision. Watering in Rio de Janeiro, though, was not recommended, because as one English captain found, water from there quickly went foul.[18]

Marrish Water, Lemons

Victuals, water and loot went hand in hand. In addition to the initial provisioning, Drake's sailors on the 1585–86 voyage to the West Indies along the way took on fish from the Barbary coast, then at Cabo Verde, coconuts, oranges, plantains, figs, dates, sugar, corn, potatoes, colesworths and onions, at the Caymans, alligators, and at the Tortugas, turtles. Drake reprovisioned and watered in the Greater Antilles before his attack on Santo Domingo. He first, though, had to deal with a mutinous Captain Francis Knollys. Drake ordered him to leave the voyage and gave him the

Hawkyns, provisioning the ship with butts of wine and meal, hides, oil, mutton, a quarter of beef and a thousand poor John (salted/dried hake). Drake then went on to sack Santo Domingo and Cartagena. Setting out for the return voyage home from Cartagena, he filled his water casks, 'which water was had in a great well, that is in the island by the harbour mouth', and baked biscuit.[19] He was chary of the Spanish colonists, as he recalled the sack of Vigo, and the possibility that the locals might have poisoned the wells. Along the Spanish Main, Drake's victuals ran low as usual. The Spanish had hidden any food and valuables in the bush, so raiding port towns yielded little sustenance. Drake resorted to seizing small coastal trading vessels. At Tolu a frigate provided maize, hens and pompions. A couple of others gave up maize, twenty-eight fat hogs, 200 hens and honey. Drake attempted to reach Matanças, east of La Havana, but after two weeks contrary winds drove him back to Cabo San António, at the west end of Cuba. There on the beach he was left to gather, powder and dry turtle's eggs, and to water the ships. He had been at sea nearly a month, and his water butts were empty:

> Our scarcity was grown such, as need made us look a little better for water, which we found in sufficient quantity, being indeed, as I judge, none other then the rain water newly fallen, and gathered up by making pits in a plot of marrish [marshy] ground, some three hundred paces from the sea side.'

To a parched throat, even brackish water was sweet. Drake set the example for his gentlemen by joining his seamen in the surf, heaving and shouldering the water butts into the ships' boats. Writes Drake's author:

> the good example of the General at this place, who to encourage others, and to hasten the getting of fresh water aboard the ships, took no less pain himself then the meanest; as also at S. Domingo, Cartagena, and all other places, having always so vigilant a care and foresight in the good ordering of his fleet, accompanying them, as it is said, with such wonderful travel [travail, exertion] of body, as doubtless had he been the meanest person, as he was the chiefest, he had yet deserved the first place of honour.

It took three days for captain and crew to water the ships.[20]

Drake was one of those generous captains who were willing to give up precious stores to other ships on the high seas or to help struggling colonists ashore. On reaching Ralegh's starving colonists at Croatoan (one of North Carolina's barrier islands) in June 1586, Drake offered them the ship *Francis* and a month's supplies looted from sacking San Agustín the week before. But just as he was preparing to send those supplies ashore, he was hit by an early severe four-day June storm. The colonists lost their nerve to stay on at the outpost and opted instead for returning to England as passengers. For want of provisions (and nerve), American colonisation was slowed by a quarter-century.

Wine 'Our Greatest Want'

Ship after ship, captain after captain, faced the problems of insufficient food, water and wood. About the time Drake returned to England in summer 1586, Sir George Clifford, Third Earl of Cumberland, set out on 26 June intending for the South Sea. Perhaps on the seas, he hoped, Fortuna or Stelamaris would grant him a prosperous voyage. Cumberland outfitted three ships and a small pinnace: 400–500 tons of shipping carrying 200–300 men. By February 1587 he had sailed to 41° S against frigid winds. Cumberland writes: 'Our bread so consumed that we have not left above two month's biscuit, our drink in a manner all spent, so that we have nothing but water, which in so cold a country as the Straits, if we should get in, and be forced there to winter, would no doubt be a great weakening to our men, and a hazard of the overthrow of the voyage.' As befitting a courtier captain, Cumberland turned back for Brazil to resupply, 'both with wine which is our greatest want, and other necessaries'. Wine was more a necessity than a luxury.

He again sailed southward and reached a height of 44° S, east of the coast of Patagonia, but with foul weather and contrary winds in colder and colder temperatures, the food, water and wine gave out. He again turned for warmer waters. At Bahia (18° S) Cumberland took four Portuguese ships and ordered a hulk from Flushing lying in the harbour to join them:

> Not daring to refuse it, he did so, and brought with him a caravel with forty or fifty butts of wine in her, and another small bark which had little or nothing in her … saving in one of them we found four butts of wine, in another two, in another one, some fish, and all the rest of their lading was on shore.

Because of reduced victuals and drink, Cumberland had to give over his idea of reaching the South Sea, and so he made for the Caribbean. At the end of July he took stock of his victuals and drink. The steward, writes the author, 'found but nine butts only, so that our captain allowed but a pint of water for a man a day, to preserve it as much as might be, wherewith every man was content, and we were then in number fifty men and boys'. Cumberland sailed directly for England. On 29 September, 'the residue reached the Coast of England after an unprofitable and unfortunate voyage'. Inexorable circumstances had again trumped Cumberland's bid for fortune. Foul weather, foul water and few victuals had proved his undoing.[21]

In 1586, just a week before Drake returned to England from the Caribbean, Sir Thomas Cavendish set out with three vessels from Plymouth on his circumnavigation, 1586–88. It was a modest but well-planned undertaking provisioned for two years, the first truly intended English circumnavigation. (Drake's in 1577–80 did not begin with the aim of sailing around the world.) In West Africa, Cavendish loaded his ships with lemons, and when he reached the Strait of Magellan, his ships reported no cases of scurvy. Cavendish's 1586–88 voyage is the first known English use of lemons to prevent scurvy, fifteen years before Lancaster, who in 1601 provisioned his voyage to the East Indies with bottles of lemon juice, and nearly 200 years before their efficacy was recognised and made policy by the

Royal Navy in 1794. Such knowledge was hardly new, as citrus fruits had been part of the diet of the Spanish sailor since at least the 1540s. On the long Pacific crossing, Cavendish lost only two men from scurvy. In Java he resupplied with eggs, hens, fresh fish, oranges and limes. Though the *Hugh Gallant's* sixteen men had been struck with an unknown disease for about a month that killed the ship's captain, almost all of Cavendish's men stepped ashore healthy at Plymouth on 9 September 1588. It was an extraordinary voyage, escaping scurvy, ague and the flux, thanks in great part to diet.[22]

Pease, Flitches, Aqua Vitae

The English voyages to the West Indies from 1588 to 1595 were, as far as is known, nearly all privateering voyages. Such ventures were more expensive than shorter and less hazardous voyages, as the ships were larger and had to be better equipped for a longer time at sea. Instead of the usual six months' victuals, ships were supplied for eight or twelve months. Nevertheless, privateering voyages were hardly a picnic. How was their fare? Andrews offers that there was 'nothing but bad food, disease, danger and the vague hope of loot'. Aboard was much drunkenness and disorder. If the booty seized were wine, the men were soon drunk. Women? Rarely, and only from dark alleyways and steamy brothels of hostile seaports. As for picking up food in the West Indies, the privateers' and pirates' journals record taking turtles and looting for bread from cassava, and hogs.[23]

In 1589, William Michelson was captain of the *Black Dogge,* sailing off the north coast of Cuba and off Campeche on the Yucatán. He took eight or nine frigates and their hens and victuals intended for the galleys defending La Havana. Most welcome were seventeen or eighteen pipes of Spanish wines, a fine prize indeed. Off Cabo San António he seized a 200-ton Spanish ship 'laden with wines and wrought iron'. Michelson records victuals and drink taken, as did most captains, alongside non-consumable booty.[24] In 1592, the corsair Christopher Newport, the seasoned captain of the *Golden Dragon* and later to be captain of the *Susan Constant,* hired by the Virginia Company to carry colonists to Jamestown in 1607, bartered with Indians on Dominica for tobacco, hens and potato roots, and then from a Spanish ship seized rice and other victuals. On Mona he procured fruits, wines, flesh and potato roots; on Saona, a store of wild beasts and swine; on Aguava, fruits; and at Truxillo, sheep, goats and poultry. On the Florida Keys, though, he was unable to find water.[25] Food first, booty second for this captain.

Captain John Chidley's voyage intended for the South Sea found him in January 1590 at the Strait of Magellan's Penguin Island and there, like most others before him, he had run low on victuals. The crew was particularly unhappy and delivered a petition to the master of Chidley's *Delight.* It put forth its grievances on 12 February:

> that whereas our Captain Matthew Hawlse, and Walter Street do begin to take into the Captain's cabin this 12. of Febr. both bread and butter (such as was put in for the provision of the ship and company) only to feed themselves, and a

few others, which are of their mess: meaning thereby rather to starve us, then to keep us strong and in health.

Sixteen of the crew had already died from not getting their allotted provision, and when inventory was taken:

there was found but five months victuals of bread, meal, greets [grit, coarse oatmeal] and pease, and also but three months victuals of beef, penguins and pork, three hogsheads of wine, ten gallons of aquavitae (whereof the sick men could not get any to relieve them), four hogsheads of cider and 18. flitches of bacon, &c. the company hath but three flitches.

This was too little food for crossing the Pacific. Captain Hawlse and the mate Street, claimed the crew, had seized seventeen pots of butter, certain cheese and a hogshead of bread for their own private use. The petition continues to say that the captain and mate:

have not only immoderately spent the company's provision in butter, cheese, aquavitae, &c. but have also consumed those sweet meats, which were laid up in the ship only for the relief of sick persons (themselves being healthy and sound, and withholding the said meats from others in their sickness).

Captain Hawlse and the mate Street were 'feeding themselves fat, which do no labour at all'.[26] It was not a moment too soon. The *Delight* came about, and set sail from the Strait in February 1590. The crew shaped a course for the Cabo Verdes, then the Azores, and Alderney in the Narrow Seas, where the remaining crew – down to just six men, four Englishmen and two strangers – first stepped ashore. The master had died, as well as the two mates and many others. The survivors then ran the ship into a port near Cherbourg, where in high winds the one anchor remaining came home, and the ship went onto the rocks. The four surviving English crew were given passage in a bark bound for Weymouth.

Water remained a desperate need, whatever the ship. James Langton was a fine captain who had the full trust of the Earl of Cumberland and led the Earl's seventh of twelve voyages of reprisal. He set out for the West Indies, 1593–94, with two ships and a pinnace, some 230 tons of shipping in all. Captain Langton was well respected by the Spanish as well as by his employer and his crew. One hidalgo describes him on this voyage as about thirty-five, good-sized, of a reddish complexion, 'with hair long in the old fashion', then goes on to compliment Langton on his seamanship. Langton watered off the south coast of Hispaniola and recounted for Hakluyt's readers the method, 'that it may hereafter be beneficial for men to know how to supply themselves in such cases'. The island of Savona has no spring, so on a small, sandy beach Langton dug a 3ft hole and lined it with a hogshead, leaving the fine sand to filter out the salt through the wooden staves of the butt as fresh water seeped inward.

Another privateer was Captain William King, who at twenty-seven was already a well-experienced mariner. He commanded the powerful privateer *Salomon*, fitted with twenty-six cannon, crewed by ninety men. When she set out in 1592 for the West Indies, she was provisioned for a full year, not the usual six months. In the Greater Antilles he watered the ship and refreshed the crew with potatoes and plantains. At Cabo Tiburón, three leagues west of Santo Domingo, he seized a small boat 'which had certain jars of molasses or unrefined sugar, with three men; which men with their boat we carried with us to Cape Tiburón, which, in respect of service done unto us in furnishing us with fresh water, we dismissed'. On Jamaica he found neither food nor loot, but at Grand Cayman he came upon:

> a good river of fresh water; and there we turned up threescore great tortoises; and of them we took our choice, to wit, fifteen of the females, which are the best and fullest of eggs, whereof two served an hundred men a day. And there with stones we might kill turtle doves, wild geese, & other good fowls at our pleasures.

At the Rio de Puercos on the coast of Cuba he took a small bark 'with four men and forty live hogs, with certain dried pork cut like leather jerkins along, and dried hog's tongues and neats' tongues, and 20 ox hides', then, near La Havana, 'took two boats laden with tortoises, which we sunk, saving some of the tortoises, & setting the men on shore'.[27]

Cassava, Beeves, Honey

Ransoms were not always paid in gold and silver. Five leagues east of the port of Santo Domingo, Langton exacted a ransom in food from the colonists to prevent their houses from being torched and to get their slaves back. 'From Francisco Ramirez and others they seized they demanded a ransom of 100 loads of cassava and 40 beeves [steers, beef] among them all (and they were many). This is what they will consume during their stay and on their voyage.' So Juan Caballero de Bazán, owner of an *ingenio* profitable for its sugar, wrote to his secretary, Anton Catalán, from Santo Domingo, December 1593. He continues: 'I have been equipping men, buying them powder. The president sent me word to spend 150 *ducatas* on the men who demanded pay and he would make them go. I offered him two boxes of sugar, which were worth more. When Gregorio de Ayala heard this he came to advise me to do nothing of the sort. He said it was better to give four cases of preserves to the two captains and the two pilots; but he says that Captain Langton is the leader to whom regard must be paid. He says that if they are given kids, melons, oranges and beeves it will please them more and save me money ... They will be satisfied; especially if in addition they are presented with a dozen loaves of sugar and another dozen jars of honey.' Bazán continues:

> Tell them that in addition to having sacked the estate twice before, they have seized two shipments of my sugar in two different years, so that, with the raids

on the plantation, I have suffered more than 20,000 ducats damage. Therefore I trust in God's mercy that the three copper pans may be returned to place and all the water jars left where they are on the estate and in the purging house.

The copper pans were essential in boiling down the sugar cane.[28]

Distilled Water from the Sea

In his 1593–95 voyage bound for the South Seas, Sir Richard Hawkyns, captain of the *Daintie*, rigged up a still on deck for making drinking water, the first known English instance of this practice:

And although our fresh water had failed us many days (before we saw the shore) by reason of our long navigation, without touching any land, and the excessive drinking of the sick and diseased (which could not be excused) yet with an invention I had in my ship, I easily drew out of the water of the sea sufficient quantity of fresh water to sustain my people, with little expense of fuel, for with four billets I stilled a hogshead of water, and therewith dressed the meat for the sick and whole. The water so distilled, we found to be wholesome and nourishing.[29]

Finding food for a square meal for the men was for privateer captains a daily matter. In 1594–95, Michael Geare took a ship near Puerto Rico for its bread, garlic, wines and oil. Amias Preston in 1595, off La Margarita, looted bacon, maize and guinea wheat from three *caravelas*, then from a fort near Caracas took two or three tuns of wine. In 1595, Sir Walter Ralegh, usually punctilious in payment and despite his distaste for stealing, nevertheless procured wine and flour by force at Santiago in the Canaries before making his westward transatlantic passage.

Scarce Victuals

Scarcity of food was a major problem not only for sailors but also for colonists left to plant Tropical America. English colonists along the Orinoco and James rivers naively counted on being fed by the local population. From the start in 1595, Ralegh's Guianans depended on ship's stores and food from the local Indians, who had barely enough for themselves. Even when the colonists could or would plant, a good harvest, even in the tropics, was by no means certain. They continued to depend on ships' stores for victuals. Any resupply generally came late if at all. A passing ship was no solution. To draw down a ship's limited and carefully rationed victuals to feed those ashore when there were fields that could be planted and harvested, was extraordinary. In 1606, William Turner, son of a London physician, writes that when he arrived in the River Wiapoco in early September, he found that the leader, Captain Charles Leigh, and thirty-five colonists had died, and that the thirty remaining 'were in great misery and extremity, both for lack of health and scarcity of victuals'. Still, the survivors had planted vegetables to sustain themselves, and to satisfy investors had planted flax and that new wonder cash crop, tobacco. This local Indian crop would be transplanted to Virginia and would eventually fund the colonists' independence from England.[30]

Robert Harcourt, an Oxfordshire man, set out on 23 March 1608 for Guiana with a ship, a pinnace and a shallop, and ninety-seven men (thirty-seven sailors and sixty landsmen, 'too great for so few ships of no greater burden'). At the barren Isla Alegranza, in the Canarias, the thirsty men found no water. So on 8 April they sailed on to Isla Tenerife. Harcourt sent the pinnace ahead to Orotavo, a town on the other side of the island, 'in hope to get some wine amongst the Merchants there; but not being able (by reason of a contrary wind) to double Punta de Nega, we altered our course from Wine to Water. And the twelfth day we passed by Santa Cruz, and watered that evening at the Calms.' In an irony, Santa Cruz, the major port on Tenerife in the Canarias, was prized for its wines. Reprovisioned, Harcourt writes that they set sail and 'stood our course for the River of Wiapoco in Guiana, having a prosperous wind, fair weather and a smooth sea. The ninth day of May, we fell into the current of the great and famous River of Amazonas, which putteth out into the Sea such a violent and mighty stream of fresh water, that being thirty leagues [90 miles] from land, we drunk thereof, and found it as fresh and good as in a spring or pool'.

Thus refreshed, the colonists arrived at the Wiapoco in May, the rainy season. As for planting: 'I found the time of the year so unseasonable for our purpose, that (by reason of continual rains) we were constrained to lie still and do nothing for the space of three weeks, or a month.' Echoing the words of Ralegh, Harcourt found Guiana a 'goodly country, and spacious empire', but with the change of season the heavy rains turned this garden of Eden into a fetid swamp.[31] On 18 August, Harcourt sailed from the Wiapoco, leaving his brother Michael in charge of twenty-two others and all the supplies and food that he could spare.[32]

Handkerchers, a Cuttworck Ruff for Water Butts

Twenty-two years after he had founded the colony, Sir Walter Ralegh finally set out in 1617 to return to his beloved Guiana. Ralegh records that he arrived at Isla Lancerota in the Canarias to rewater and revictual. Shots were exchanged after the governor mistook Ralegh's fleet for Turkish-Algerian corsairs. Ralegh still needed water and sailed on for Isla Gomera, where, on anchoring, the English were again given a hot reception. When Ralegh's twenty demi-culverin returned fire, Ralegh and the governor soon came to an agreement:

> I for my part should promise on the faith of a Christian not to land above 30 mariners without weapons to fill water we were within a pistol shot of the wash of the sea, myself farther promising that none of those should enter their houses nor their gardens. Upon this agreement I sent my boat ashore.

In case of any further misunderstandings, Ralegh armed the few going ashore and 'brought six ships with their broadsides towards the town which I would have beaten down in 10 hours if they had broken the agreement'.

To get his water he sweetened matters with a touch of gallantry. He sent the governor's countess '6 exceeding fine handkerchers [handkerchiefs] and 6 pair of gloves' and later two ounces of ambergris, an ounce of amber extract, a 'great glass of rose water', and 'a very excellent picture of Mary Magdalen, and a cutwork ruff'. It worked. He left the Canarias well watered.

But some weeks later when becalmed in the Doldrums, the *Destiny* had only enough water left aboard for six days. Ralegh was still 400 leagues, some 1,200 miles, from his landfall. Providentially, a week later on 29 October, enough rain fell to fill three hogsheads (about 300 imperial gallons). The usual two-week Atlantic crossing had nearly tripled to thirty-eight days. When Ralegh's ships reached the River Wiapoco on 11 November, their water and victuals were again nearly gone. Three days later, the *Destiny* re-anchored. Many crew and Ralegh were suffering the bloody flux or an ague. Ralegh had to be carried ashore. Under a tent he was fed bits of local pork and armadillo. He delegated command to his old friend, Lawrence Keymis. Keymis and Ralegh's young hotheaded son Wat went in search of gold. Wat was cut down by Spanish lead shot while rashly charging the Spanish at San Thomé. Before the year was out, Ralegh was to meet his own death on the block.[33]

It may have been that Ralegh, in that sear autumn in London, 1618, read these words from Isaiah (30.20) in the staunchly Protestant Geneva Bible, 1560, before taking the final sacraments of bread and wine: that the Lord has given the 'bread of adversity, and the water of affliction, thy rain shall be no more kept back, but thine eyes shall see thy rain'. From the first English voyages by William Hawkyns to Ralegh's last one, it took prosperous winds and a safe voyage to outface the breads of adversity and the waters of affliction.

Notes

1 Smith, 112. See also G. B. Harrison, *England In Shakespeare's Day* (London: Routledge, 2005), vol. 3:101.

2 Quoted in Kenneth Andrews, 'The Elizabethan Seaman,' *The Mariner's Mirror*, vol. 68 (1982), 245–62.

3 *EP*, 40.

4 Nathaniel Boteler (Boeteler, Butler), *Six Dialogues about Sea Services. Between an High Admiral and a Captain at Sea*. London: Moses Pitt, 1685, rpt. W.G. Perrin (ed.) as *Boteler's Dialogues* (London: Navy Records Society, 1929), 56–60. *Boteler's Dialogues*, written in 1634 and published 1685 shed much light on the early Stuart navy.

5 Smith, vol. 3:96–7.

6 Smith, vol. 3:11, 97, 112; *EP*, 17.

7 Quoted in Mary Freer Keeler (ed.), *Sir Francis Drake's West Indian voyage 1585–86*, Ser. 2, No 148 (London: Hakluyt Society, 1981), 46–7. *Sir Francis Drake's West Indian Voyage 1585–86*. Abbr. *DW*. This list is more extensive than the victual allowance calculated for four men for twenty-eight days, as printed from State Papers 1581 in Sir Julian Corbett (ed.), *Papers Relating to the Navy During the Spanish War, 1585–1587* (London: Navy Records Society, 1898, rpt. 1987), 263.

8 Kenneth R. Andrews (ed.), *The Last Voyage of Drake & Hawkins*, Hakluyt Society, Ser. 2, No 142 (Cambridge: Cambridge University Press, 1972), 50, ff. *The Last Voyage of Drake and Hawkins* Abbr. *LV*.

9 *EP*, 40–50.

10 Daily rum ration, 1 pint (0.47 litres).

11 After the Battle of Trafalgar, 1805, rum was quickly elevated in name to 'Nelson's blood' when a rum cask into which the admiral's body had been placed for preserving was opened back in England. The spirits had been drained off at the bung and quaffed by crew. 'Splicing the mainbrace' means a double ration. Grog is rum cut or mixed with beer or water (the pirates' bumbo), a dilution with water, lime or lemon introduced 1740 in the Caribbean by 'Old Grog', Admiral Edward Vernon. Only in 1970 in its concern for sailors operating machinery did the Royal Navy abolish the daily rum ration.

12 *EP*, 236–83.

13 *PN*, 10:9–63; Irene A. Wright (ed.), *Spanish Documents Concerning English Voyages to the Caribbean 1527–1568, Selected from the Archives of the Indies at Seville*, Ser. 2, No 62 (London: Hakluyt Society, 1929), 76–108. Abbr. *SD*; James A. Williamson, *Hawkins of Plymouth*, 1949, 2nd edn (London: Adam & Charles Black, 1969), 70, note 1. Abbr. *HP*.

14 *PN*, 10:9–63; *HP*, 70, note 1; *SD*, 76–108.

15 *PN*, 10:64–74.

16 *PN*, 9:398–444.

17 *PN*, 11:227–90.

18 *PN*, 10:97–134.

19 *PN*, 10:126–7.

20 *PN*, 10:126–8.

21 *PN*, 11:202–27; *PP*, 16:5–7.

22 *PN*, 11:290–376.

23 *EP*, 21–31.

24 *EP*, 53–6.

25 *EP*, 193.

26 *EP*, 68–9.

27 *PN*, 10:190-3; *EP*, 209–18.

28 *EP*, 236–83.

29 *PP*, 17:90. Nothing new under the sun here, for Aristotle (*c.* 350 BC) had described the process of distillation in *Meteorologica* (II.3.358b16).

30 *PP*, 16:338–57.

31 *PP*, 16:391–2.

32 *PP*, 16:358–402; Thomas Southey, *Chronological History of the West Indies*, 3 vols. (London: Longmans, 1827), vol. 1:242.

33 Robert H. Schomburgk (ed.), 'Sir Walter Ralegh's Journal of his Second Voyage to Guiana', in *The Discovery of the Large, Rich, and Beautiful Empire of Guiana … by Sir W. Ralegh, knt.*, Hakluyt Society, Ser. 1, No 3 (London: Hakluyt Society, 1848), 184. Abbr. *DG*. This early Hakluyt edition, written during the age of sail, retains a valuable perspective too lacking in the engine room.

3

Western Winds
– a Tropical Rutter

'Western Wind, when will thou blow,
That the small rain down can rain?
Christ, if my love were in my arms
And I in my bed again!'

Anonymous, sixteenth century

This chapter sets forth for the first time the sailing directions, what the sixteenth-century English pilot would call a rutter, for navigating from England to the American Tropics and back. It presents descriptions of climate and weather in the words of the early mariners. As their conditions were roughly similar to those today, an appendix provides tropical climate and weather in terms of present-day science. This chapter, together with the pilot atlas charts and the analytical scientific appendix, form the rutter.

☙

The Little Ice Age

The Little Ice Age, from about 1300 to 1850, had minimal effect in the tropics, though it did affect North Atlantic sailing and colonisation along the North American coast. In Europe and on the North Atlantic, the winters were stormier, the summers colder, and in North America droughts were common. Such weather was the worst in many hundreds of years, and it continued off and on throughout the period, as archeologist-mariner Brian Fagan has noted.[1] Given the adverse conditions, a sailor was lucky to be blown safely home on a favourable western wind.

The Greenland ice cap, the Antarctic ice shield, tree rings and records of grain and wine harvests provide evidence of the extremes. Bitter winters, droughts or torrential rain in the summers became common. Climate changes varied from place to place, but the two unusually cold decades between 1590 and 1610 were global. The sailor, once south in the Trade Winds off the Canarias or the Cabo Verdes, and certainly once he had reached the West Indies, found a climate still warm, indeed, hot. As for the North American coast, rings in cypress trees record that severe droughts occurred between 1560 and 1612. The most severe droughts in 800 years were between 1587 and 1589, precisely when the Spanish and English were trying to settle along the North American coastline. Spanish colonists had founded Santa Elena (on present-day Parris Island, South Carolina) in 1565, but because of poor harvests they were forced to abandon their colony in 1587 and resettle back at San Agustín, Florida. In 1584 Ralegh had dispatched an expedition that determined Roanoke (near present-day Nags Head on the Outer Banks of North Carolina) would be suitable for colonisation. Within a year, in 1585, Ralegh had sent out a second fleet of five ships led by Sir Richard Grenville, who landed 107 colonists led by Ralph Lane in August that year. These did not fare well, and when Drake appeared in 1586, returning from the Caribbean, he brought the colonists home with him. In 1587, the year the Spanish were abandoning their northerly post, Ralegh sent out 150 more settlers, led by John White. White returned to England for more aid, leaving behind ninety men, seventeen women and eleven children. But because of the Spanish attack on England in 1588 and subsequent threats, he could not return until 1590. On arrival he found that the colonists had vanished. the site was deserted, the word 'Croatoan' (present-day Hatteras Island) had been carved on a post, and the fort had been dismantled but not destroyed. In the interim, the area suffered the worst years of drought in nearly a millenium. What happened remains a mystery. In any case, the Croatoan Indians, without food themselves, could hardly feed the English, nor could the few fields planted by the English yield much.[2]

The severe weather of climactic extremes that began in the 1590s was Europe's coldest decade in the sixteenth century. Extreme weather was to last for over two centuries. From 1591 to 1597 there were six consecutive years of poor harvests, during which European farmers got good harvests only 40 per cent of the time. There were food riots. The polar ice cap marched southward, and anticyclones battered England with frigid northeasterly winds. The winter of 1607 was England's coldest in 700 years. Low temperatures and frost split the trunks of many ancient trees.[3] The Jamestown colony, England's next attempt at colonisation (after the settlement at St John's, Newfoundland, 1583), this time on the Chesapeake Bay, fared not much better in 1607. Its colonists had left a frigid England in December and waded ashore in May to face a drought along the banks of the James River, just north of the Dismal Swamp. During those critical first years for the colony, the American eastern seaboard was in the midst of the driest seven seasons in 770 years. Droughts continued until 1613. One hundred and four colonists came ashore to plant Jamestown in 1607. A year later, only thirty-eight were still alive. Between 1607 and 1625 some 6,000 English came to Jamestown. Over 4,800 of them died of malnutrition, water shortage, contaminated water and related illnesses.[4]

In South America a few years earlier, there had been a major natural disaster. For three weeks in 1600, from 16 February to 5 March, around 4 miles from Arequipa in Perú, the 4,800m volcano Huanyaputina erupted. Ash fell on Lima, La Paz, Arica and elsewhere, killing more than a thousand souls. Sediment in the upper atmosphere in summer 1601 darkened the sun so that the entire northern hemisphere experienced its coldest summer since 1400 and western North America its coldest summer in 400 years. The phenomenon was not isolated; similar volcanic eruptions brought cold summers in 1641–43, 1666–69 and 1698–99.[5]

The seafarer found it a stormy time to be sailing the North Atlantic. For over 100 years the weather had grown increasingly worse, affecting not only sailors but fish as well. Consider cod. *Gradus morrhua*, the 'beef of the sea', the Portuguese and Galician fisherman's *bacalão*, had long been a staple of the English diet. Cod was plentiful. It is 80 per cent protein, easily salted and dried. It had been commonly caught in the North Sea and in the Bay of Biscay, but by the mid-fifteenth century colder sea temperatures sent both fish and fisherman west and farther offshore. By 1500 cod fishing on the Newfoundland Banks had become a major industry. By 1550 more than 2,000 Basque were there. English doggers with crews of some ten men would sail in February against current and wind to the warmer waters of Iceland and the Newfoundland Banks. They would reach the Banks, fish all summer, then return to England in October and November to sell a cargo of some 30 tons. As for herring, the other staple of the English fishmonger's stall, in 1588 historian William Camden found that thanks to the colder water, Norwegian herring was now swimming off England's east coast (a steep thermal gradient was at that point located between 50 and 65° N). The fish, then, was more than the early Christian symbol of faith, for it sustained both body and soul. When the separatist Pilgrims sailed in *Mayflower* to New England in 1620 they did so to 'serve their God and to fish'. God and cod drove them westward.[6]

Records of wine harvests in Europe show that the continent had a period of warm springs and summers from 1520 to 1560, but before and after those years, summers were colder and wetter.[7] On the high seas, cyclones grew stronger during the sixteenth and seventeenth centuries. Particularly severe was the gale of 11–12 November 1570 that brought on the famous All Saints Flood (the *Allerheiligenvloed*), the worst flood in Dutch history. It inundated five-sixths of Holland and drowned more than two thousand people. Exceptionally high tides and sea levels caused the North Sea coastal water to rise over 4m above normal. In all, there were four particularly severe All Saints Floods in the south end of the North Sea, all in early November: the year 1170 in the Netherlands, 1304 in Pomerania, 1436 in Frisia, and, as noted, 1570 in the Netherlands. Gales persisted throughout the 1580s, with winds of 40 to 60 knots. It was these storms that destroyed much of the Spanish Armada off the west coast of Ireland in late summer–early autumn 1588.

After 1590, mariners experienced an increase of eight times more full gales in winter than in summer. Rough seas occurred every four days, and gale-force winds were common from May to September. North Atlantic Oscillations

(NAO) produced frequent lows (barometric low pressure systems). The sailor also faced anticyclones (high pressure systems) both in the Atlantic and the North Sea. In Europe the summers from 1617 to 1650 were especially cold and harvests were poor. Not surprisingly, malnutrition, hunger and unemployment fomented social unrest, sending landsmen out onto an indifferent and cruel sea. Storms increased 85 per cent in the second half of the sixteenth century, most occcuring in winter. Severe storms rose 400 per cent.

A Tropical Rutter

Early transoceanic navigation coincided with this stormy period. Such rough conditions at sea tested the skill of the best navigators, who at best worked with few tools. The English navigator had tide tables for local waters, a compass, sounding leads, hour and minute glasses, an astrolabe or cross-staff or later a back-staff, a chip log and a traverse board. With these he could figure latitude (but not yet longitude) reasonably accurately and could safely get from England to the tropics and back.[8]

How did the mariners do it? The captain had a rough idea of the months to make transatlantic passages, the times of severe storms, the position of the Doldrums at different seasons, the prevailing winds and currents both offshore and coastal, and some limited information on ports, rivers, bays and gulfs across the ocean. For the rest, he would often kidnap a Portuguese or Spanish pilot and steal his charts and instruments.

By contrast, a modern mariner piloting a coastline or navigating offshore has volumes of information in both digital and hard copy to aid him. In the United Kingdom and the United States, for example, the governments provide charts, pilot charts or atlases for the world's oceans five regions, and for each region, twelve pilot charts, one for each month. Each chart has a synopsis, and for each month gives averages of wind directions and forces, currents, air and sea temperatures, wave heights, ice limits, visibility, barometric pressure and other weather conditions. The mariner also has sailing directions for use en route that give coastal and port-approach information subdivided into sectors or regions, with information on coastal weather, currents, ice, dangers, features and ports. He also has light lists and notices that update charts and other publications.[9] As logbooks and charts of the period have not survived, data for this book must come largely from journals and depositions by mariners using a few instruments and tables.

An early rutter, like today's pilot atlas, was organised geographically. Here, the geographies under consideration are the North and South Atlantic, Caribbean (including the Gulf of Mexico), the Strait of Magellan and the east coasts of the South and North Pacific. The rutter provides a synopsis of tropical weather and gives examples of weather encountered on early voyages. The ordering follows a transatlantic voyage: south from England to the northeast Trade Winds, west on the Trades to the Caribbean, around the west of Cuba, east in the Gulf to Florida, north then north-east to Bermuda or Newfoundland, and back to England by catching the west-southwesterly winds and currents of the gyre generated by the Icelandic Low and the Azores High. Or if the voyage is to the Pacific via the Strait of Magellan, the course is from England south to the Cabo Verdes, west then south across the Doldrums, south-south-west down the coast of South America to the Strait, and return (either back eastward or across the Pacific westward). Illustrations of pilot atlas charts show the routes found in the text below.

North Atlantic Ocean, Caribbean Sea (and Gulf of Mexico)

Given these general conditions, the early seventeenth-century galleon captain would normally leave England for the Canaries or the Cabo Verdes in November to catch the constant northeasterly Trade Winds to cross the Atlantic. Once in the Caribbean, the weather remains dominated by the northeast Trades, and the mariner would find stable conditions except during hurricane season, June to November. Then as now, though, there can be hurricanes as early as May and as late as December.

The worst months for storms are from August to October, with twelve over Force 8 (F8) (a gale, over 34 knots or 40mph), during this period, of which half become hurricanes. September is the cruelest month, with 4.5 storms, of which half become hurricanes. In the Caribbean, east winds prevail, with the strongest winds from December to May, when chances of storm are slight. Summer and autumn are rainy and stormy, with high temperatures and humidity. Weather in the Gulf of Mexico, although it is often in the path of hurricanes spawned in the Caribbean, is driven mainly by continental North American weather. It is not strongly affected by the northeast Trades, but by the continental land mass that generates Northers, strong gales of F7–9, 28–47 knots (32–54mph), in winter, and cyclones from June to November.[10]

To make a North Atlantic passage westward, the English galleon's captain would sail south in November (when the Trades are fully developed) to about 15° N, the Canaries, or to 28° N, a point some 150 miles north-west off the Cabo Verdes. He needed to gain the northeast Trade Winds and the westerly current to drive his ship across the ocean. The northern limit of the Trades in winter is about 25° N.[11]

Once across the Atlantic and in the Caribbean intending for gold and silver in Panamá, the galleon will continue westward along the Spanish Main, carried along in the Guiana Current (0.75–1.5 knots setting west or west-north-west, somewhat stronger in winter and spring). She will stay with the northeast Trades, most constant in winter, light and variable in March, and from August to October. They are strongest within 150 miles of the north-west Colombian coast from January to March, in part because of the coastal mountains, an area where gales and hurricanes are rare, though squalls are common near land.

In the south-west corner of the Caribbean the northeast Trades and the westerly currents meet the land mass of Panamá. The winds continue easterly, but the current swirls in an opposing anticlockwise gyre, making for wind against current and large-scale circular eddies of both current and wind in some places. Such conditions continue up the eastern coast of Central America, where the winds are typically east-north-east F4, and the current is west-north-west at 0.5–1.0 knots. The current sets north-north-east from the Gulf of Honduras to the Yucatán Channel at a rate of 1.5–2 knots. The axis of the strongest current flows 35 miles off the Yucatán coast. The humid rainy season from May to December produces frequent thunderstorms.

A current in the north Caribbean sets west at 0.5 to 1.0 knot from west of Jamaica to the Gulf of Mexico, where it increases to 3 knots. There are easterly variable counter-currents of 0.75 knots in the bight of south-west Cuba, just as there are from Cartagena to Panamá. Counter-currents also occur off the western half of Hispaniola, and on the north side of the island the set of current in the Windward Passage, where the current is south-west, 0.75 to 2 knots. The closer currents are to the coast, the more they are affected by tides. The early mariners knew little of this from books, though they did observe and noted the details in their accounts, something which was to serve mariners in later centuries.

South Atlantic, Strait of Magellan, E. South Pacific

If sailing from Europe to the South Atlantic or Pacific via Cape Horn, the mariner must consider when and where to cross the Doldrums, or the Intertropical Convergence Zone (ITCZ). Once his galleon has reached the Cabo Verdes at 15 ° N, and if bound southwards in December or January, the best longitude to turn south is at 29° W Long., and if in August, farther east at 23° W. Between these months, he will cross somewhere between those longitudes (likely figured by dead reckoning). The winds in the ITCZ vary with the season and the band's position. North of it the Trades are east-northeast and average F3, and south, east or southeasterlies F3–5. In the South Atlantic, gales are infrequent, though squalls do occur along the coast, mostly between April and September south of 5° S Lat. The best time to go south along the Brazilian coast is during summer, that is, from October to February, when a broad reach puts the northeast winds off the stern quarter.[12]

Observations from the Deck

'Blow, winds, and crack your cheeks! rage! blow!' So Shakespeare wrote in *King Lear*, 1605–06, in the middle of the stormy decades raging out in the North Atlantic. What was the weather as seen from an Elizabethan galleon's deck? Was there 'occular proof', as another of his characters would insist, recorded in the journals of the time?

Not all winds were foul. More often than not, the Trade Winds co-operated in a passage, as they did for Drake in his 1572–73 Caribbean voyage. On Whitsunday Eve, 24 May 1572, Drake in the *Pascha* and *Swan* sailed from Plymouth for Nombre de Dios in Panamá. The winds were northeast, and in the standard expression of the age, they were 'prosperous and favorable'. The passage was fast, 'without any alteration or change', writes Drake. On 3 June he reached Porto Santo, in the Madeiras, and within twelve days, the Canaries. Once in the Trades, he reports, 'we never struck sail, nor came to anchor, nor made any stay for any cause, neither there nor else where, until 25. days after, when we had sight of the island of Guadeloupe [28 June], one of the islands of the West Indies, goodly high land'.[13] Typically, the journals record any storms encountered. (See the pilot atlas illustrations for the major storms encountered during the period.)

Doldrums, Hurricanes, Currents, Rivers

Sir John Hawkyns faced contrary winds and storms on his second slaving voyage, 1564–65, to Sierra Leone and the West Indies. Leaving Sierra Leone in Africa for the West Indies in late January, Hawkyns first had to sail through the ITCZ. In January it ranges in a 4–5° band from 7 to 3° N off the Ivory Coast south-westerly to 2 to 3° S off the mouth of the Rio Amazonas. Once reaching the Doldrums, Hawkyns lost the steady following winds. 'For the space of eighteen days,' writes Hawkyns' author John Sparke, 'we were becalmed, having now and then contrary winds, and some tornadoes, amongst the same calm, which happened to us very ill', and many feared never reaching the Indies, but the 'the Almighty God, who never suffereth his elect to perish, sent us the sixteenth of February, the ordinary breeze, which is the northwest wind [read northeast], which never left us, till we came to an island of the cannibals, called Dominica, where we arrived the ninth of March, upon a Saturday'.[14]

Hawkyns sold his slaves along the Spanish Main, and on 31 May sailed north for Hispaniola, for more hides, and then home. He was soon set westward by the Caribbean Current. Here may be the first mention by an English mariner of that current. Sparke writes:

> The fourth of June we had sight of an island, which we made to be Jamaica, marvelling that by the vehement course of the seas we should be driven so far to leeward: for setting our course to the west end of Hispaniola we fell with the middle of Jamaica [an error of at least 2°, 120 miles or more], notwithstanding that to all men's sight it showed a headland, but they were all deceived by the clouds that lay upon the land two days together, in such sort that we thought it to be the headland of the said island.

Hawkyns' ships could not go to weather well, and so he was unable to come about and beat back to fill the rest of his hold with hides. Profit was lost.

Later on that same voyage, leaving the Spanish Main and sailing north Hawkyns felt the strength of the Florida Current and the Gulf Stream. His was the first known English notice of those currents. John Sparke writes:

> The twelfth day [of July 1565] in the morning we fell in with the islands upon the cape of Florida, which we could scant double by the means that fearing the shoals to the eastwards, and doubting the current coming out of the west, which was not of that force we made account of; for we felt little or none till we fell in with the cape, and then felt such a current [6.5 knots at Fowey Pt.], that bearing all sails against the same, yet were driven back again a great pace.

The ships' boats were off watering when night came on, and the sailors lost sight of the fleet:

> When they departed, the ships were in no current; and sailing but a mile further, they found one so strong, that bearing all sails, it could not prevail against the same … whereupon the captain sent the *Salomon*, with the other two barks, to bear near the shore all night, because the current was less there a great deal, and to bear light, with shooting off a piece now and then, to the intent the boats might better know how to come to them.

In time the boats rejoined the fleet, and the fleet could continue eastward.[15]

Captain Edmund Barker writes in his 1594 account of the voyage of the *Penelope*, the *Merchant Royal*, and the *Edward Bonaventure* about the strong currents in the Golfo de Paria, between the River Orinoco and the island of Trinidad. Barker had heard that Chidley's ship had had refreshment at Trinidad, and, writes Barker's author, the captain:

> directed his course to that island, and not knowing the currents, we were put past it in the night into the gulf of Paria in the beginning of June, wherein we were 8 days, finding the current continually setting in, and ofentimes we were in 3 fathoms water [a seagoing ship of that time might well draw 16ft], and could find no going out until the current had put us over to the western side under the main land, where we found no current at all, and more deep water; and so keeping by the shore, the wind off the shore every night did help us out to the northward.

Many a ship has been caught in the currents of the Golfo de Paria. With the aid of offshore winds and slack currents Barker was barely able to escape the gulf.[16]

By the early 1500s, European sailors had been recording ocean currents and tides. These they understood in terms of the zodiac. In 1516, a French pilot had passed on to Sir John Yorke his observations on currents in the South Atlantic:

> Whensoever the sun is any of these signs he governeth the tides as followeth. The sun being in Taurus, Gemini, Cancer, the tide hath his course northwest. The sun being in Leo, Virgo, Libra, no current. The sun being in Scorpio, Sagittarius, Capricorne, the tide hath his course south-east. The sun being in Aquarius, Pisces, Aries, no current.[17]

As for voyages for the Strait of Magellan (and similar attempts to seek the Orient via the Northwest or Northeast passages), contrary weather in the high southern latitudes was a constant factor. Portuguese captain and pilot Lopez Vaz writes: 'The seeking of these Straits of Magellan is so dangerous, and the voyage so troublesome, that it seemeth a matter almost impossible to be performed, insomuch that for the space of thirty years no man made account thereof; until of late one

Francis Drake an Englishman' did so. Drake was lucky. He transited the Strait in a quick twelve days. Once through, though, a fierce storm battered him on 8 October 1578, separating his fleet. He had started with six vessels. At this point he was left to carry on around the world alone in the *Pelican* (now renamed the *Golden Hinde*).

On sailing north along the coast of Chile and Perú in 1579 during what was to be his circumnavigation, Drake benefited from Perú's Humboldt Current (Perú Current) and southerly winds. This was reason enough for Drake not to sail back through the Strait eastward for England. Another was that the Spanish were laying in wait for him at the Strait. From 16 April to 3 June Drake sailed northwards. Once off North America, he bucked the wind and current of the south-flowing Japanese Current. In search of the western end of the Northwest Passage, his crew complained on reaching 43° N (near today's southern Oregon) that it was too cold to continue. He turned back and landed in June 1579 at 38° N Lat., in Alta California (near present-day San Francisco), which he claimed for England, naming it Nova Albion. Drake chose to return to England by carrying on westward across the Pacific, following the route of the Spanish Manila galleons, favouring the Trade Winds of the North Pacific Circulation. In his hold lay a fortune, and on his return to England, the riches carried in that one galleon bought Drake a knighthood.[18]

The power of American rivers was far beyond what Europeans had known. In 1518 Spaniard Martin Fernandez de Enciza, writing on tropical riverine flow, observes that:

> From this river Marannon [the upper reaches of the Rio Amazonas], unto the river which is called the sea of fresh water, are 25 leagues; the river hath 40 leagues of breadth at the mouth, and carrieth such abundance of water that it entereth more than 20 leagues into the sea, and mingleth not it self with the salt water.[19]

So powerful was that current that ships could refill their fresh water casks at sea, well off the coast.

Merchant Robert Tomson provides what is likely the first extensive description in English of a North American tropical storm, one that included St Elmo's Fire. In the Gulf of Mexico, January 1556, a month supposedly free of storms, the Spanish fleet in which he was sailing was hit by a Norther. His ship sank, and seventy-five men drowned. During the storm Tomson writes that at night he saw St Elmo's Fire, *Cuerpo Santo*, on the top of the main yard and mainmast, where it flew from mast to mast for three hours. The light, explains Tomson, 'was but a congelation of the wind and vapours of the sea congealed with the extremity of the weather, which flying in the wind, many times doth chance to hit on the masts and shrouds of the ships that are at sea in foul weather'.[20]

The voyage of James Langton, the well-respected general commander for Sir George Clifford, third Earl of Cumberland on the Earl's seventh voyage,

1593-94, called at Hispaniola's Cabo Tiburón at the island's south-west point, and, as author Richard Robinson writes:

> from thence they went to the Bay of St Nicholas … thinking to have ridden there some time for fear of the hirrocano [hurricane]: which hirrocano is a violent strong wind, and though it come not every year, yet when doeth come is most commonly in November and December and is so furious that no ship is able to resist the violence therof unless in very good harbours.[21]

The appendix on tropical climate and weather considers how to survive such Caribbean hurricanes.

Hawkyns' 'third troublesome voyage', 1567–68, shows the power of a hurricane.[22] Hawkyns left Plymouth on 2 October 1567 with six vessels in fair weather, to trade slaves, as before. Four were his vessels, two were the Crown's. En route to Africa he was soon battered by a storm off Cabo Finistere. He loaded slaves, sailed to the Spanish Main, where he sold his slaves. He left Cartagena in July 1568, hoping 'to have escaped the time of their storms which then soon after began to reign, the which they call Furicanos'. He was correct: August and September have nearly twice the number of cyclones and hurricanes than all the other months combined. On 12 August in the Gulf of Mexico he was hit by an 'extreme storm', no doubt an August hurricane. For four days it battered the fleet including the royal *Jesus of Lubeck*, his 700-ton admiral:

> We cut down all her higher buildings, her rudder also was sore shaken, and withall was in so extreme a leak that we were rather upon the point to leave her then to keep her any longer, yet hoping to bring all to good pass, we sought the coast of Florida [Mexico], where we found no place nor haven for our ships, because of the shallowness of the coast: thus being in greater despair, and taken with a new storm which continued other 3 days.

Hawkyns took refuge in San Juan de Ulúa, then the Gulf port for the Viceroyalty of Mexico. A Spanish fleet carrying the new viceroy and with orders to hunt down and capture Hawkyns had also been battered by the same tempest. The Spanish fleet entered the harbour a few days after the English, on 17 September. Antonio Delgadillo, captain and inspector for the island, writes that 'it was winter and the season for north winds' (read late summer, the height of hurricane season).[23] The Spanish soon attacked. Hawkyns and Drake fought their way free with just two ships, Hawkyns' *Judith* and the royal *Minion*. Four other ships, including the *Jesus of Lubeck*, their cargoes and cannon were abandoned to the Spanish.

Diurnal winds saved the English. Drake had already escaped in the small 50-ton bark *Judith*. Hawkyns observed that Drake 'the same night forsook us in our great misery'. Hawkyns in the *Minion* moved two bowshots length from the Spanish and rode there throughout the night. On the offshore breeze before dawn, he was able to reach an island a mile from the Spaniards, likely the northerly island off the mainland. But Hawkyns found himself on a lee shore. There 'took us a north wind, and being left only with two anchors and two cables (for in this conflict we lost three cables and two anchors) we thought always upon death which ever was present'.[24] One of Hawkyns' sailors, Job Hortop, writes:

> At night when the wind came off the shore, we set sail, and went out in despite of the Spaniards and their shot, where we anchored, with two anchors under the island, the wind being northerly, which was wonderful dangerous, and we feared every hour to be driven with the lee shore. In the end when the wind came larger [no longer hard on the wind, but full and by, a reach], we weighed anchor, and set sail.

The northerly wind (likely the left or back side of what remained of the hurricane) saved the English from pursuit, for after midnight the wind had shifted to the north and the Spanish could not follow, according to a deposition by the new viceroy of Nueva España, Martín Enríquez de Amanza. One of the officials, Francisco de Bustamente, confirmed that on the night that the English ships withdrew outside the harbour, 'the wind shifted to north and the north wind blew Friday and Saturday following', keeping the Spanish from pursuing the English. At last, writes Hawkyns, 'the weather waxed reasonable, and the Saturday we set sail, and having a great number of men and little victuals our hope of life waxed less and less'.[25]

The survivors were now free from the Spanish but not from storms. On 8 October Hawkyns' *Minion* was off Tamaulipas, at 23° 30' N (just south of the current Texas–Mexico border, state of Taumalipas) when he was hit by yet another hurricane or a severe storm while filling water casks ashore. It was 'an extreme storm, so that in three days we could by no means repair aboard our ship: the ship also was in such peril that every hour we looked for shipwreck'. Along that coastline they could find no navigable cuts through the barrier islands to the protection of a sheltered sound. Finally, on 16 October, Hawkyns had 'fair and prosperous weather', and after a month entered the Atlantic Ocean.

But once there, more foul weather followed. 'The wind being always ill for us to recover England, we determined to go with Galicia in Spain, with intent there to relieve our company and other extreme wants'. Hawkyns reached Ponte Vedra, north of Vigo, on 31 December. When the ship reached Mounts Bay, Cornwall, on 25 January 1569, his men were weak and feeble.[26] Drake, in Hawkyns' smaller but faster *Judith*, had already arrived home a month earlier. Hawkyns concludes his account: 'If all the miseries and troublesome affairs of this sorrowful voyage should be perfectly and thoroughly written, there should need a painful man with his pen, and as great a time as he had that wrote the lives and deaths of the martyrs'. The year 1586 was a stormy one on the Atlantic, in the Caribbean and in the Gulf.

Mariner Sir Walter Ralegh had weathered stormy Elizabethan politics long before 1592, the year he secretly married a pregnant Elizabeth Throckmorton, one of the queen's ladies-in-waiting. When they were discovered, both were locked away in the Tower. Later, on James Stuart's accession in 1603, Ralegh was alleged to be part of the Main Plot, convicted of treason, and once again was sent to the Tower. On release under parole in 1616, he sought redemption in the sea and his tropical colony, Guiana. There he hoped to find enough gold to buy the favour of the king. In summer 1617 – the start of very cold summers in Europe that lasted until 1650 – he set out for the Caribbean. Ralegh kept a meticulous journal of his outbound passage on what was his second transatlantic voyage, 1617–18. Leaving Cork (after an earlier start from Plymouth on 19 August, the winds were prosperous, but reaching the Canaries, 28 degrees 57 minutes north, he was hit by what he calls a 'hurricano' (it was at least a severe storm, as though it was hurricane season, it would be rare for one to be found so far east). He reached the island of Bravo in the Cabo Verdes, 14° 48' N, 24° 44' W, on 1 October. There he experienced a 'tornado'. Once in the Trades he set his course westward towards Guiana. His fleet of thirteen was set by contrary currents flowing a half point west of south-west by west. Ralegh, writes an early editor, Robert Schomburgk, had encountered 'the great current from the north-west [which] changes immediately after passing the Cape Verde Islands; it becomes first southerly and sets afterwards to the west'.[27]

In October, the Doldrums' northern limit is at about 13° N Lat. off Senegal and Guinea and lies in a 3° band westward to 5 to 2° N between the Rio Amazonas and Guiana. Ralegh likely had sailed into the Doldrums, for on 8 October at 11° 39' N (his latitudes were frequently in error about 4° high), the day had started calm, then turned to rain and gusts, followed two days later by a dark sky with the makings of a squall. Light, variable winds were followed by a small gale from the north-north-west, and then calms, rain, and a morning rainbow. Even in this area, generally clear of hurricanes, the weather between August and October is nevertheless still unsettled. On 17 October the wind blew 'horrible with violent rain'. Ralegh lay ahull. The wind, he writes, 'doth continue this Saturday morning and [I] think that since the Indies were discovered never was the like wind found in this height, which we guess to be about 9 deg.: for we could not observe since Monday last'. He writes that on 12 October the *Destiny* was 'in miserable estate not having in our ship above 7 days water, 60 sick men and nearly 400 leagues [1,200 miles] off the shore, and becalmed'. The day of 13 October was dark. The next one blew a fresh gale. It was that day that Ralegh saw the first of many rainbows in the midst of rain and winds from the south of east, south-east, and south-south-east. Rainbows to Ralegh, as any seaman knows, are not signs of good fortune but harbingers of foul weather.

The passage was extremely hot, calm, with rain, occasional gusts, waterspouts and more rainbows. One night he saw 'Magellan's Cloud round and white which riseth and setteth with the stars'. Magellan's Cloud is a cluster of small galaxies visible in the Southern Hemisphere.[28] On 24 October, at 7° 20' N, Ralegh was concerned that his water casks were again nearly empty. But that afternoon a gale with violent winds brought some water. On 28 October, at 7° N, 48.5' W, Ralegh notes compass variation of 3° (whether east or west he does not say, but it was likely east). On 29 October the wind was large (off the beam) and light. Ralegh's position was 6° N, on course for Guiana. That morning he saw a double rainbow, and the evening of that day there was rain and wind, thunder, lightning, then calm. That night, there was a circle around the moon; bad omens all.

Two days later, 11 November, Ralegh made his landfall near the Cape of Wiapoco (Cape Orange and the Rio Oiapoque, Brazil's border with French Guiana). He had made his passage near the end of the hurricane season outside their typical track. Conditions should have been better. His passage would normally have been fast, but for the Doldrums. Caught there, his crossing was fraught day after day of light variable winds or severe storms. From the deck of the *Destiny* Ralegh could see but could never reach the end of his rainbows.[29] The day before the *Destiny* anchored at Punto de Gallo, Trinidad, Ralegh wrote in his journal that on 16 November alone he had seen fifteen rainbows, including one that was a perfect circle (the bottom part in such a rainbow is formed by the sea spray), and two wind galls (secondary, broken rainbows). All were omens signalling an ill-fated voyage. On his return to England he brought back no chests of bullion, only 'a Guiana idol of gold and copper' and a few samples of gold and silver. As a mariner, Ralegh well understood the meteorology of the rainbow, but had hoped desperately to the end for the luck of the Irish, that at least one rainbow might lead him to a pot of gold.

Notes

1 Brian Fagan, *The Little Ice Age: How Climate Made History, 1300–1850* (New York: Basic Books, Perseus Books Group, 2000), 47–97. Abbr. *LI*. Fagan's study has provided valuable scientific and historical data for this chapter.

2 *LI*, 96–7.

3 *LI*, 103.

4 *LI*, 96–7.

5 *LI*, 104.

6 *LI*, 78.

7 *LI*, 151–5.

8 A narrative of these voyages is found in the author's *Tropics Bound: Elizabethan Seadogs on the Spanish Main* (Stroud: The History Press, 2010). Abbr. *TB*.

9 If today a mariner is sailing to the American Tropics from England, he might consult the volumes (UK or US) for the west coast of Europe and northwest Africa (US pub. 143), the pilot atlases and sailing directions of the North Atlantic Ocean (including the Gulf of Mexico) (pub. 186), the Caribbean Sea, vols. 1 and 2 (pubs. 147, 148), the east coast of South America (pub. 124), and the west coast of South America (pub. 125) The US Government recently announced that it would no longer print charts, but only offer electronic ones. In the United Kingdom the mariner will find information at www. ukho.gov.uk, and at the United Kingdom Hydrographic Office, Admiralty Way, Taunton 2A1 2DN. In the United States, he might check online at www.msi.nga.mil/ and the National Geospatial-Intelligence Agency, 4600 Sagamore Road, Bethesda, MD 20816. Non-governmental commercial companies such as Imray, Adlard Coles, Hughes, Reed, RYA, and similar US firms also provide similar information in the form of paper and electronic charts, chart plotters, cruising guides, almanacs, and more.

10 James Clarke, *Atlantic Pilot Atlas, Including the Caribbean & Mediterranean* 4th edn (London: Adlard Coles Nautical, 2006) 44–67. Abbr. *AP*.

11 *AP*, 36.

12 *AP*, 32–42.

13 *DE*, 74.

14 *PN*, 10:9–63.

15 *PN*, 10:9–63.

16 *EP*, 287–91; *PN*, 6:403–7.

17 *PN*, 11:72–3.

18 *TB*, 70–1.

19 *PN*, 11:19–22.

20 *PN*, 9:338–58.

21 *EP*, 236–83, an edited version of Purchas' condensed version of Richard Robinson's account of the voyage, printed in *PP*.

22 *PN*, 10:64–74.

23 *SD*, 131–52.

24 *PN*, 10:72–3.

25 *SD*, 131–52; *PN*, 10:73.

26 *PN*, 10: 64–74; *TB*, 36–42.

27 *DG*, 189–90.

28 Schomburgk writes about the latitude of the Doldrums, the 'Rains' with its calms, rains, thunder, lightning, waterspouts, which in August can reach 15° N: 'Although Ralegh gives us no intimation of his longitude [latitude?], we doubt not from his description that he was engulphed in that zone'. *DG*, 194–5.

29 What of Ralegh's rainbows? Rainbows are not objects, and cannot be reached. They are chimeriae, unattainable. They cannot be measured as being located at any specific distance from the viewer, as they are in fact water droplets seen in relation to the sun's rays (generally 42° from the direction opposite the sun). The sun, at a low altitude and shining behind the droplets, mist or rain, produces the rainbow first by refraction, then reflection, then refraction. The light breaks up into different wavelengths of colour. The Judeo-Christian belief is that a rainbow appeared after the Flood, and that it signified that God would not destroy the world, a good sign. Aristotle, in the third century BC, wrote the first scientific treatise on the qualities of the rainbow. Issac Newton in 1672 identified the rainbow's five primary colours, which he soon expanded to seven. The human eye finds in the rainbow a spectrum in bands ranging from red, to orange, yellow, green, blue, indigo and violet. Irish legend – Ralegh's fleet, after poor weather, finally disembogued on this last voyage from the Irish port of Cork – has it that a pot of gold is at the end of a rainbow, guarded by a shoemaker leprechaun, a fancy dresser in a red suit, sometimes wearing an Elizabethan ruff and cuff frills of lace (not unlike the fastidious dresser Ralegh, who in happier days had owned a 40,000-acre estate near Cork). *DG*, passim.

4

Stars for Wandering Barks

'the star to every wandering bark,
Whose worth's unknown, although his height be taken.'
William Shakespeare, Sonnet 116 *(1609)*

In 1603, Captain Bartholomew Gilbert sailed on 10 May in the 50-ton bark *Elizabeth* from Plymouth for Virginia. On 26 May he was at 32° N, expecting the island of Madeira, 32–33° N Lat. But somehow he missed it, and on 1 June, simply 'haled over to the West Indies'. Fifteen days later he saw land, and announced that he had fetched the Bermudas (about 32° 20' N Lat.) He was, in fact, at St Lucia, 13° 15' N Lat., an error of some 17°, more than 1,000 miles off course, an example of what D.W. Waters calls 'courageous ignorance'. This was error, a gross one in measuring his height or altitude.[1] Fortunately, most navigators were more accurate than Gilbert.

What went into fixing a position at sea? What was navigation to the Elizabethans and Jacobeans? The era encompasses an extraordinary merging of science and sea from late medieval to early modern times. At the start, thirteenth-century Italian portolan charts (Ital. *portolano*, regarding ports) provided distances and bearings to Mediterranean ports. Early northern European rutters used kennings – that is, sailing from one headland to the next (Anglo-Saxon *cennan*, to recognise by sight), noting significant landmarks. With tide tables to show rise and fall, ebb and flow, and the speed and direction of tidal currents the seaman could make his way along a coastline. But from the end of the fifteenth century, when sailing went offshore, the seaman needed the skills of navigation as well as those of coastal piloting. What follows is organised into two parts: the first treats the technical aspects and instruments of navigation, and the second, the process of bringing to England the Continental sciences of fixing a position at sea by means of celestial navigation and by calculating the interaction of time, speed, distance and direction.

Mariners had long used dead reckoning (deduced reckoning) – solving for time, speed or distance when knowing two of the three elements. For distance, they figured from the time travelled and from the speed. Time was counted with hour-glasses and minute glasses, and speed by streaming a chip log from the stern on a knotted line for a set period of time. Direction was figured with the compass, the ancient Chinese invention in use in Europe since the twelfth century. Before the mid-sixteenth century mariners helped their calculations by using a circular traverse board. This board marked out the thirty-two compass points around its circumference, and had holes radiating from the centre with pegs to record time sailed on a specific heading. Latitude was figured by measuring the height or alti-tude of the sun or stars at a given time each day. For this, the mariners could use the Arabic kamal or the European astrolabe, then later, the Portuguese cross-staff, later modified by the English to a back-staff. Accurate calculation of longitude was to come well after the Tudors and Stuarts.

The second half of the discussion below takes up the Englishing of the Continental science of navigation: translating texts, correcting them, writing original ones, then joining mathematics and navigation. The discovery of loga-rithms brought the invention of the slide rule, a significant advance that naviga-tion offshore easier and more accurate.

Fixing a Position at Sea

Piloting and Navigation

Dr John Dee, the great Elizabethan mathematician, defined navigation in 1570 as the art by which 'the shortest good way, by the aptest direction, & in the shortest time, a sufficient ship, between any two places (in passage navigable) assigned: may be conducted: and in all storms, & natural disturbances chancing, how, to use the best possible means, whereby to recover the place first assigned'.[2] Prolix to be sure, but still accurate. Piloting is conventionally thought of as a matter of headlands, depths and currents along coasts. Navigation is done offshore, out of sight of land, where fixing a position uses the stars, sun, moon and time. Both can use dead reckoning (as noted, finding of a position by advancing from a known position to a new one by figuring course steered and distance run by employing the elements of time, speed, direction and distance).

The Renaissance's development of offshore or celestial navigation began with zodiacs, astrolabes and tide tables. Additionally, writes Dee, the master pilot must know hydrography, astronomy, astrology and horometry (chronometry) and their common bases, arithmetic and geometry. To aid him in establishing position far out to sea, the mariner measures the altitude or height of the sun, moon or stars by means of a quadrant, an astonomer's ring, staff or astrolabe, then consults tables to calculate the position of planets for any given hour of any day. To fix his position on the map, he uses a hydrographical globe and hydrographical charts (with true, not parallel, meridians). To determine direction, he employs a set of compasses: a common sea compass, a compass with variation and proportional and paradoxal compasses.

Coastal Sailing

Any voyage, any offshore navigation, begins and ends with coastal piloting. The pilot consulted a rutter (Port., *roteiros*; Fr., *routiers*), the sailing directions for both coastal and offshore that included prominent landmarks, elevations and harbour plans to aid in fixing a position, and other information once offshore. Rutters were first circulated as manuscripts, then later were printed as books. The best of these Continental texts were translated into English. The Elizabethan reader wanted the details about the new American Tropics, and Hakluyt's *Principal Navigations* supplied them. One example is a chapter on the currents of the River Amazon and the West Indies, rivers that might lead to the gold of El Dorado. Such is *A short description of the river of Marannon or Amazones*, 1518, by Martin Fernandez de Enciza.

Enciza writes that the Amazonas is 'a great river, and hath more then fifteen leagues in breadth eight leagues within the land. It hath many islands, and in this river within the land forty leagues there is near to the said river a mountain' which has a grove of incense trees. As for the coastline near its mouth, 'from the Cape of S. Augustine unto Marannon [Rio Maranhão] is a clear coast & deep, but near to the river are certain shoals towards the east part. And by the west part the river is deep, and it hath a good entry'. The author decribes the flow of the Amazon far into the sea:

> From this river Marannon, unto the river which is called the sea of fresh water, are 25 leagues; the river hath 40 leagues of breadth at the mouth, and carrieth such abundance of water that it entereth more than 20 leagues into the Sea, and mingleth not it self with the salt water; this breadth goeth 25 leagues within the land, and after it is divided into parts, the one going towards the southeast, and the other towards the southwest. That which goeth towards the southeast is very deep and of much water, and hath a channel half a league of breadth, that a carrack may go up through it; & the tides be so swift, that the ships have need of good cables. The river of this port is very good, and there have been some that have entered 50 leagues within it, & have seen no mountains.[3]

Here was a river far greater than the Thames or the Severn, or anything the Continent had.

Fixing a position in coastal waters can be done by measuring the sea bottom's depth and identifying its nature. To find depths, the mariner had long and short lead-lines armed with tallow to identify the nature of the bottom. In shoal waters of less than 20 fathoms the sailor used a shorter and thicker line, with the lead's cavity armed with tallow to pick up bits of sand, rock or mud from the ocean floor. A pilot with local knowledge counted the knots, felt the grit, smelled the bottom mud. From the lead line he could determine his location with remarkable accuracy. He sailed short coastal routes in small clinker-built vessels under 100 tons, running from cape to cape in kennings of 20 miles (14 miles in Scotland, where visibility was often more limited), finding his way by means of seabeds, shoals, currents and tides. This was the time-tested way to sail close to shore.

Offshore, the pilot used the long line or deep-sea (dipsie) lead and line was used to sound to 100 fathoms, as when coming off the North Atlantic onto the continental shelf at the Western Approaches to the English Channel. Off soundings, beyond 100 fathoms, the lead line was put away.

Tides

Along coastlines, the rise and fall of tides (following a sine wave curve) affect the depth, the direction and force of tidal flow. Given Britain's great range of tides, such tables showing the heights of tides and tidal flow of particular places throughout the day, month and year are of particular value. Tides were then and still are essential knowledge. Not surprising, tide tables were the first nautical observations compiled and printed. The earliest known example is those compiled by the monks of St Albans in the thirteenth century. These were first printed in England around 1540, a century after the invention of moveable type. So much are the tides to English life that they are proverbial. Both sailor and landsman well understood that 'tide and time tarry for no man'. Shakespeare's Brutus in *Julius Caesar*, 1599, urges Cassius to join him against Octavius and Antony, for 'there is a tide in the affairs of men, which, taken at the flood, leads on to fortune'.

Tidal currents, essential for safe coastal sailing, are less relevant offshore, though there are ocean currents that affect navigation. These and winds are the essentials offshore. Hakluyt includes a note on currents in the South Atlantic written, he says, sometime early in the sixteenth century, about the time the English started navigating offshore. The author is a French pilot who links currents to the zodiac, as was then commonly done. In 'A special note concerning the currents of the sea between the Cape of Buena Esperanza and the coast of Brasilia', we learn that the information had been given by the pilot to 'Sir John Yorke knight, before Sebastian Cabote; which pilot had frequented the coasts of Brasilia eighteen voyages'. The French pilot writes that in this part of the South Atlantic, 'the sun hath the like dominion over the tides there, as the moon hath over our tides here', an early hypothesis. He further finds that it is the zodiac that determines tidal flow:

> Whensoever the sun is any of these signs he governeth the tides as followeth. The sun being in Taurus, Gemini, Cancer the tide hath his course Northwest. The sun being in Leo, Virgo, Libra, no current. The sun being in Scorpio, Sagittarius, Capricorne, the tide hath his course southeast. The sun being in Aquarius, Pisces, Aries, no current.[4]

Was it unreasonable to think that the zodiac, which was believed to affect human actions, might also affect tides?

The Spanish navigator Martín Fernández de Enciza's (Enciso), *Summa de Geographia*, 1519, is one of the earliest accounts of the New World. The author writes about the tidal currents in the Golfo de Paria, west of Trinidad, which he locates at 6.5° N Lat. (actually 10–11° N Lat.; his latitudes are often low by 4–5°):

And from this fresh water sea unto Paria, the coast lieth west northwest, and it so full of shoals that the ships cannot come near to the land. There are from this river to Paria 250 leagues. In this fresh water sea, the tides do ebb & flow as much as they do in Brittany, and it standeth in 6 degrees and a half. Paria standeth on the other side of the Equinoctial toward the north, in seven degrees: In Paria the sea floweth but little, and from Paria towards the West, the sea doth not flow. It hath in length 25 leagues, and as many in breadth, and standeth in eight degrees, and is inhabited of many people, and is yet not under subjection.[5]

In 1518, when Enciza was writing, Trinidad was still Indian and not yet controlled by Europeans. By the time Hakluyt printed Enciza's account in 1598–1600, Trinidad was most firmly Spanish, and the myth of El Dorado, somewhere nearby, was not yet discounted.

Charts

The chart, the card's horizontal latitude and vertical longitude lines, allow the mariner to fix his position numerically, an ancient system first used by Hipparchus and later by Ptolemy. But it was only in the period of the English long transoceanic voyages that the problem of reconciling a spherical globe to a planar surface required a solution. The hot pursuit of profit in South America demanded reliable navigation. Such was the voyage made in 1527, when two Englishmen in the company of Sebastian Cabot sailed with a Spanish fleet to the Río de la Plata, separating Uruguay from Argentina. As with the Amazon and Orinoco rivers, that could lead to El Dorado, so the River Plate might lead to the wealth of the Incans. This important river, write the Englishmen, is:

> situate in 35 degrees of southerly latitude; together with an exact rutter and description thereof, and of all the main branches, so far as they are navigable with small barks, by which river the Spaniards of late years have frequented an exceeding rich trade to and from Peru, and the mines of Potossi, and also to Chili [Chile], and other places.

The captain intended for the Mollucas (Malukus) by way of the Strait of Magellan but reached only the River Plate, discovered the previous year by Sebastian Cabot. Charts held the secrets to finding wealth. The two Englishmen were 'somewhat learned in cosmography', and had been ordered to bring back:

> certain relation of the situation of the country, and to be expert in the navigation of those seas ... Seeing in those quarters are ships and mariners of that country, and cards [charts] by which they sail, though much unlike ours: that they should procure to have the said cards, and learn how they understand them, and especially to know what navigation they have for those islands [the Moluccas] the sea doth extend without interposition of land to sail from

the north point to the northeast point one thousand seven hundred or one thousand eight hundred leagues, they should come to the new found islands that we [the English] discovered, & so we should be nearer to the said Spicery by almost 200 leagues then the Emperour, or the king of Portugal are.[6]

The Spice Islands were the goal, Spanish charts the means. The great land masses of the New World prevented reaching those rich spiceries. It was such commerce that drove the English to spare no effort to get those 'different' and superior Spanish 'cards' or charts. With them they could steer them around the Americas, seen as impediments to Oriental spices and silks.

In time, the Americas themselves would be seen as a source of wealth. The far-reaching William Hawkyns made voyages to Africa and Brazil in 1530, 1531 and 1532, and likely in other years as well. Perhaps there was no need to reach to the Orient. Africa had pepper, elephant tusks and other exotics, and America had woods, dyes, Brazilian kings and commodities that could be sold back home. His voyages were usually profitable, but not always. In his only known surviving letter, the elder Hawkyns petitioned in 1536 for Crown support to aid his 'poor affairs', despite having made at least three successful passages to Brazil. Reason? Navigation. Though most of his vessels had returned safely, 'albeit by four parts not so well as I suppose it should if one of my pilots had not miscarried by the way'.[7] Profit was lost when navigation went awry.

Time, Distance

Besides charts and tide tables, the navigator needed almanacs or calendars. These are based on the astronomer's highly accurate ephemerides (Gk, *ephémeros*, daily), the calculations of the motions of planets and stars in months, days and hours give the positions of the sun, moon and selected stars. Adapted, they aided in fixing a ship's position at sea. The first English calendar was the popular *The Kalendayr of shyppars*, 1503. Shortly afterwards, the Portuguese bound together in one book the nautical almanac and the manual of navigation. Such was the *Regimento do estrolabio e do quadrante*, 1509. Another was Frenchman Pierre Garcie's *Le routier de la mer*, published 1502–10 (Englished and printed by Robert Copland as *The Rutter of the Sea*, 1528). The first truly original English rutter – not a translation – came nearly fifty years later: William Bourne's *A Regiment for the Sea*, 1574.

Knowing the date, the hour and the minute is primary to celestial navigation. Dee writes that the mariner used a sundial or sandglasses of three-hour, hour, half-hour and half-minute sizes. To keep track of the sands of time flowing during a watch on deck, the pilot used the traverse board's holes and pegs to mark the bearing and time elapsed. First noted in hours, after 1600 the pegs marked each half hour, in one of the eight holes along a spoke marking the thirty-two points of the compass. Eight holes neatly covered a four-hour watch. Once the ship's estimated position was entered in the log, the board was cleared for the next watch. Pilots would then correlate degrees of latitude with miles sailed north or south. The progress would be recorded in the ship's log.

Robert Hues, in *Tractatus de Globis*, 1594, writes of vessels bound south from England for the Cape of Good Hope in terms of sailing a degree a day – that is, 60 miles in twenty-four hours. Using a Portuguese or Spanish traverse table, they would 'raise or lay a degree of latitude' (where distance = difference of latitude/cosine of the course). In the words of one mariner:

> if sailing directly north or south, then each 60 miles equals one degree. If sailing at a different course, then you have to go 60 miles divided by the cosine of the course to cross one degree of latitude: 1/cosine (course) = secant (course). So you have to go 60 miles secant (course) to cross one degree of latitude.[8]

Following the usual land-based practice, the English system first reckoned the nautical mile as 5,000ft, but this measurement, when determined as a function of latitude to be short by a sixth of a mile, was later changed to 6,076ft (one minute of latitude at the earth's centre, also figured at 6,080').

Speed

The log and line, probably an English invention, dates from before the 1570s. It was first noted in print in English in 1623, and was later described by Samuel de Champlain in 1632 in 'Traitté de la Marine', part of his *Les Voyage de la Nouvelle France Occidentale*. Champlain, from a distinguished seafaring family, notes that the log and line were earlier 'used by several good English navigators'.[9] To run freely, the line itself must not be too thick. At its end is a small flat board of chestnut wood, weighted at the bottom and measuring 12in x 6in. To get beyond the ship's wake the seaman deploys 8 to 10 fathoms of 'stray line' from the taffrail to reach the measured line. One sailor deploys the chip as another measures a half minute with a sandglass, turning the glass as the first knot passes the taffrail, then when the sand has emptied the top of the glass, counts the number of knots run out.[10] Then as now, the mariner compensated for whether the ship is running, reaching or beating (the log and line overreads on a beat, underreads on a run). The speeds, notes Champlain, were recorded on a board 3ft high by 15in wide and divided into thirteen parts long and five parts wide. In the first column hours were entered for the twenty-four-hour day. The second column noted the number of knots, the third the fathoms, the fourth and fifth the rhumbs of the winds (directions of the four primary and other winds shown on portolans). From knowing the elapsed time and speed, the distance travelled could be figured: $D = S \times T$. Similarly, when S is in knots, D is in nautical miles (1,852m or 6,076ft. based on 1' at 45° Lat.) and T in hours, the time component is found using the formula $T = D/S$ and speed, $D = S \times T$., based on 1' at 45° Lat.

Direction (Bearing and Heading)

The compass was and still is the single most important navigational instrument for maintaining a course. By the early 1400s this essential device was found mounted in the binnacles of European ships. But was it constant like Caesar, 'constant as the

Northern Star'? When sailing great distances westward, mariners soon noted an anomaly. The compass showed 'easting' or continual variation of magnetic from geographic north. Chart north and compass north did not agree. Over long distances such differences mattered.[11]

Calculating Altitude

Determining latitude is easy. Measure the height of a celestial body on a given day and the time of day, and from that, fix the position north or south of the equator. Astrolabes, kamals and cross-staffs or back-staffs were commonly used to measure altitude. The astrolabe was known to the ancient Greeks, then to the Moslems in the ninth century and the Spanish in the eleventh century. The Arabic kamal, a brilliantly simple device invented in India in the ninth century, consists of a length of taut string with knots to mark one *issabah* (Arabic, finger, here the width of a finger, $1°$ 36', a fist is about $10°$). The knots correspond to degrees of elevation. The pilot slides a plate or transom along the string. He sights along its top to measure the heavenly body by holding one end in his teeth, as he stretches the string taut, and slides the plate along the string. Away from his eye, the elevation decreases, and when he moves it in, it increases, as measured by the knots. This simple and effective instrument was used by Vasco da Gama's Arabic pilot to cross the Indian Ocean in 1498. These instruments gave way to another by the end of the sixteenth century.

The Portuguese cross-staff (introduced by John Dee to England in the 1550s) is a staff marked in degrees, along which vertical sticks (vanes or transoms) slide. It measured the height of the object by sighting it directly. If that object were the sun, gazing directly resulted in errors. John Davis, using Thomas Hariot's idea, devised the back-staff (also called the Davis Quadrant) in 1594. With it, the sailor looks away from the sun by means of mirrors. With these mirrors, the pilot can look at the heavenly body as a reflection, and the elevation reads from the arcs and scales much more accurately. Improved models could measure to $90°$. Much later came the octant, invented by three Englishmen and a Frenchman at the end of the seventeenth and start of the eighteenth centuries, and still later came the sextant, invention of another Englishman in the mid-eighteenth century.

Some measurements of celestial bodies can be made with simple instruments. To find the height of the Pole (North) Star or the zenith of the sun at midday the sailor would take a number of sights and find the one with the highest altitude. The reading with the greatest height would be made at noon. Knowing the precise time is thus unnecessary. From such calculations the astronomer measures his natural day from one midday to the next midday (and is the mariner's traditional noon-to-noon run). The sun was more useful than the moon or stars as the heavenly body to measure. The moon, though close at hand and easy to find, moves too fast to guarantee a good record of its height. Stars were also used but they were harder to find. Once found, they too, like the moon, moved quickly from their calculated positions. The sun was much easier to measure, but as it is so large, the navigator must take its size into account, by adding a factor to bring the reading to the centre of the sun.

Finding longitude, the east–west factor in solving the navigational triangle, was quite a different matter and was largely beyond sixteenth and early seventeenth century navigation. It calls for translating angular distance into planar distance (in miles or leagues run east or west) and requires very accurate measurement of time, or equally accurate measurement of the angular distance between celestial bodies. Clocks were still far too inaccurate for the first approach. For the second, no instrument was at that time fine enough to measure angular distance of celestial bodies. Early navigators understandably still relied on dead reckoning for figuring longitude, aided by the traverse board as the present position was advanced from the previous one.

Englishing Navigation

Why were the English so slow in developing deep-sea skills, decades after the Portuguese and Spanish? George Best writes in his *True Discourse*, 1578, that the English lagged behind because their nobility lacked liberality (they were tight-fisted), that there was little if any royal support (not true), that their mariners lacked navigational skills, and their ships were unsuitable for pelagic waters.[12]

By the mid-fifteenth century the Portuguese *caravelas* had already navigated first to the Madeiras and the Azores and had doubled Africa's Cabo Bojador. Before the end of that century they had discovered the Cabo Verdes and had doubled the Cabo de Tempestades (later euphemisically renamed Cabo de Boa Esperança, Good Hope) and reached India. Henry the Navigator, Duke of Viseu, 1394–1460, in the early decades of the fifteenth century invited navigators and sea captains to confer and study at his Vila do Infante, near Sagres, in what was perhaps the earliest Continental navigational school. Overseas Portuguese trade centres were established from 1434. At home, after 1482, the Portuguese formed the Armazém da Guiné e Índias, the naval arsenal. About 1501, sea merchants set up the Casa da Índia, an administrative centre, in Lisbon's Praça do Comércio. Portuguese commerce and profit called for new technology to advance their far-flung empire (as centuries later it would be so for the English). The Spanish case was different from the Portuguese, as profit for them was more heavily flavoured by religion. Theirs was a *reconquista* led by the cross against infidels, first Moslem then American Indian. About the same time as the Portuguese, they established their house of trade, the Casa de Contratación, in Seville in 1503. It licensed captains and pilots and regulated the flow of Spanish manufactures sent out to the colonies, and on the return brought gold and silver from the Americas.

In England, there were similar moves to organise shipping. For centuries England's economy had centred on exporting wool and manufactured goods to Europe, especially the Lowlands, in what was essentially costal trade. Following the Portuguese and Spanish examples, Trinity House was established in 1514 to license pilots, set up a system of navigational aids, and oversee other nautical matters.

Unlike the Iberians, though, the English at that date had no overseas trade, nor
was there as yet much need for offshore navigation. The thought was coastal.
Robert Copland writes in 1528 in his Prologue to *The Rutter of the Sea* that in
order to 'conduct a vessel as a blind man in a desolate wilderness doth walk til he
be lost' he needs instruments: 'the card, compass, rutter, dial and other, which by
speculate practise showeth the plat, that is to say the coasts, havens, roads, soundings, dangers, floods, ebbs, winds, kennings, courses and passages from land, to
land.'[13] In the 1520s, even after their first voyages to the Caribbean, the English
were still thinking locally.

Not surprisingly, in 1540 when the *Barbara* sailed to Brazil, her English captain
had to rely on a French pilot to guide him. Similarly, it was under the eye of a
Portuguese pilot that Thomas Wyndham sailed to Africa in 1553 with two ships
and a pinnace on his ill-fated thirteen-month voyage to Guinea and Benin.[14] In
his circumnavigation of 1577–80, Drake bragged that he had successfully sailed
7,000 leagues since leaving England, but he failed to mention that it was accomplished by kidnapping foreign pilots along the way. During that voyage he had
seized the Portuguese pilot and captain, Nuno da Silva, in the Cabo Verdes, and
in Santiago Spaniard Juan Griego, and off the South American western coast one
Colchero, a Spanish pilot on the treasure ship *Cacafuego*. Da Silva reports that
Drake used, besides his English charts, a Portuguese world map. Da Silva observed
further that 'the first thing he [Drake] did when he had captured a vessel was
to seize the charts, astrolabes and mariners' compasses which he broke and cast
into the sea … He is a very skillful mariner'.[15] Skillful, perhaps, but prudent?
Kidnapping a pilot and stealing his charts was the common English way.

Navigation in Europe

Mathematics and the arts of navigation and cartography came late to England.
Consider numbers. Though Arabic figures had entered Europe in the twelfth
century, Tudor stewards were still keeping their household accounts in Roman
numerals until the mid-sixteenth century. It was still later, not until the seventeenth century, that plus, minus and equal ($+$, $-$ and $=$) signs were universally
adopted in England. In the 1590s logarithms were still unknown, and simple division was not yet used.[16]

As for navigation, Portuguese and Spanish navigation was throughout the
period generally far superior to English. As late as the 1630s the standard manuals
of navigation were still Spanish. Even farther from the stamp, 'made in England',
were the practical instruments for measuring altitude at sea – the astrolabe, kamal
and cross-staff. These were Islamic inventions, though the English were to make
refinements to the last two by developing the back-staff, the octant and later
the sextant.

The Dutch had long been in the vanguard of scientific thought, but in the
sixteenth and early seventeenth centuries Spanish rule over the Lowlands had
stunted the growth of navigation, especially cartography. It was not until the
1580s when the United Provinces broke free from Spanish rule[17] that the Dutch

began to take the lead in hydrography. Then things progressed fast, so that by 1602 with the foundation of the Dutch East India Company the growing power of Dutch merchant adventurers was evident.[18] Trade was propelling science forward.

As for cartography, at the end of the 1590s the prime meridian of longitude was located in the Isla del Meridiano in the Canarias, as it had been for many centuries. It marked the westernmost extension of a Ptolemaic Europe–Africa. Meridiano had been considered the westernmost reach of Europe since the second century AD. Logically, Pope Alexander VI used it as the line of demarcation between Portuguese and Spanish spheres of influence in the Treaty of Tordesillas, 1493. It made further sense as a prime meridian, for it was here that ships bound transatlantic generally turned west into the Trades. Edward Wright's chart of 1599 illustrates Cumberland's last cruise,[19] and shows that track. The site was reaffirmed as prime meridian by France's Louis XIII in 1634. It was not until 1884, once Britain's Royal Navy clearly ruled the seas, that it was moved to Greenwich. But in both the first and second great ages of English sail – Drake's and Nelson's – navigation was still calculated from a prime meridian on a Spanish island using instruments of mostly Islamic origins, pricked out on Iberian charts.

Translated Texts

In the 1550s and '60s, the first printed English navigation books were translations of the best Spanish ones. These began appearing in the London book stalls. Martin Cortes' *Breve Compendio de la Sphera y de la Arte de Navegar*, 1551, was translated by Richard Eden as *The Art of Navigation*, 1561.[20] William Bourne published the first English original manual on navigation, *An Almanac and Prognostication for iii Yeres, with Serten Rules of Navigation*, only in 1567 (no copies extant), followed by another edition in 1571. This was followed in 1576 with Thomas Digges' *Errors in the Arte of Navigation as Commonly Practized*, which corrects well-known errors in the originals and carried into the translations: 'They neither have true rules to direct themselves, the nighest course, nay yet treading their beaten paths can assuredly decide of their certain place. For reformation of these errors and imperfections, new charts, new instruments and new rules must be prescribed'.[21] To make offshore sailing less a matter of guesswork, Sebastian Cabot had directed in his *Ordinances*, 1553, that in the north-east voyage to Cathay that those who can write shall keep a log, day and night, of 'the points, and observation of the lands, tides, elements, altitude of the sun, course of the moon and stars' of the said ships, and the 'like order to be kept in proportioning of the cards, astrolabes, and other instruments prepared for the voyage'.[22] Small advances, but advances to be sure.

Lack of knowledge is reflected at sea. Despite the translations and small advances made from the 1550s to the '70s navigation at sea was no sure matter. In the 1560s even a seasoned Sir John Hawkyns had his troubles. In his 1564–65 voyage, John Sparke the Younger, later to be twice mayor of Plymouth, provides an account of Hawkyns' troubles. The Caribbean Current set Hawkyns' fleet to leeward so much so that he drifted down from his intended landfall, Hispaniola, and found himself at Jamaica.[23] This error in longitude was no doubt made in the dead reckoning. The drift was greater than estimated. Local knowledge was of little help. Writes Sparke:

> A Spaniard being in the ship, who was a merchant, and inhabitant in Jamaica, having occasion to go to Guinie, and being by treason taken of the Negros, & afterwards bought by the Tangomangos, was by our captain brought from thence, and had his passage to go into his country, who perceiving the land, made as though he knew every place thereof, and pointed to certain places which he named to be such a place, and such a man's ground, and that behind such a point was the harbour, but in the end he pointed so from one point to another, that we were a leeboard of all places, and found ourselves at the west end of Jamaica before we were aware of it, and being once to leeward, there was no getting up again.[24]

Later on that voyage, Hawkyns was given more bad advice, this time about Cuba from a Frenchman:

> This hill we thinking to have been [at] the Table [a prominent landmark] made account (as it was indeed) that Havana was but eight leagues to windward, but by the persuasion of a French man, who made the captain believe he knew the Table very well, and had been at Havana, said that it was not the Table, and that the Table was much higher, and near to the sea side, and that there was no plain ground to the eastward, nor hills to the westward, but all was contrary, and that behind the hills to the westward was La Havana.

Hawkyns was persuaded to sail to leeward for a week, but:

> finding no habitation, nor no other Table; and then perceiving his folly to give ear to such praters, was not a little sorry, both because he did consider what time he should spend ere he could get so far to windward again, which would have been, with the weathering which we had, ten or twelve days' work, & what it would have been longer he knew not, and (that which was worst) he had not above a day's water and therefore knew not what shift to make.[25]

Here was another error in longitude and erroneous local knowledge. Reaching the intended destinations in these waters depended on local knowledge and measurement of drift. Hawkyns, unawares, on the same voyage had twice missed his destinations. After twelve days Hawkyns reached Florida, and, seeking water, found himself in swift currents and off a shoal lee shore, new to him. Without specific knowledge of the Caribbean and Gulf of Mexico, sailing was living with the unknown, even for seasoned mariners such as Hawkyns. Drake, for one, bragged about his navigational skill, but in 1577–80, sailing up the west coast of North America (likely in fog) he missed San Francisco Bay, at 37° N, just as the surveyor Captain James Cook in 1778, two centuries later, would sail in fog and poor weather and miss the Strait of Juan de Fuca, at 48° N.[26] Here, the errors were in latitude, made in poor weather.

Though New World navigation in the higher latitudes often had to deal with extreme tidal ranges (at times over 50ft), in the tropics, seasonal water depth was a factor to be considered. Hakluyt prints a translation of an undated anonymous Spanish account placed in *Principal Navigations* just before Hawkyns' 1567-68 voyage to the Caribbean. It is the first known description in English of the navigable depths for ports along the Pacific coast of Nicaragua, important to the Spanish because of the Manila silk trade. A Spanish transpacific galleon could easily draw 16ft. The small port of Tecuanapa, at the mouth of the River Tlacamama, was excellent for building, repairing and stocking ships sailing the Pacific, but the river had the usual sand bar. The Spanish author writes that in the dry summer months the channel has 'little less then one fathom at low water, and at full sea one fathom and a half: in the time of rain, with the increasing of the land-water it hath three fathoms and more',[27] – even then hardly enough depth for sea-going vessels. As for navigating the River Tlacamama, it is navigable for canoes and lighters for eight months of the year but not the other four:

> because that the sands of the plains do soak and drink up the water in such wise, that there remaineth so little, that there is no passage … [Yet once inside] this small harbour of Tecuanapa being seen and viewed, seemeth very commodious for to build ships in, by reason of the great abundance of mountains full of good timber for that purpose, with the commodities of rivers, and with the service and victuals from the towns thereabout, which be very good for coast towns.[28]

Some ports were good, others not. Hakluyt printed the accounts of Lopez Vaz, who writes that Cuba's La Havana, well-protected, is a fine port and its 'townsmen are very rich by reason of the fleets that come from Nueva España, and Tierra Firma which touch there'.[29] More difficult is the 'river of Marannon' (Rio Amazonas), mighty and golden, for 'none can pass up this river because of the greatness of the current which commeth down, as also there are many shelves of sand lying in the mouth thereof'.[30]

Contrary winds, currents and few harbours were the case in sailing to the Pacific. Vaz comments on transiting the frigid Strait of Magellan, lying at 52° S: 'Howbeit the cold is not the cause why navigators frequent not the same, but the westerly and southerly winds, which blow most furiously on that coast, and that oftentimes out of the very mouth of the straits, and so continue for the most part of the year.' Ships enter the strait so battered by storms so that when they 'come to the mouth thereof they have been hindered by the current and wind, and so have been put back again'.[31] The current can run so strong that anchors drag, and the first harbour is 30 leagues into the strait. There were few safe harbours near the strait for fueling, victualling and watering. The good ones were held by the Spanish. So dangerous and inhospitable are the waters of the Strait that it was thirty years after Magellan's transit before another accomplished it: Francis

Drake, who made it through thanks to the sharp eye of his kidnapped Portuguese pilot, Nuno da Silva.[32] Once through, on the Pacific coast of South America, the first port north of the strait is Castro. But 'the harbour belonging to this town is compassed about with so many shoals, that it will serve but to receive small barks only'. Other hindrances encountered sailing north along west coast of South America are strong southerly winds and the north-flowing Humboldt Current. Vaz was arguably the first to recognise the Humboldt Current, and he writes that when Francisco Pizarro sailed there in 1513, it took him not fifteen days but eight months to sail southward against wind and current along the coast. But then he was exploring the coastline in some detail.[33] Vaz comments on the contrary current and wind: 'But from Panamá by sea to the coast of Perú they could not trade in a long time, because of the southerly winds blowing on this coast almost all the year long, which are a hindrance to ships sailing that way'. Francisco Pizarro, sailing south in the 1520s and '30s had met 'contrary winds and rain'. Vaz comments that 'not knowing the right course', Pizarro 'ran into every river and bay that he saw along the coast'.[34]

Mathematical Navigation

In 1574, William Bourne had published his *A Regiment for the Sea*, a 'rule' or manual 'for the simplest sort of seafaring man'. In contrast to Dee's scholarly proof, Bourne wrote from first-hand experience at sea. He had voyaged to Russia at age sixteen. Later he sailed with Frobisher to Arctic North America in 1576, and drew the chart for that voyage. On it he noted the positions of irregular magnetic variation, which incidentally showed Frobisher's ship's course.[35] He is author of *The Art of Shooting in Great Ordnaunce*, 1578, the first English book on gunnery. In it, he also treats 'martial affairs by sea', making it also the first English book on naval tactics. That same year the prolific Bourne published his *The Treasure for Travellers*, one of the earliest examinations of ocean currents. Bourne left the sea to become Comptroller of the Navy, 1581–99, yet he still found time to devise a diagram for determining how many miles are in a degree of longitude at any given latitude. This seemingly simple stroke still remains a brilliant piece of practical work.[36]

Thomas Harriot (Hariot) was another extraordinary mathematical mind. In 1579, the polymath Harriot came down from St Mary Hall, Oxford, to become Ralegh's accountant, tutor in mathematics, astronomy and astrology, his adviser in navigation, and his naval architect. By 1584, he had written a manuscript on navigation, titled 'Articon', now lost. In 1585, Ralegh sent him on the Virginian voyage, during which Harriot made astronomical navigational calculations for the captain, Sir Richard Grenville. His account of the voyage appeared later as *A briefe and true report of the new found land of Virginia*, 1588.[37] The manuscript 'Articon' survives in part in Hariot's later manuscript, 'Instructions for Raleigh's Voyage to Guiana, 1595', written for Ralegh's sea captains for his first overseas voyage. In it, Harriot stresses the importance of measuring the sun's meridian altitude and the height of Polaris with a cross-staff or, better yet, with John Davis' new invention, the back-staff. (The idea was Harriot's, but Davis published a diagram of his version in 1594 and, by making the device, Davis gets the credit.) Harriot writes that because of magnetic variation, the ship's course should be checked about every twelve hours. He warns of parallax error in using the cross-staff, and that the coloured glass found at the upper edge of the cross-staff's transom produces refraction. To correct that error, 16 minutes (half the sun's diameter) should be subtracted from the observed altitude. He accounted for dip, the correction made for the height of the observer's eye above sea level and atmospheric refraction, as well (though Harriot's adjustment is consistently high), and noted that the precession (the westward or backward shift of equinoctial points along the ecliptic) that causes the equinoxes to occur earlier each sidereal year, rotates westward of the equinoxes and affects magnetic variation and thus the position of the seemingly ever-fixed Pole Star (Kochab, Ursae Minoris, Polaris, Stella Maris or otherwise called the seaman's star). Harriot's manuscript, 'The Doctrine of Nauticall Triangles Compendious', 1594, calculated meridional parts before Wright's calculations and before Gunter had applied a line of those parts onto his cross-staff.[38] Harriot was to become the founder of the English school of algebra.

Gresham College, the Traverse Board

The 1580s saw further advances. Following the Iberian example and to supplement the work of Trinity House, Hakluyt in 1582 and 1584 urged establishing a lectureship in navigation in London. His call was answered in 1598 when Gresham College was founded to teach the mathematics of practical navigation. Another advance in the '80s was in cartography. A year before Drake sailed for the West Indies in 1585 an important compilation was published in Holland. Dutchman Lucas Janszoon Wagenaer, pilot for some twenty-five years and later collector of port dues in Holland, brought out his *Spieghel deer Zeewaerdt* in 1584 and 1585, translated as *The Mariners Mirrour*. These charts were the first that could be confidently used at sea. So good were they that a 'Waggoner' has since been a synonym for 'sailing directions'. The year 1585 also saw the decimal system made generally known when the Flemish mathematician and military engineer Simon Stevin published his *De Thiende* (the Art of Tenths), later Englished as *Decimal Arithemetic*, 1608, by Robert Norton.[39]

The accounts of Drake's 1585–86 West Indies voyage show the way navigation was carried out at sea. A journal records that regularly 'the boards were cleared'. These were the traverse boards used to track time sailed on a particular heading. For example, Drake's latitude, or height, on 18 September 1585 'at a reasonable guess was 52 minutes. The elevation being 39 [degrees] 10 minutes'.[40] A few days later the journal begins: 'At noon time the board was cleared as followeth 16 pins southwest and … her way southwest 6 leagues, 32 pins south, southwest, her way good south west and by south 6 leagues'.[41]

Pilots, chart and rutters were essentials at sea, of far more practical value than gold. Thomas Fuller, master of the *Desire* and part of the fleet on Cavendish's circumnavigation, 1586–88, assembled his lists of 'heights' (the latitudes) of capes, islands, rivers, ports and bays of the Barbary coast, then Brazil to the South Sea, Chile and Perú, New Spain (México) and the Orient. He next gives information on soundings along the Barbary Coast and Guinea, then Brazil, Chile, New Spain, the 'lying of the land' in the Strait of Magellan, the South Sea and the coast of East Africa – in short, the world encompassed. He keeps some of the old ways of the portolan in showing compass headings and distances: along the coasts of Chile and Perú, New Spain, 'from the coast of America unto the westwards', the Orient, the Cape of Good Hope to the west and north. Along the coast of New Spain at 12° N Lat., Fuller observed one point (11° 15') E magnetic variation. He records places to anchor, and the 'finding of the winds'. Fuller's log is a raw prosaic distillation of the facts necessary for navigating a ship, just the type of information a captain needs.[42]

The year after Fuller's and Cavendish's return in 1589, East Anglian Thomas Blundeville, from Norfolk, invented his most useful tool, the protraction, a half circle with lines inscribed, similar to the mariner's fly. His *Exercises*, 1594, was the first canon of trigonometric functions published in English: the sine, tangent and secant (a line that cuts a curve at one or more points, also the ratio of the hypotenuse to the shorter side adjacent to an acute angle in a right-angled triangle). Or, more simply, one divided by the cosine.

The decade of the 1590s was a particularly active time at chart tables at sea and desks ashore. The best efforts combine the work of seaman and scholar. An example of the successful seaman is William Parker, who made reprisal voyages to the West Indies each year from 1590 to 1597.[43] In his 1592 and 1593 voyages this gentleman from Plymouth used surprise attacks with small forces, the same tactic favoured by John Oxnam and Sir Francis Drake. In 1596 he was described by Ralegh as 'sometime my servant and now attending on your lordship' (Charles Howard, Lord Admiral and First Earl of Nottingham). Parker probably knew as much as any Elizabethan sailor about the Caribbean, though the location of El Dorado he had given Ralegh proved useless. The Spanish rutter for the West Indies, though, was of value. Parker was to be named mayor of Plymouth in 1601, was a founding member of the Virginia Company in 1606, and in 1617 was made vice-admiral of an East Indies fleet.

Large gaps still remained between the scholar's desk and the ship's chart table. As late as 1593 during Sir Richard Hawkyns' voyage, printed in 1622, the currents and tides so important to a passage are not detailed. Because no navigator could regularly determine longitude, a problem not solved in practical terms until John Harrison perfected his chronometers in 1764, a captain could not determine the speed of an ocean current nor its east–west limits.[44] In the 1560s Hawkyns had encountered them in the Caribbean, and had considerable drift. He could not accurately determine longitude. In his 1595 voyage to Guiana, Ralegh meticulously records latitude but, like others, he omits longitude. No matter that mathematician Thomas Harriot was in Ralegh's service and that Harriot in 1583, and still earlier Dee in 1575 in 'The British Complement of Perfect Navigation', 1575, a manuscript now lost. These mathematical solutions to the longitude problem mathematically were too laborious and arcane, true still in the 1590s, when the instruments had improved, but still not fine enough to measure angular distance with enough accuracy.[45] Another geographer-mathematician-seaman of the 1590s was Robert Hues. His *Tractatus de Globis*, 1594, came about from sailing with Thomas Cavendish on his last voyage, 1591–92. Hues combined theory and practice on globes, and his *Tractatus*, dedicated to his friend Sir Walter Ralegh, would become the standard work for the next 100 years.

Davis, Practical Navigator

In that same year, 1594, another experienced seaman, one who had sailed both the Arctic and Antarctic, published a practical book. Captain John Davis, on returning from sailing the Strait of Magellan, wrote his *Seamans Secrets*. Davis' book marks the start of the period of the greatest advances in English navigation. This greatest period in English navigation would run to 1631, when Richard Norwood published his *Trigonometrie*, the clearest explanation of logarithms to that date. Norwood's is the first known logbook laid out in the familiar columnar form. It gives date, latitude (observed altitude), course, leagues sailed, wind direction and observations. The early years 1595–96 were especially important for both navigational theory and practice. In 1595 Ralegh undertook his first transatlantic voyage to the Caribbean, and Drake and Hawkyns made their last. It was the year that the word 'trigonometry' entered the English language and the year that Sir Richard Hawkyns noted certain errors in navigation.[46] Davis' was the best account of navigation to date, and written in terms that a tar could understand. He was the first navigator to define course and traverse clearly and to distinguish three sorts of sailing: 1. horizontal or plane (plain) sailing, assuming the earth to be flat, though known to be a sphere; 2. paradoxal or rhumb line sailing (a line of constant compass heading); and 3. great circle sailing (the shortest route on a sphere between two points, which is 'the circumference of the circle which joins them and whose centre is at the centre of the sphere'.[47]

His is the earliest discusion of parallax error caused by using the cross-staff. Davis eliminated parallax error with his invention of the back-staff in 1595 (following Harriot's earlier idea). Its mirrors allowed the pilot to make his measurements without having to look directly at the sun, thus reducing error. Further, the back-staff or quadrant was able to measure altitude to 90 degrees and could be used in equatorial waters. Davis shows why plane sailing could be done only for short distances. He explains the paradoxal compass and made a circumpolar chart that views the world down from above the poles and made sailing in higher latitudes feasible (still used today). It was he who is credited with inventing the protractor (though Thomas Blundeville had devised a similar instrument in 1589).

From 1595 to 1600 two further aids to the mariner appeared. One was Hakluyt's greatly expanded second edition of *Principal Navigations*, brought out first in 1589, the year following the Spanish Armada, then greatly expanded and published incrementally between 1598 and 1600, while England was still at war with Spain. It contains two rutters for the West Indies, valuable at least for the general reader, as they drew attention to deep-sea navigation. These rutters consider the best times to make an oceanic passage and the routes to follow. On leaving England, the captain should go south to catch the Trades at the Canaries or Cabo Verdes, make the ocean passage, and return from Havana and sail thorough the Florida Strait.[48] The study of mathematical navigation begun at Gresham College in 1598 was to gain further respect when Henry Briggs left Gresham and was named Savilian Professor of Geometry at Oxford in 1619 (Cambridge was to follow in 1663 when the Luscasian Chair of Mathematics was established).[49] In 1619, then, navigation had been firmly accepted as an academic discipline.

Wright on Mercator's Errors

The greatest advance in marine cartography was made by the Flemish cartographer Gerardus Mercator (Gerhard Kramer). It is Mercator's projection, devised in 1569, that first transferred a spherical surface onto a flat plane.[50] Within thirty years his projection and other advances made long-distance sailing reliable, but only after mathematician Edward Wright corrected errors in Mercator's projection. Wright, in *Certaine Errors*, 1599, asserts that it was his own ideas published in 1594 and 1597 that made Mercator's 1569 projection useful because it was he who provided the way to translate angular distance into planar nautical miles, a necessary step for practical navigation. Why did Wright wait until 1599 to assert his claim? As early as 1592, Wright had submitted to George Clifford, Earl of Cumberland, a finished draft of his *Errors*. Its information had been published (with Wright's permission) by Blundeville in 1594 and later by Barlow in 1597. These publications and Wright's draft came into the hands of navigator Abraham Kendall, tutor in navigation to Robert Dudley, later Duke of Northumberland (himself later an author of a book on navigation and other matters in *Dell'arcano del Mare*, 1646–47). Kendall was pilot for Dudley's voyage to Trinidad and Guiana in 1594. Though Kendall, like Drake, died of disease and was buried at sea in January 1596 off Portobelo, Wright's manuscript lay safely on board at the bottom of his sea chest. When the West Indian fleet returned to England, Kendall's copy of Wright's manuscript was given to Cumberland, who logically assumed it was Kendall's own work. Cumberland passed it on to Wright for an assessment, and Wright with horror and indignation quickly saw that the words he read were his own words, the very words of his own *Errors*, not Kendall's. To make matters worse, about the same time Dutchman Jodocus Hondius published maps based on Wright's projection (Wright had freely given him details), and Hondius had credited Mercator but failed to mention Wright. It was high time, thought Wright, that matters were set right. Thus it was in 1599 that Wright published *Certaine Errors* along with the account of Cumberland's 1589 voyage, graciously dedicating the volume to Cumberland. Correcting Mercator turned out to be, as Prince Hamet might have observed, one of indirections finding directions out.

The Elizabethans were also fond of saying that to be of any use, ideas needed to be joined to action. So it was here. A Wright (Mercator) chart projection allowed the rhumb line spiral to be drawn as a series of straight lines if calculated at short

10' intervals. In this way, for the first time the pilot's chart could plot positions accurately in the higher latitudes, outside the tropics. Yes, it is mathematically incorrect, but it works. *Certaine Errors* includes a chart showing Cumberland's voyage to the Azores in 1589 and incidentally is the first published chart employing the Wright-Mercator projection.

Wright's mathematical solution to navigating marked a major turning point. Mathematics had joined practical navigation. That same year, 1599, also found Simon Stevin, at the prompting of his Dutch friend, Maurits van Nassau, Prince of Orange, publishing his *Hafenwinding*. Stevin's book was translated that year by – again – Edward Wright as *The Haven-Finding Art, Or, the Way to find any Haven or place at sea, by the Latitude and variation*, 1599. Stevin's work gives the latitude/ longitude of locations having magnetic variation.[51]

Magnetism, Shipyards, Tides

The next decade, 1600–1610, saw many advances in navigation as well as changes in politics. The sea chest of navigational items grew larger. Near the end of Queen Elizabeth's long reign, one of her physicians, Dr William Gilbert from near Norwich, was drawn not only to her bedside for physic, but to magnetism as well, which figures in navigation. His *De Magnete*, 1600, the first truly scientific English treatise on the subject, contains, almost as an afterthought, what is arguably its most useful contribution to the pilot. On the very last page he sets out in columns the angle of dip for every degree of latitude between 1° and 90° (not to be confused with the dip caused by refraction or the height of the observer from sea level). That one page alone made it most useful at sea.

Even shipbuilding came under the mathematician's rule. In 1578, with the spurt in building and rebuilding of ships to race-built design, shipwrights had complained to the Crown that 'as all kinds of vessels are greatly increased, so are the artificers likewise augmented, only in number, but less in skill'.[52] Even the best shipwrights typically needed three times more timber than first estimated. Help came when a generation later shipwright joined scholar in Richard More's *Carpenter's Rule*, 1602.[53] In writing his book, More had consulted the Gresham College mathematicians to help calculate tonnage and to estimate how much timber was needed to building a ship. He also tackled the problem of the tender, crank Jacobean vessels. He proposed girdling – that is, putting an extra skin onto the hull to increase the vessel's beam and gain stability. Shipbuilding had for too long been non-scientific, complained Captain George Waymouth in his manuscript on shipbuilding and navigation, 'Jewell of Artes', 1604. Shipwrights, he writes, built too much by estimate, not enough by measurement.

The decade 1600–10 brought with it events both great and small. Elizabeth Tudor died in 1603 and Scottish James Stuart acceded to the English throne that year. Navigation, in contrast, proceeded more quietly, correcting small errors one by one. In 1605, Richard Polter published *The Pathway to Perfect Sayling*, a popular if not a particularly original work, but still important. Polter observed the error of calculating tides on a forty-five-minute daily change, and points out that because of the eccentricity of the sun and moon, the daily change was a bit longer, and should be based on forty-eight minutes daily. Those three minutes make a significant difference.[54]

Gunter's Navigational Triangle

In 1605–06, a year before the Jamestown settlement, Edmund Gunter wrote his manuscript, 'Sector and Cross-staff' (not published until 1623), in which he shows how to find a ship's position by mathematics. Others, such as Dee and Harriot, had earlier solved the navigational triangle, but their methods were too advanced for their time, nor could their complex methods be used at sea.[55] Gunter lays out how to solve the navigational triangle by geo-trigonometric means, making it useful at sea.[56] In what Waters calls 'one of the great contributions to navigation', he showed the relationship between the course and distance sailed, and the resultant difference in latitude, departure, and difference of longitude.

Gunter sets forth three propositions. To paraphrase Waters: 1) that the latitude and distance scale anywhere on a Mercator chart is proportional to the secant of the latitude; 2) that the length of a degree of longitude (in miles or leagues) on a parallel of latitude is equal to a degree on the equator multipled by the cosine of that latitude; and 3) that the distance to be sailed along the rhumb line to raise or lay a degree of latitude is found by dividing the length of a degree of latitude by the cosine of the rhumb (course).[57] Gunter's practical traverse tables took the error out of doing calculations, thus reducing pilot error at sea. Though Dee in the 1570s, Harriot in the '80s, then later Davis had proposed mathematical solutions to the navigational triangle, and though Wright in *Certaine Errors*, 1599, had first published the formulae, it was Gunter's tables that made arithmetical navigation useful, at least in theory and on land if not yet at sea.[58] It was not until Ralph Handson, a student at Gresham College and friend to Hakluyt, published his *Trigonometry* in 1614 (a translation of Bartholomaei Petisci, *Trigonometriae*, 1600), with its improved tables, that such navigation could be used on deck. So good are his tables that they are in essence the ones still used today.

The Prospective Glass

The invention of the 'prospective glass' or telescope was proposed as early as 1294 by Roger Bacon, though the first one dates from 1608, made by Dutchman Hans Lippershey. Right away, the Dutch started manufacturing prospective glasses. Soon after, Tycho Brahe's pupil Johannes Kepler looked through a telescope and announced his two laws of planetary motion in 1609 and third law in 1618, then his Rudolphine Tables (Ephemerides) in 1627. On 25 August 1609, Galileo demonstrated his telescope to Venetian lawmakers. Months later, January 1610, he turned his eye to Jupiter, and was the first to see the planet's moons.[59] No idle observer, Galileo published his observations on Jupiter's moons the same year, and further, he found that longitude could be determined by measuring the angular distance between those moons. Correct, yes, but he noted that no instrument at the time could measure the angles so finely.[60] By 1610, too, telescopes were being manufactured in London. Thomas Harriot bought one that year, and that December became the third man to record sunspots, after Raphael Gualterotti (who had seen them with the naked eye) in 1604 and Henry Hudson on 21 March 1609. Galileo's observations of sunspots followed in 1611. Telescopes were quickly adopted for sea use, though even to the end of the seventeenth century, telescopic sights were not included as essential to a ship's inventory.

Baffin, Scientific Mariner

The decade 1610–20 brought more scientific advances and their applications at sea. In 1613 William Baffin, sailing north-east for the Muscovy Company, noted that his compass showed magnetic variation of 5½°, and recorded it in the way that is still used: as deflection of the north end of the needle in degrees east or west. Incidentally, Baffin was the first mariner to record his course in degrees, not in the rhumb of the winds (where primary and lesser wind directions are shown as radiating lines). In doing so, he shifted cartography from the Mediterranean portolan to the modern chart. He was also the first English captain to set out his journal (as opposed to a logbook) in columnar form. He recorded daily his longitude and latitude, the course made good and the distance run. Baffin kept a *Brief Journal* (a traverse book and log book in one) with entries for each day's sailing. Baffin's *A True Relation*, a précis of his *Brief Journal*, set down his observations in narrative form. In this he was not the first, as Sir Hugh Willoughby in 1553 and Christopher Hall in 1578 had each penned their narratives this way. Baffin, in 1613, recorded longitude while under way at sea in a mix of dead reckoning and bearings in degrees. On fixing the position of Resolution Island, in Hudson Strait, at 61° 33' N, 65° 00' W, his longitude was only 6' out, an astoundingly accurate calculation.[61] Baffin was truly what Waters calls him – the 'scientific seaman'.[62]

In 1614 Robert Norman published his *Newe Attractive*. It is the first published explanation in English of arithmetical navigation and the clearest one to that date.[63] Norman postulated that if any two of certain factors were known – latitude or departure (or the difference in longitude), distance sailed, or true course – then from the tables of the sine, tangents and secants, one could find the other two.[64] In that same year, 1614, one of the greatest advances in mathematics took place, arguably the most significant discovery of the entire period: logarithms.

Napier's Logarithms

In 1614, Scotsman John Napier published in Edinburgh his *Mirifici Logorithmorum Canonis Descriptio*. In it, he not only employs the decimal point (a recent advance, though decimals themselves are ancient) but much more importantly, he invents logarithms. 'Probably no work has ever influenced science as a whole, and mathematics in particular, so profoundly as this modest little book', writes Waters.[65] Logarithms abolished the need for long division, multiplication, and of finding the power and root of numbers. These shortcuts helped on a hot deck or heaving sea. Napier's logarithms are not today's Naperian or hyperbolic logarithms. These follow from a set of trigonometric functions printed that same year, 1614, by John

Speidell in *New Logarithmes*, and derive further from yet another man's work that year, Henry Briggs' *Table*.

Edward Wright, who nearly two decades earlier had advanced Mercator's projection, quickly set out to translate Napier's Latin text, believing it would be, as he advertised it, 'of very great use for Mariners ... a book of more than ordinary worth, especially for Sea-men'.[66] Wright travelled to Scotland and got Napier's approval to translate the Latin text, but before he could finish it he died in 1615, aged fifty-four. Henry Briggs completed Wright's work, and Wright's son saw it published as *A Description of the Admirable Table of Logarithmes*, 1616. Here is a remarkable example of scientific co-operation. The son dedicated his father's translation of Napier's work to the East India Company, which employed 'so many Mariners in so many goodly and costly ships, in long and dangerous voyages' and for them the 'little book' would be 'chiefly behooveful'.[67]

Logarithms were far more than a mere academic exercise. Logarithms made navigation easier and more accurate. Napier went on to invent a calculator using a set of sticks, known as 'Napier's bones', a prototype of the modern calculator. His last work, *Mirifici Logarithmorum Canonis Constructio*, 1619, explains his logarithmic tables, left unfinished when he died of gout on 1 April 1617 at 62. Henry Briggs edited and published them.[68] In 1617, the same industrious Briggs published his own common or decimal logarithms in *Logarithmorum Chilias Prima* (followed in 1624 by his more extensive *Arithmetica Logarithmica*). These books made logarithms still easier to use. Meanwhile, Briggs' friend Edmund Gunter published the first common logarithms of the trigonometric functions in *Canon Triangulorum*, 1620. Gunter's invention of his Sector or Scale, in which the logarithmic scale is laid out as a 'Line of Numbers', and describes it in his *De Sectore & Radio*, 1623. This device was to become a later age's slide rule – most useful at sea and land until supplanted by the electronic calculator, then satellite positioning in the latter twentieth century.

The next two decades in English politics, 1620–40, were fractious ones. There was the long-standing Scottish-English rift (the Act of Union was not ratified until 1707), the Royalist-Puritan split, the king versus Parliament, inflation and poor harvests. But on this turbid ebb and flow floats the extraordinary story of mathematical collaboration between England and Scotland, between friends, between generations, that took place within the six years from Napier's disvovery of logarithms in 1614 to Gunter's refinement of them as common logarithms in 1620.

These were important years for mathematics, the advancement of navigation, and for colonisation. Napier, Wright and Briggs were at work on logarithms, just one of many brilliant scientific advances in England and Scotland. It was a different story in North America. Colonists at Jamestown and Plymouth were desperately trying to avoid starvation, scratching out poor harvests, living in wattle and daub cabins with dirt floors in Virginia swamps or in pig huts dug into rocky, barren hillsides in frigid New England. Sir Walter Ralegh's Virginia colony on the Carolina coast had first begun as a private capitalist venture in the 1580s, but failed. It took fresh root in the Chesapeake in 1607, then faltered its way into the 1620s. In its death throes it was taken over by the Crown. This commercial enterprise was followed in 1620 by a religious one. The Separatists started the religious Plymouth Plantation, a theocracy that for years was to sputter on before becoming viable.

Ralegh's Heights and Variation

Before the time Gunter published the first common logarithms in 1620, Ralegh had been released on parole from the Tower in 1616, had sailed once more for Guiana, and had returned England and met the headsman's axe in 1618. The man-uscript of Ralegh's journal of 1617–18 records in his own hand the outbound passage from England to Guiana and catches the flavour of early navigation just prior to logarithms. Ralegh left finally from Cork on 19 August 1617 at six in the morning, 'having the wind at N.E. we set sail in the river of Cork, where we had attended a fair wind 7 weeks'. After a good start, the wind died, 'so as between 10 in the morning and 4 at afternoon we made not above 2 L'.[69] Ralegh is careful to record the ship's heading, wind direction, and time and distance run for each heading, factors needed for dead reckoning. After two days of sailing south-west in light winds, on the 21st the winds increased. On 22 August he calculated his latitude. 'Taking the height, we found ourselves in 48 degrees wanting 10 min-utes.' That put the *Destiny* off the north end of the Bay of Biscay.

By 27 August, Ralegh had reached Cabo Finisterre. A sight taken the next day showed the ships at 42° N, 'wanting 10 m'. The day after they 'were in 40 wanting 30 m. August 30th'. His record of noon sightings reads that 'from 12 the 29 to 12 the 30 we ran on 30 leagues south: and brought Lisbon east-northerly', latitude about 38° 40' N. The log shows the usual daily course run from 1200 hours to 1200 hours, the sun's height taken at its zenith. Following common practice (but unlike Baffin in 1613), he did not attempt to calculate longitude. Ralegh found the northeasterly Trades at the Canaries, but sailed on south for the Cabo Verdes at 16–17° N Lat., where the winds are generally more constant. At that latitude he could still measure his height from the North Star, though the Cruzeiro do Sul or Crux is at that point visible once south of 18° N. Off the island of Bravo (14° 48' N, 24° 44' W), Ralegh finds a current at the bay Furna, which 'sets very strong from the south to the north and runs in effect all ways so'.[70]

Progress was slow. The fluky winds of those latitudes slowed Ralegh's ships. Ilness soon beset him and his men. The entries for 11 and 12 October read: 'From Saturday the 11 day at 12 to Sunday at 12 we had all calms as before', seldom seen in such passages, so that he was not able to progress more than 6 leagues a day. On 28 October, Ralegh writes that 'we found the compass to vary 7 deg.'[71] Landfall was on 11 November at the Wiapoco, and in December, he reports: 'I embarked my men in five ships for Orenoke, to with 400 soldiers, and sailors', anchoring the *Destiny* and the rest of the fleet off the coast awaiting the party's return from inland.[72] Ralegh's journal abruptly ends in February 1618, on learning the bad news of the English attack on the Spanish in which his son was killed. Ralegh's contribution to seventeenth-century navigation ends there too, as he lost his own life to the executioner in October that year.

The Slide Rule

While Ralegh was sailing the *Destiny* in tropic waters, Johannes Kepler, on 8 March 1618, announced his third law of planetary motion, confirming it on 15 May. In that year appeared the second edition of Wright's translation of Napier's *Descriptio*. Next year, 1619, Gunter published his tables and, incidentally, coined the terms cosines and cotangents in his *Canon of Triangles*, 'one of the fundamental books of arithmetical, or modern, navigation', Waters writes.[73] Earlier in 1607, the year that Gunter invented his sector, John Speidell had invented a plain scale or ruler with lines to calculate distance. His *A Geometricall Extraction*, 1616, advertised an improved model of such a scale in brass or wood, which could be purchased at his house, he writes. In 1624, John Aspley published *Speculum Nauticum*, in which he describes his own plain scale, an instrument similar to Speidell's.[74]

Seamen needed a logarithmic tool that was cheap, strong and could stand up to weather and salt spray. Brigg's folio-sized tables would not do. But Gunter's solution, set forth in his *Canon of Triangles*, 1619, described a tool made of wood, ivory or brass that did work. This was the 'Scale', or 'Gunter' as it was commonly known, a straight ruler about 2ft long and 2–3in wide, modified somewhat if used on a cross-staff. Gunter described this Scale in describing a cross-staff: the staff was a yard in length on which were lines, one for measure and protraction, one for observing angles, one for the sea chart, and four others for working proportions. On the stick were Briggs' logarithmic numbers, like a modern slide rule.[75] The first published description of the Gunter in rule form came from Paris, 1624, and is described by the English mathematician Edmund Wingate in his *L'Usage de la Reigle*, 1626, a second edition translated to English in 1628 as *The Construction and Use of the Line of Proportion*. The Gunter, writes Wingate, is 'a mechanical Table of Logarithms',[76] a practical invention. Before Gunter's Scale, invented in 1623, there was no simple process for fixing a position. Gunter describes it in his *Sector* that same year.[77] Like Wright's work, Gunter's *Sector* brilliantly addressed the problem of correlating geographic or planar distance sailed (in leagues and miles) with angular distance (in degrees and minutes).

His version of the traditional log-line, another application of logarithmic relationships, could be made into a line of proportion (a log scale of numbers) to give a direct reading of miles run in an hour. His system was quickly adopted. Knots tied into the taff-rail line were common by the 1630s. The log-line was generally deployed every two hours (on some ships, every hour), so that each noon the pilot could calculate the 24-hour run for the day. The data were entered in the traverse-book or log-book. From the last sight, the mariner noted the difference in latitude and departure, corrected for wind, wave and point of sail, and a fair entry was made in the log-book.[78] Gunter provided the formulas for calculating the running fix and cross-bearing fix. Gunter preferred scales to tables, as did any seaman. He came up with a cross-bow to measure altitude, but before he could realise that invention, he died at age 45, in 1626.

From about 1620 to the 1640s mathematics texts become more a matter of the library rather than chart table. Astronomy and mathematics were established at the universities, and the Royal Observatory at Greenwich aided in finding what Waters calls the 'navigator's most intractable problem – longitude-finding'.[79] Navigation on the high seas was still very imperfect. For instance, as the lay of the coastline from New York to Boston was east-north-east to south-west, navigation was at least half a matter of longitude. Calculating longitude was guesswork. When the captain of the *Mayflower* set out for the New World, he intended to disembark his passengers at the mouth of the Hudson River, then the northerly limit of the Virginia patent. His navigation was off, and the Pilgrims were landed at Plymouth instead, an error of some 200 miles that would change the course of early American history.

Books for Velvet Breeches

The seventeenth century found a pressing need for practical books that could be understood not only by the ordinary tar but also by the new breed of gentleman captains. In 1616 the lawyer, sailor and pirate Captain Sir Henry Mainwaring returned to England from the high seas. He had sailed under the pirate's bloody flag, and commanded a fleet of eight based in Newfoundland. Out of gratitude, and receiving the king's pardon for his piracy, Mainwaring wrote his *Discourse of Pirates*, 1618, advocating the suppression of their (and his) nefarious practices. Around 1620–23 he wrote *Nomenclator Navalis* or *Seaman's Dictionary* designed for the new breed of captains in velvet breeches.[80] The book circulated in manuscript before being printed years later.

As Mainwaring the seasoned sailor was quick to point out, no book of sea terms could substitute for sea time. He had recently seen first-hand the nautical ignorance of his friend George Villiers, Duke of Buckingham, James I's favourite, appointed Lord High Admiral in 1619.[81] The war with Spain, 1625–30, showed the English the need for such primers. Books like those of Smith and Mainwaring are not original. The Spanish had been publishing such books since the 1520s for land commanders who found themselves at sea, swamped by terms they did not understand.[82]

England was again at war with Spain in 1624, a war that lasted to 1630. Then came the Anglo-French war, 1627–29, during which England suffered defeat while supporting the Huguenots in the Siege of La Rochelle, 1627, partly because of poor leadership from the quarterdeck. Long gone was the Tudor model of a captain who thoroughly knew his ship. The Navy was no longer lucrative work. A new breed of mariner had come aboard, not up through a worn hawsepipe, but up a varnished gangway. The new gentleman captains were young and inexperienced, and relied on their more seasoned officers, those few who had the respect of the tarpaulin sailors, to take command in the absence or death of the captain.[83] The standards of the Navy had seriously deteriorated.

About this time, Thomas Addison, in *Arithmeticall Navigation*, 1625, provides the first example published on the solution to navigation problems by means of logarithmic tables, using Napier's difficult logarithmic tables. The more convenient common logs were to come some six years later.[84] Addison's is the earliest navigation manual devoted solely to arithmetical navigation, putting him in a class with Cortes, Bourne, Blundeville and Davis. Unfortunately, unlike his famous literary namesake, Joseph Addison in the next century famous for his balanced style, this earlier Addison's prose is largely incomprehensible.

In 1625, King James I died and his son Charles acceded to the throne of England. That year also saw the publication of *The Sea Mirrour*, and an English translation of Willem Janszoon Blaeu's charts, *Seespiegel*, published in Dutch in 1623 and 1624. Its six books provided the most recent and best coverage of Europe's coastlines, a datum for depths and tidal flows, given in knots. Captain John Smith, a soldier of fortune and friend of Sir Walter Ralegh, was a castaway and pirate in the Mediterranean, surveyor of the Chesapeake and New England, and 'sometimes Governor of Virginia, and Admiral of New England'.[85] His credentials as a worldly soldier of fortune were solid. Smith further knew something of the sea. In 1604, he had been crew on an English vessel at Safi that had engaged two Spanish warships in a desperate battle. He returned to England, and with the Virginia Company sailed to Jamestown in 1607. He returned to England in 1609, then in 1614 sailed for 'North' Virginia, which he named New England. He sailed for New England twice again in 1615, and on the second voyage was taken by French privateers. En route for Alexandria, the French ship captured a rich Venetian prize. All this for Smith before the age of 45.[86] His *Accidence*, 1626, was expanded as the popular *Sea Grammar* in 1627. It draws heavily on Mainwaring and Bourne to explain the way of a ship to young gentlemen and is the first printed example (but not the first manuscript) in English literature of a 'sailor's word book'.[87] Writes Waters:

> The *Sea Grammar* in fact did for ships and seamanship what had already been done by other writers for navigation and gunnery; it collected, collated, codified, defined, and explained the ordinary workaday knowledge of seamen and their ships; how they built, rigged, manned, victualled, armed, handled, fought, and sailed a ship at sea.

Discs to the Scaffold

The appointment of Villiers as Lord High Admiral in 1619 had prompted Mainwaring to write his primer. English support of the Hugenots in 1627 resulted in yet another sort of sea book, this time in the field of medicine. John Woodall's *Woodalls Viaticum: The Path-way to the Surgions Chest*, 1628, was advertised as for the 'younger sort of surgeons now employed in the service of His Majesty for the intended relief of Rochell ... Intended chiefly for the better curing of wounds made by gun-shot'.[88] As Mainwaring and Smith had done, so Woodall wrote in response to events of his time, this time in support of the English help for the Huguenot French in 1627.

Politics again enters, albeit tangentially, in touching another navigational invention. The first description of a slide rule specifically for use at sea is found in Richard Delamain's *Grammelogia*, 1630. His invention operated not as sliding rulers but as rotatable discs. It was an instrument so prized that Charles I is said to have closely clutched his sea discs as he mounted the steps to the scaffold in 1649.[89]

In 1631, Richard Norwood published *Trigonometrie*, the clearest explanation of logarithms to that date. He gives a vivid (and highly readable) example of charting a course by the great circle route from the Bermooths (Bermudas) to the Lizard.[90] A big problem was finding the great circle route in the middle latitudes, where most sailing was (and still is) done. It was easier to figure the great circle route when sailing the higher latitudes. Until the advent of logarithms, great circle navigation had been too complex, as Norwood had explained in his *Seamans Practice*, 1627. It was Norwood who made another incremental advance by setting the nautical mile at 6,120ft (just over the current 1,852m or 6,076ft (rounded to 6,080ft), far more accurate than the long-standing 5,000ft statute mile.[91] Additionally, he was the first to consider ocean currents as a practical factor in navigation. He further sketched out the form of a log to be kept on a ship's bridge.[92]

In sum, Waters puts navigation's basic problem clearly:

> One of the basic things that a navigator is concerned with is distance – the distance between places, the distance he has sailed, the distance he has to sail. Gunter – correctly – considered that the first essential was to establish clearly the relationship between the basic unit customarily used to express distances in lengths and the basic unit used to describe angular distance on the globe. This, of course, is of fundamental importance when a ship's position is fixed astronomically.

It also requires 'measuring the length of a degree along a meridian on the earth's surface'.[93] Angular distance between celestial objects, converted to radians to make use of the trigonometry of sight reduction, has to be reconciled with the spherical distances (that are seemingly flat), as traversed by a ship at sea. These vagaries and those of a pitching deck, hot sun and weather were faced by Hawkyns, Drake and Ralegh. They still matter today.

Notes

1 The English league was set at 3 miles, where 60 nautical miles = 1 degree of latitude, 1 minute = 1 mile. D.W. Waters, *The Art of Navigation in England in Elizabethan and Early Stuart Times*, 1958, 2nd edn. (Greenwich: National Maritime Museum, 1978), 257–8, 377. Abbr. *AN*. This chapter is indebted to Walters' brilliant and authoritative book. See also G.D. Dunlap and H.H. Scufeldt, *Dutton's Navigation and Piloting* (Annapolis: Naval Institute Press, 1972); and Nathaniel Bowditch, *The American Practical Navigator*, 1837 (Bethesda: Defense Mapping Agency Hydrographic/Topographic Center, 1995).

2 Quoted in *AN*, 521.

3 *PN*, 11:19–22.

4 *PN*, 11:72–3.

5 *PN*, 11:21–2.

6 *PN*, 11:91–2.

7 Quoted in Michael Lewis, *The Hawkins Dynasty, Three Generations of a Tudor Family* (London: George Allen and Unwin, 1969), 46–7.

8 A.G. Dean, editorial comments (Raleigh: North Carolina State University, 15 April 2013).

9 *AN*, 425.

10 Translation of Champlain in *AN*, 592–3. Today, sailors can do the same in a shorter time by tying a knot every 8ft 6.5in, counting 10 seconds, and observing how many knots have been run out, with allowance made for the point of sail.

11 *AN*, 521.

12 *AN*, 177.

13 Robert Copland, *The Rutter of the Sea*, 1550 edn., quoted in *AN*, 501.

14 *PN*, 6:151.

15 Quoted in *AN*, 536.

16 *AN*, 244–5.

17 The seventeen provinces of the Netherlands were declared a separate united entity from the Holy Roman Empire and France by Charles V in the Transaction of Augsburg, 1548. Further wars and treaties continued to 1648, when the Peace of Westphalia finally gave the Dutch full independence from Spain. The Union of Utrecht, 1579, brought about the United Provinces, and the Act of Abjuration, 1581, established northern Netherlands as Protestant and free from Spanish rule.

18 *AN*, 328.

19 *AN*, 550, 552.

20 *AN*, 501.

21 Quoted in *AN*, 125.

22 Quoted in *AN*, 509; see *PN*, 2:195.

23 *PN*, 10:9–63; *SD*, 76–108; *HP*, 70, note 1.

24 *PN*, 10:43.

25 *PN*, 10:46–7.

26 Barry Gough, *Juan de Fuca's Strait: Voyages in the Waterway of Forgotten Dreams* (Madeira Park: Harbour Publishing, 2012).

27 *PN*, 9:466.

28 *PN*, 9:466–73.

29 *PN*, 11:227–90; *PN*, 10:75–7.

30 *PN*, 11:241–3.

31 *PN*, 11:256.

32 *PN*, 11:260.

33 *PN*, 11:273–80.

34 *PN*, 11:279.

35 *AN*, 528.

36 *AN*, 140.

37 *AN*, 546. See Stephen Clucas, 'Thomas Harriot's A briefe and true report: Knowledge-making and the Roanoke Voyage', Kim Sloan (ed.), *European Visions: American Voices* (London: British Museum, 2003), 17–23.

38 *AN*, 584–91.

39 *AN*, 345.

40 *DW*, 73–4. Though Keeler believes that Drake probably measured latitude with an astrolabe, it was more likely a cross-staff, but not a back-staff, which appeared about ten years later.

41 *PN*, 10: 97–134; *DW*, 73–4.

42 *PN*, 11:348–76.

43 *EP*, 219–24.

44 *AN*, 266.

45 *AN*, 535–6, 372, 584–9.

46 AN, 313, 340.

47 Peter Kemp (ed.), *Oxford Companion to Ships and the Sea* (London: Oxford University Press, 1976), see plane, paradoxal, great circle sailing.

48 *AN*, 264.

49 *AN*, 235, 553.

50 *AN*, 121.

51 The extraordinary Prince Maurits (1567–1625) was a brilliant general of his day. It was he who made the northern part of the Netherlands Protestant. This eldest half-brother of Philip William was so well regarded that the island of Mauritius was named for him. In 1624 Henry Hudson named the Mauritius River (later changed by the English to the Hudson River) after him. Another member of the illustrious family was Prince Johan Maurits van Nassau-Siegen (1604–79), grand nephew of William the Silent, the father of Maurits van Nassau. Yet another family member was Johan Maurits, Governor General of Netherlands Brazil for the Dutch West India Company. From 1637 to 1644 this Calvinist administered the area from Maranhão to the Rio São Francisco, an area at that time larger than Brazil, the area to the south. He rebuilt the fazendas and sugar mills destroyed in Holland's war with Portugal, and made that region's sugar mills the most productive in the world. To the regret of many of his Brazilian fazendeiros in Maranhão, Prince Maurits returned home to the Netherlands in July 1644. His departure marked an end of the early Dutch presence in Brazil.

52 Quoted in *AN*, 295.

53 *AN*, 295.

54 *AN*, 302.

55 *AN*, 372–3.

56 *AN*, 358–66.

57 *AN*, 380, and Table 12, 381.

58 *AN*, 381–93.

59 *AN*, 297–8.

60 AN, 299–300. Only with the invention of the satellite Global Positioning System in the 1980s and '90s was Galileo's method made truly useful. Its measurements of the positions of satellites at a given moment obviated the need for declination tables, almanacs, complex mathematics, accurate chronometers, and instruments for measuring celestial bodies.

61 *AN*, 276–83.

62 *AN*, 282.

63 *AN*, 559.

64 *AN*, 399–400.

65 *AN*, 402, 594.

66 Quoted in *AN*, 404.

67 Quoted in *AN*, 405.

68 *AN*, 406.

69 Note: 20 leagues = 1°. 1 L = 3' Lat. 1 nm =1' Lat. (an average, figured at the middle latitudes).

70 Editor Schomburgk's note: 'This remarkable observation of Ralegh's has since been confirmed. In no part of the ocean have mariners been more perplexed in accounting for currents than near the equator, chiefly between the meridians of twenty-five degrees

and forty degrees west. The effect of the African monsoon, if the periodical wind prevailing during the changes of the season may be called so, is to divert a great portion of the equatorial stream to the north, north-north-east and north-east, even beyond the Cape Verde islands …This passage in Ralegh's journal confirms our high opinion of the acuteness of his observations of whatever related to seamanship; hence no wonder that he rose to a reputation as a navigator which, after the death of Drake and Hawkins, was enjoyed by very few of his contemporaries'. On 7 October he encountered another current that set him west of south-west by west. Schomburgk continues: 'The great current from the north-west changes immediately after passing the Cape Verde Islands; it becomes first southerly and sets afterwards to the west'.

71 East variation. Ralegh's noon sight put him at 7° N, 48.5° W, at the meridian of Pará, accounting for +3° E variation for that year.

72 *DG*, 177–203.

73 *AN*, 408.

74 *AN*, 437.

75 *AN*, 416–19.

76 *AN*, 420.

77 *AN*, 429.

78 *AN*, 436–7.

79 *AN*, 411.

80 He completed his manuscript by 17 May 1623, dedicating the surviving copy to his friend the Marquis of Buckingham, who the next day was made a Duke. The *Seaman's Dictionary* circulated in manuscript and was finally published in 1644. Formations and tactics came naturally to Sir Henry Mainwaring (pronounced 'Mannering') (1587–1653), B.A. Brasenose College, Oxford, 1602, where he studied under no less than John Davis. Mainwaring had sailed some years as a privateer and pirate before he was pardoned in 1616 by James I. In thanks, he presented his 'Discourse of Pirates' to the king in 1618, the same year he was named a Gentleman of the Bedchamber and knighted by the king. Nefarious, notorious, he now gained a knighthood. He was elected MP for Dover, 1621–22. In 1630, Mainwaring was named Master of the Corporation of Trinity House, and in 1637 was promoted to Rear Admiral and then Vice Admiral in 1639, when he finally left the sea. To crown this man's extraordinary life, in 1643 he was awarded the degree of Doctor of Physic at Oxford. A Royalist in the Civil War, he left for France during the Commonwealth, where he died a pauper in 1653. His remains were later reburied in London. *AN*, 271.

81 *AN*, 594.

82 *AN*, 466.

83 *AN*, 463.

84 *AN*, 447.

85 *AN*, 474.

86 *AN*, 467–8.

87 *AN*, 457, 462.

88 Quoted in *AN*, 477.

89 *AN*, 478.

90 *AN*, 482.

91 *AN*, 488.

92 *AN*, 491.

93 *AN*, 423.

5

The Way of a Fighting Ship

'Things hid from me, the waie of a shippe in the middes of the sea.'
Geneva Bible, 1560

The 'way of a ship', whether armed merchantman or warship, includes matters in common: tempests and hurricanes, open–ocean and coastal navigation, navigating lee shores, sandbars, ocean currents, steering, keeping a fleet together, setting and shortening sail, tacking and wearing ship, beating, running, going roomer (falling off the wind), lying ahull, anchoring, repairing sprung masts and yards, tallowing the hull, making casks, cleaning ship, organising the crew, maintaining discipline, punishing prisoners, extracting ransom, surviving mutiny or shipwreck. It means battle and risk, cannon and gunnery, formations and tactics, and amphibious operations. The ship's captain also had to negotiate the wild waters of domestic and foreign politics.

To examine Elizabethan ships, this chapter will consider first galleons, pinnaces, frigates and galley-frigates used against other navies, privateers and pirates, then examine their ordnance, especially iron and bronze cannon. Then it will take up formations and tactics, including close and open order, single column ahead, getting the weather gage, boarding and employing amphibious operations. It ends by looking at the seafaring manuals written to introduce the ways of the sea to new sailors and readers ashore.

◊

England at the start of the sixteenth century was a marginal maritime nation with coastal but no transoceanic experience, in contrast to Portugal and Spain, the world's dominant maritime powers. Over the century, though, England's royal and merchant navies came to challenge Spanish hegemony in Europe and the Americas, thanks to capital ship construction, regular maintenance and ship rebuilding carried out according to the newest designs. The superiority that the English gained over the Spanish, writes Geoffrey Parker, was above all because for almost a century, but especially under Elizabeth, the English, unlike the Spanish, had been investing steadily in the navy. Thirty per cent of the defence budget was allocated to the navy, he writes, an amount unparalleled by any other nation. In contrast, Philip II started building a Spanish high-seas fleet only in the 1580s, at the point Spain took up the Portuguese crown and her fine navy in 1580.[1]

England's aim was to catch up with Spain and to break her prohibition of trade with England (or any other country) in Spanish America. She had been on a war footing with Spain since before the 1520s (over a decade before Henry VIII broke with the Pope in the 1530s) though 1585 is the date generally given as the start of the Anglo-Spanish war. Numerous hostilities by land and sea had peppered the years leading up to 1585.

Vastly outnumbered and outgunned, the English needed a different sort of navy. Superior artillery was one answer. More powerful artillery allowed for firing at longer range, clearly better than boarding larger and more heavily manned enemy ships. In this, England was following the lead of her long-time commercial ally, Portugal, which had protected commerce by arming her merchant ships with long-range cannon to keep pirates and other boarders in the Arabian Sea and the Bay of Bengal at a distance. The underdog Elizabethans pragmatically realised that it was enough to disable the enemy from a distance. This new idea was adopted first by England's merchant mariners, who saw destroying a ship as a waste of a ship and her cargo. The Spanish, in contrast, felt that relying on artillery alone was not chivalric – that artillery has no conscience and is not man-to-man combat. This medieval view would yield to modern thinking during this first great age of fighting sail. The change from from seeing ships as ferryboats for boarding by marines to seeing them as moveable artillery platforms for destroying an enemy fleet at a distance was profound.

Ships

Race-Built Galleons
Improved artillery called for improved design for the English galleons, now working as mobile artillery platforms. The old carrack's substantial fore- and stern castles as on Sir John Hawkyns' *Jesus of Lubeck*, was by the 1560s still a mighty fortress, but outdated. She had been built in the 1540s when grappling and boarding were common. The lesson Hawkyns brought back in 1568 from his defeat by Spanish land artillery and boarders at San Juan de Ulúa was that her high fore- and sterncastles had proved useless. She was moored next to the Spanish ships, and under the guns of the fort that had been retaken by the Spanish and turned on the English. Two points became clear. First, the carrack design of the *Jesus* was poor. A new design that stressed speed, strength and manoeuvrability was needed. Second, her bronze cannon needed to be the standard on warships, to be able to destroy the enemy from long range. Within ten years of San Juan de Ulúa, Hawkyns saw that nearly all of the navy's capital ships had had their high hampers cut away – ships were now 'race-built' or 'race-rebuilt'. As for

long-distance gunnery, the new bronze culverins, though more expensive, were clearly more powerful and more accurate than the older iron cannon.[2] The technologies of armament and ship design affected each other. Race-built galleons were faster, more seaworthy, more handy and more powerful than the old design, so much so that the Portuguese commander in the 1588 Spanish Armada, Dom Diego Pimentel, said that the English could 'tack four or five times in the time it took us to go about once'.[3] And, her batteries could fire three or four times faster than Spanish cannon.

Pinnaces and Frigates

If the galleons were main battle ships of the day, the smaller pinnaces and frigates were the Tudor navy's powerful escorts. The pinnace was variously called a galliot, bark, galley, launch, shallop, frigate, ship's boat or an advice boat. The seventeenth-century governor of Bermuda, Nathaniel Boteler, touches on pinnaces in a set of literary dialogues between an admiral and a captain. His captain finds ships, frigates and pinnaces the same, except in bulk and burthen:

> unless it be in that they have no decks, nor bulkheads, but are all hold below; for otherwise they have the same masts, yards and shape. And these vessels are much in use with the Spaniards, especially in the West Indies, and so have gotten the denomination of Spanish frigates. And the most of these are very good sailers afore the wind, but not so good by a wind' (running versus beating).[4]

The pinnace was generally between 20 to about 70 tons displacement, square-rigged on the fore- and mainmasts, and fore-and-aft rigged with three or four jibs, a fore-staysail and a lateen mizzen sail. The craft was well armed, fast and strong, and normally carried from sixteen to forty cannon. During a passage, pinnaces would often be stowed below in pieces, then assembled once at the cruising grounds. If making a transoceanic passage on her own keel, she would either be towed or sailed independently. She was seaworthy enough to navigate the Strait of Magellan, could be rowed in the light airs of the Caribbean, or with her shoal draught, could navigate rivers such as the Amazonas or Orinoco. No experienced English captain would set out on a transatlantic voyage without at least one pinnace to serve as the ship's boat or tender to reconnoitre anchorages and rivers, fetch water and wood, fight sea battles and to lead raids ashore.[5]

Shipwrights are a conservative lot. The venerable galley, the primary warship for some 2,000 years from the Greeks to the Venetians, remained so in the minds of Spanish administrators in Seville. What other vessel could manoeuvre independent of the wind and maintain close battle formation? What other could ram and board? Only recently, had not the Holy League's galleys decisively defeated those of the Ottoman Empire at Lepanto in 1571? What no one could foretell in the 70s was that the Mediterranean war galley had fought its last great battle of the oars. But the Mediterranean Sea, *mare nostrum*, was not the open ocean. In tall ocean swells, her ram was useless, her bow chasers inaccurate, and with oars, she had no artillery battery to deliver a broadside. Her low freeboard meant that ocean waves easily swamped such a vessel. Against the seaworthy and powerful pinnace the galley stood no chance. W.L. Rodgers writes that in 1588, 'the English introduced a new type of battle, relying on great guns in sailing ships rather than on boarders in rowing ships, so that in this year we see the birth of a system of tactics'. New tactics followed from new technology.[6]

Yet despite repeated objections from its New World colonials, Seville time and time again insisted that galleys should defend Caribbean ports (and Spanish ones such as Cádiz) against corsairs and French and English attacks carried out with pinnaces. Colonial governors wrote back to Spain to say that galleys were expensive to maintain, and had to stay in port in all but calm seas. Though fast, their bow chasers were out-gunned by broadsides from pinnaces. After all, these colonials had sixty years' experience in failing to defend Caribbean ports against French corsairs like Le Têtu or Englishmen such as Drake. These raiders knew the value of a better vessel. Drake crossed over to Panamá in 1572 with two heavily armed ships, the *Pascoe* and the *Swan*, both 'richly furnished, with victuals and apparel for a whole year'. Despite such fine ships, he went to some trouble on an island off Panamá to assemble 'three dainty pinnaces' that he had carried prefabricated in the hold. He left his ships anchored, and set out in these smaller craft to attack Nombre de Dios. With muffled oar, he surprised and overcame the Spanish.[7] He used pinnaces in 1587 in the successful sack of Cádiz. The Spanish galleys stationed to protect the fleet moored in the harbour were powerless against the firepower of a pinnace. Off Gravelines in '88, it was the pinnace's powerful artillery, maoeuvrability and speed that helped the English win the day.

Lancaster's Galley-Frigate
James Lancaster used a ship's tender to lead the sack of the Brazilian port of Olinda in his voyage of 1594–95. His small fleet consisted of three ships and a crew of 275. His galley-frigate (that is, a pinnace) was brought out in pieces from England, assembled on site and launched to lead the attack while his sea-going ships remained behind at anchor. John Clerk of Eldin, writing in 1782, points to Lancaster's example, and writes that Lancaster thought of this galley-frigate and other boats as disposable landing craft. 'Before Fernambuco, in the Brazils,' where 'seeing great numbers of enemy on shore, he 'ordered his men to row their boats with such violence against the shore, as to split them in pieces. By this bold action he both deprived his men of all hope of returning, unless by victory, and terrified the enemy, who fled after a short resistance'.[8] Drake once had gone further. To spur small boat attack on Panamá in 1572, he cut off his crew's retreat by secretly scuttling then setting fire to their pefectly sound ship, the *Swan*.

Pett's Whelps
In 1625, at the start of Charles I's reign, 18,500 tons of navy vessels had not been able to protect the English merchant navy against Dunkirk pirates and privateers, harassing the English and Dutch since the 1590s. A new design was needed.

Shipwright Phineas Pett at Chatham, thought to have taken the lines from a French pinnace, built four frigates, ranging in size from small armed sloops to 200–300-ton vessels, heavily armed with twenty to thirty guns. These frigates or pinnaces were light, built with a lean length-to-beam ratio of 3.5 to 1, and could be both sailed and rowed. So successful were they that in 1628 the government commissioned ten more of what became known as Lion's Whelps. The Whelps originally had one gun deck, a quarterdeck and a spar deck, but later ones had additional decks.[9]

After Dunkirk, the Whelps were used to crush the Salé pirates of the North African Barbary coast. In 1610, Phillip III had expelled, with no right of appeal, a million *Moriscos* (Spanish Moors of mixed blood), many of whom had lived for generations in the mountains of Andalusia. It was the *reconquista* of 1492 a century later. The exiles had gone to Rabat (now renamed New Salé), at the site of the ancient Phoenician port city of Salé on the Barbary Coast. In a *jihad* against the Christian Spanish and others, the *Moriscos* allied themselves with the pirates of Algiers and Tunis and took their wrath against the Christians into the Atlantic as far north as Iceland, Ireland and England. Within seven years, 1609–1616, they had seized 466 English merchant ships, and by the 1640s had enslaved more than three thousand English men and women.[10] In early summer 1625 Islamic Barbary corsairs took the fight to Britain's home waters. Over twenty sail attacked Cornwall, seized nearly thirty British ships and a thousand skiffs, and carried off a thousand villagers into slavery.

The Moorish vessel in these attacks was the *xebec* (*zebec*, Arabic *shabbāk*, Catalan *xabec*). The *xebec* was small (to 200 tons), fast, low to the water, two- and later three-masted, with lateen sails, a long bowsprit and boomkin and broad-beamed to carry such a large sail plan. They, like the pinnace, were both sailed and rowed by oars or sweeps. *Xebecs* were armed with up to forty cannon. The crew (when attacking) numbered three or four hundred (for boarding, her primary tactic). She could beat to weather well and when becalmed could attack or retreat using her oars. She would make a lightning attack with musket shot, grapple, then board hundreds of corsairs, and with axes, cut away rigging, stun and quickly take the prey. A *xebec* close-in presented a low freeboard, presenting a a minimal cannon target at medium to long range. Close in, they were below the maximum depression of a galleon's ordnance. So fearsome were they that a later tar described how these pirates would close with the Christian vessel, board and terrorise 'more like ravenous beasts than men'.[11]

What could the English throw against the swift and powerful *xebec*? The pinnace, very similar, except that she was sea-going and strong, and used her strength and long-range artillery rather than hoardes of men for boarding. Like the *xebec*, the shallow-draught pinnace could also navigate where sea-going vessels could not, and with oars and sail could maintain a formation and concentrate her firepower, essential to winning, wind or no wind. To go against the Salé pirates, the Crown ordered built two 300-ton pinnaces having a length to beam ratio of 3.46 to 1. Long-range artillery won out over muskets and men. So successful were

these vessels that after years of preying on Christians, the Barbary corsairs sued
for peace in 1637. Long employed in the Caribbean both as a tender and raiding
vessel and sometimes flying a dubious flag, the pinnace had proved herself an
effective enforcer of English interests off Dunkirk and the Barbary Coast.

Pinks and Penecho Carvels

The second decade of the seventeenth century found pirates plaguing England
in small pinks (small flat-bottomed, narrow-sterned coastal fishing boats). Their
tactics took advantage of these vessels' capabilities. Sir Henry Mainwaring, pirate
and privateer (earlier considered as a lexicographer in Chapter Four), comments
in 'Discourse of Pirates', 1617, that these pirate pinks 'commonly go well, and
are of good burthen, as between 180 and 200 ton; and [with] ... such a ship well
manned they quickly overbear any small Ship with a few great Ordnance, and
so by little and little reinforce themselves, to be able to encounter with a good
ship'.[12] The corsairs with 'the wind being westerly, they may, with one or two
wherries in the night, go aboard and enter them, and put to sea before a wind, so
that they cannot be stayed or prevented'.[13] A small, fast, well-armed vessel could
surprise and overcome a larger one. It was the lesson of Drake and Mainwaring,
well-versed in guerilla tactics.

Once the pirate captain Mainwaring had reformed, he disingenuously revealed
his pirate tactics to his king and public in a pamphlet:

> In their working they usually do thus: a little before day they take in all
> their sails, and lie a-hull, till they can make what ships are about them; and
> accordingly direct their course, so as they may seem to such ships as they see to
> be merchantmen bound upon their course ... If any ships stand in after them,
> they heave out all the sail they can make, and hang out drags to hinder their
> going, that so the other that stand with them might imagine they were afraid
> and yet they shall fetch them up.[14]

Mainwaring in this was like the notorious Elizabethan writer Robert Greene,
who practiced coosenage alongside London's con-artists, card sharks, pimps and
felons of the 1580s then exposed his mates in his best-selling conny-catching pamphlets. In Greene's case his exposé brought no reward from a grateful monarch.

The pirates of Algiers, Mainwaring advises the king, could be stopped with:

> 'floaty ships, good sailors ... of reasonable good force in regard that the Turks of
> Algiers go in fleets some 8 or 9 sail together with 20 or 30 pieces of ordnance
> each of them. I am verily persuaded that some of your Majesty's ships, and some
> small advisers, that went with sail and oars, being employed to those places
> where they resort, might cut off most of them in a short time.[15]

A 'floaty ship' he writes elsewhere, is one 'which draws but little water'.[16]
Mainwaring recommends that accompanying a ship 'must belong a nimble

pinnace, such as a Penecho carvel, which may with sail and oars quickly turn to windward'. Penecho *caravelas*, another small, fast vessel, came from Peniche, south of Lisbon, and was more than a match for most vessels. According to Monson, 'there were few ships but they could fetch up, and then keep sight of them both night and day'.[17]

Ordnance and Gunnery

These smaller, faster vessels, from the smaller race-built galleons to pinnaces, called for smaller, lighter, but still powerful ordnance. Gun and ship design influenced each other. On the eve of England's first transatlantic voyage, Henry VIII's Royal Navy in 1515 had twenty-four vessels, of which ten were over 400 tons. But besides size or speed, Henry VIII insisted on substantial firepower. The early iron cannon were heavy, thick, and were often cast with imperfections. The thicker walls and heavy weight of brittle iron cannon and their propensity to explode made them inferior to bronze ones. But iron cannon did not overheat or distort. Bronze cannon did, but overall, the bronze alloy was found superior. Henry armed his navy with these latest cannon, and contracted the Flemish artisan, Hans Poppenruyter of Mechlin (Mechelen) to fabricate the new bronze cannon.

Bronze is about 90 per cent copper and 10 per cent tin.[18] This alloy, though more expensive than iron, was ideal for naval cannon. It resists corrosion, is remarkably strong, and has little metal-to-metal friction (asit fires its iron cannonball out of the bore). Bronze cannon can take the force of discharge better than iron because though the barrel quickly heats fast and expands, its flexibility (hysteresis) allows it to return quickly to its original shape. Bronze is also easier to cast than iron, and can be more finely wrought.[19] Yet iron casting was improving. Developments in refining and casting iron had reduced the sulphur and phosphorus so that when the molten ore was poured, there were fewer air bubbles. Despite these improvements, though iron cannon were improved and were cheaper (in 1570 iron cost £10–£20 per ton, bronze £40–£60), about 1575, the Navy gave up iron for bronze ordnance.

What kinds of weaponry worked best? Culverins or demi-culverins? How many of each? A year later, the Navy adopted 'Sir William Wynter's Proportion of 1569', based, writes Waters, 'upon the scale of armament with which Hawkins in the *Jesus* had fought himself free of the Spanish toils … It vindicated Hawkins's tactics and the armament with which he had fought the *Jesus*',[20] writes D. W. Waters. The *Jesus of Lubeck* had twenty battery guns (the larger culverins, according to Sir Walter Ralegh, needed at least four gunners per gun), and thirty-four secondary guns – in total, sixty-one cannon. Seventeen of these were culverins, of which nine were long range, and eight demi-culverins, medium range. The proportion on this ship's total ordnance was that 15 per cent were periers for closing in and firing fragmentation shot and 85 per cent divided between long-range culverins (45 per cent) and medium-range culverins (55 per cent). Had the battle at San Juan de Ulúa been fought at sea at greater range instead of within a small, crowded harbour, moored fore and aft next to the Spanish ships, a sitting duck directly under the hostile guns of the fort, Waters believes the *Jesus* would have survived 'unscathed'. She certainly had sufficient firepower to defend herself.

By 1575, although the cheaper iron cannon were considered satisfactory and safe to use in the field and at sea, bronze was preferred. After 1588, bronze culverins were cast yet more robustly, and if loaded with the more powerful 'mealed' or harquebus powder, they had a greater range and punch. The powder was usually made up in paper or canvas cartridges to speed reloading, to provide an accurate charge, and to prevent fire. Whether iron or bronze, all these cannon were heavy. Shot alone weighed from eighteen to sixty pounds (commonly used were 10-, 16- and 24-pound shot). Inaccurate firing was bad enough, but the heavy mass of the cannon increased instability (the higher centre of gravity induced rolling in these top-heavy vessels). That, and significant recoil, were serious problems.[21]

Tudor Cannon

How many guns per ship? What sorts? In the early sixteenth century the common ratio was one ton of artillery to fifteen tons of ship. English capital ships in the early sixteenth century carried more than 100 guns (though most of these were of lighter calibre). The *Henry Grâce à Dieu* (the *Great Harry*), 1,000 tons, sometimes called the first British battleship, carried 184 guns when launched in 1514, increased to 251 after her rebuild between 1536 and 1539. Twenty-one of the large guns were bronze and 230 iron. There were 100 hand guns.[22]

By the late sixteenth century English ships were armed with three classes of naval artillery: culverins, cannon and perriers. Based on bore-to-length ratio, the culverins were the longest and perriers the shortest. Culverins included pieces about 30 bore diameters (calibres) long, including the culverin, demi-culverin, saker, falcon and falconet. Culverins had thick walls for long-range firing. Cannons (of various sizes) were about 15–20 calibres in length, their shot usually 10 pounders or heavier. The perrier (*petrero*, *pedrero*, cannon *pedro* or stone thrower) was 16 to 8 or less calibres in length, with a large bore for its length. It fired stone at low velocity. Perriers included petards, mortars, trabuccos or howitzers. Sir William Wynter, Master of Naval Ordnance and author of 'Wynter's Proportion', balanced the variety of ordnance a vessel carried. Wynter's Proportion called for arming nineteen of the queen's thirty-four ships with 80.4 per cent culverins – the newer longer-range cannon, preferably bronze. By the time of the Armada in 1588, twenty-three vessels carried cannon of which 85.3 per cent were the new bronze culverins.

A 12–14ft bronze full-length culverin fired an 18-pound shot. This shot was found to be too heavy and the barrel too long for the narrow race-built galleons. In the early 1580s William Wynter, Master of Naval Ordnance, ordered them shortened. Demi-culverins of 9ft fired 8-pound shot, and these weapons were 500–1,500 pounds lighter. They proved as powerful as the older ones if charged with more potent powder. They could be reloaded and refired more quickly than full culverins or the long Spanish cannon. A few full-length culverins were still kept as chase guns, where their power at their extreme range was thought to be advantageous. Ralegh, however, found the full-length culverins to be largely useless: on a pitching deck, he observed, the fire of these chase guns was wildly inaccurate, and noted that batteries of the new shorter demi-culverins were more effective.[23]

To the Tudor and Stuart gunner, just how far off was long-range firing, what then was called 'stand-off gunnery'? Hughes writes that even later (1650–1805), the effective gun range was limited to well within 300 yards at point blank range – that is, with flat trajectory, no elevation and fired point 'blank' (or 'blanc' because a French target's bullseye is traditionally white). In that period, the maximum significant gun range was 800 or 900 yards. The sweep of the firing arc continued to be limited to about 25° fore and abaft the beam, about 50° in all, whatever the gun carriage. The superior narrow and smaller naval truck carriage used on English ships allowed gunners to traverse the guns more easily than that of the Spanish, who continued to use the wider field carriages, with large wheels and with trails (like field artillery towed on land). The English naval carriages proved more manoeuvrable, and in running the muzzle-loading cannon in and out for loading and firing, an English cannon on the smaller carriage could be reloaded faster and swiveled more easily through its arc. As training a gun was so slow and awkward whatever the carriage, guns were often aimed by manoeuvring the ship itself. Rotating gun turrets were long in the future.

So valued was naval artillery to the English that their gunners in the Armada battles outnumbered Spanish gunners per ship.[24] The English put their men where they did the most good – in naval artillery. Following the Portuguese example, English merchant vessels were powerful floating fortresses of mobile firepower. In contrast, the massive Spanish Armada augmented its massive galleons designed for defence or to board, by augumenting the fleet with lightly armed merchantmen normally employed in the *flotas* bound for the Americas to serve as troop and materiel carriers. Hughes observes that as the Anglo-Dutch and French wars of the seventeenth century were principally over trade and not politics, the flight of an enemy ship from battle was counted as enough. It was not necessary to sink or capture the ship. To achieve this new objective, the commander wanted fast, concentrated fire to drive the enemy into retreat. Moreover, writes Hughes, 'firepower was increasing the rate of fire and by keeping station at close interval with superb seamanship'.[25] Rate of fire was different for Spanish and English gunners. Faster reloading meant more concentrated firepower. In Henry VIII's time thirty shots a day was thought good. But by 1588, English cannon and culverin could fire eight shots per hour. Spanish records from 1588 state that the English bombardment of the Armada was relentless and that the English could fire three rounds to their one.[26]

To increase the density of firepower, cannon were stacked vertically on two or three gun decks. Ships were commonly defeated by a firepower kill – that is, by knocking out guns and gunners and crushing morale with an initial broadside. Afterwards, the rate, accuracy, concentration of firepower and shot penetration determined victory. In the age of fighting sail, the art of command lay in accomodating for the wind to allow the ship's batteries to concentrate overwhelming firepower on the enemy.

English naval tactics changed in a few decades, so that when Drake fitted out the *Elizabeth Bonaventure* in 1585 for his West Indies expedition, he dispensed with defensive guns altogether. Instead, he added two cannon periers, two full culverins and four demi-culverins, increasing his firepower from 406 pounds to 522 pounds of shot, and thus gaining both more power and also greater range.[27] Hawkyns' changes that began in the 1570s continued into the '90s. The *Warspite*, launched in 1595, was the last of the galleons built to Hawkyns' race-built specifications. She was the beamiest of the race-built galleons, with a ratio of 2.5. Her beam gave greater buoyancy and stability and allowed her to take heavier artillery (her offensive artillery shot was a total of 444 pounds). Galleons built from about 1595 to 1599 began to be loaded down with still heavier culverins. These proved too heavy for Hawkyns' narrower race-built vessels, so about 1600–02, race-built galleons grew fatter, and returned to the length-to-beam ratio (about 2:1) of the pre-1570 design. Given the other race-built modifications in superstructure and sail plan that were kept, it was a reasonable trade-off. In exchange for greater strength and buoyancy, these vessels remained nimble and lost only a small fraction of their speed.[28]

Boarding versus bombarding? When Drake singed the beard of the Spaniard in the Cádiz raid of April 1587, the Spanish had counted for defence on their galleys to ram, board and engage in hand-to-hand combat. The ancient warships and tactics that had worked so well now proved useless against powerful pinnaces. Galleys in Spain proved as useless as they were in the Caribbean. Rodgers (echoing Alfred Thayer Mahan) points out that in the 1587 Cádiz raid, 'the English meant to make a gun fight, whereas the Spaniards regarded the guns as auxiliaries. So we have another example of the great tactical advantage of so managing the battle as to make the victory turn on the superiority of the weapon in which the victor is strongest'.[29] By means of artillery, at Cádiz Drake destroyed eighteen vessels, took six prizes and revictualled his fleet. It was a loss of 172,000 ducats according to the official Spanish reckoning. The Spanish were fighting today's war using yesterday's technology and tactics.

Manoeuvrable race-built galleons and quicker broadsides meant that the English could risk closer engagement. One Spaniard wrote that they would dart into close range, 'within musket shot and sometimes arquebus shot', fire quickly and fall off.[30] Rodgers writes that in 1588 'the English introduced a new type of battle, relying on great guns in sailing ships rather than on boarders in rowing ships, so that in this year we see the birth of a system of tactics'.[31] The weaker side exploited its superior gunnery and faster galleons. The technique continued to be used in the West Indies by the same commanders of 1588: 'Much the same pattern marked Drake and Hawkins' last expedition to the Caribbean' in 1595, notes Parker.[32] One should add that when the English returned to San Juan in 1598, there was no element of surprise, nor could the batteries of demi-culverins match San Felipe Del Morro's powerful land batteries.

Off the Portland Bill and in the shoal waters off Gravelines, Charles Howard, Lord High Admiral from 1585 to 1619, accounted his demi-culverin to be his most effective weapon for hitting and running. In contrast, the culverins fired an 18-pound shot and the demi-culverins a more handy 9-pound shot. The demi-culiverins were quick-loading and when loaded with a more powerful charge, a barrel with finer casting, and bronze giving a tighter fit for the projectile, the demi-culverin had an extreme range of 2,500 paces, over a mile. The foundries of England and Sweden, countries with rich iron deposits, had both the raw materials and the expertise for superior manufacture. Ordnance manufacture in England and Sweden had by 1600 surpassed Spain's arms industry. By 1603 nearly all the English royal ships had the superior bronze guns.[33] Spain had chosen the cheaper but heavier iron cannon, though they recognised the superiority of bronze, and used it when possible.

The next 100 years saw smaller, lighter and more powerful cannon, followed then by a return to larger ones and beamier ships to accommodate them. By the early seventeenth century the English navy had changed from iron to cast-bronze, but within another twenty years with more guns per ship, the cheaper cast iron cannon, now better-designed and built, returned.[34]

Formations and Tactics

This section follows the order of a naval engagement: from sailing to the site of battle, to ordering the fleet in formation, deciding on tactics, gaining the weather gage and engaging the enemy at close or long range.

Keeping Station

Tacking (crossing the eye of the wind across the bows) and wearing or gybing (crossing the wind across the stern) in a closely ordered fleet called for discipline to prevent a collision. Losing station by falling to leeward was a common problem, and for this reason British fleets, when close-hauled, would steer seven points off the wind (nearly 80 degrees off the wind), even though steering six points was possible. The extra point was to allow ships that had fallen off to work their way back to station. Well-trained French fleets, when sailing close-hauled, could manage six points off the wind (about 67 degrees). None of this was easy, even considering that fleets in battle formation moved slowly, perhaps making no more than four knots. Tunstall writes that 'it is difficult for modern readers to visualise the agonising slowness of most seas battles under sail'. Even under ideal conditions the attacking ship could not advance directly onto the enemy without disabling its own batteries, whose arc of fire was limited. He outlines the options:

> Systems of naval tactics were thus inevitably designed to bring fleets into action as rapidly as possible while exposing them to as little hostile fire as possible. This could be done by approaching the enemy's line end on, so that the enemy was prevented from firing his batteries; by an oblique approach which allowed the

ships to begin firing on part of the enemy line even if they had to shift targets as they advanced; or by a bold head-on charge at the enemy line, as at Trafalgar, which reduced the time of exposure to long-range enemy fire.[35]

Wind and Weather Gage

In the age of sail, wind was the determining factor. Fighting sail required special considerations not so critical in oar or machine-powered vessels. As Tunstall has said, given the inability to point into the wind, over half the compass was off limits, and in a dead calm with the fleet dead in the water, the entire compass was useless.[36] Oars freed a ship from the mercy of the winds, just as later in the late eighteenth century, engines were to do, first in commercial vessels and then in naval ships.[37] As Tunstall has observed, prior to engaging in battle fleets would try to gain the windward gage (the usual spelling for this nautical sense). 'Weather gage', being upwind of the enemy, provides a better position for exploiting the wind. A fleet could only form in battle order if the wind and weather were favourable. Besides affording greater speed and manoeuvrability, being upwind of the enemy also meant that smoke from the guns did not mask the signal flags of the admiral and, if his squadron overlapped the enemy, he could order his van or rear to double or bracket the enemy line. A further advantage of windward gage is that the admiral could deploy fireships downwind onto the enemy.

That said, there are still some advantages to taking up the leeward position, as the French pointed out. Attacking from below the enemy meant that an enemy ship, once disabled, would drift down and could be captured, and if she were an attacking ship and damaged, she could simply bear away. When firing broadsides from downwind and in the lee of the enemy, the lower gunports on the weather side could be kept open even in a seaway and the guns could fire longer. As a close-hauled enemy could not escape to windward, attacking from leeward could force him to engage in battle on the terms dictated by the attacker.[38]

In truth, most early commanders maintained formation going into battle, but once engaged, broke formation and fought ship against ship. John Paul Jones, the Scottish captain fighting as an American commander against the English, observed in 1783: 'A captain of the line "must" at this day be a tactician. A captain of a cruising frigate "may make shift" without having ever heard of naval tactics.'[39] What was true in the eighteenth century was doubly so in the sixteenth and early seventeenth centuries with less manoeuvrable ships and the privateering tradition of one-on-one engagements.

From his experience, the privateer admiral Sir William Monson (1569–1643) understood tactics better than many. He had sailed against the Armada in the Channel and later, under Cumberland, fought the Spanish in the Caribbean. Monson was captured in 1591 by Spanish, spent a year in galleys and in prison at Lisbon Castle. On release, he successfully engaged the Spanish off their own coast. In his manuscript *Tracts* (c. 1603), he opposed De Chaves' idea of fixed battle formations (1530) as being unmaintainable. Monson writes that 'ships which must be carried by wind and sails and the sea, affording no firm or steadfast footing, cannot be commanded to take their ranks like soldiers in a battle by land'.[40] A commander must, he writes, gain the wind before any action. Monson approved of maintaining close order to within a cable, 100 fathoms, between ships – that is, when closing with but not when engaging the enemy.[41]

Monson took command in the Narrow Seas in 1603, the year he may have written his *Tracts*, and the last year of the protracted Anglo-Spanish War. As for battle tactics, he writes that before engaging, the commander should divide the ship's company into three groups – boarders, those firing small shot, those firing cannon – but they must stay able to help each other, whiich was later to be Ralegh's advice. Before joining combat, the ship is to be brought by the sailors to her short or fighting sails. These were the foresail, mainsail and foretopsail. These three sails provide enough steerage way and result in only small heel in a breeze, making the cannon fire more accurate. The ship's way can be regulated by shivering or throwing aback any of these sails, usually the topsail. All the other sails are to be bent and ready for setting. The vessel has already worked her way to weather using her fore and aft sails. Once there, these are furled. No fore and aft sails are to be set when going into battle. Monson observes that flush-decked ships, race-built, good in attack, are poor against boarders, as there are no bulk-heads or fore- or sterncastles for defence.[42]

In the age of fighting sail, no victory could come about without first work-ing wind and wave to advantage. 'Naval tactics are an admiral's art, and in a fleet propelled by wind and sails he exercised his art with difficulty. At no time could he make use of more than five-eighths of the sea around him, and when a calm prevailed he could not move his fleet at all', writes Tunstall. Square-riggers can sail close-hauled only to five or six points off the wind. He continues: 'Since the weather gauge automatically conferred some measure of tactical advantage, especially in the choice of whether, when and how to attack, the manoeuvres preliminary to a battle were often concerned with keeping, gaining or disputing the windward position.' Futher: 'Everything depended upon the wind and the weather and, unless these were favourable, no battle could take place, nor could either fleet be formed in battle order ... The larger the fleet the more difficult it was to control, and the longer it took to carry out evolutions.'[43]

Close and Open Order

Nathaniel Boteler in his 'Dialogical Discourse Concerning Marine Affairs', writ-ing about 1634, observes that a fleet can be put in either close or open order. If close, there is the danger that one ship may collide with another. When firing a broadside, the better sailers, 'being nimble and yare [quick] of steerage,' can veer or tack to bring the opposite battery to bear on the enemy. But 100 bad sailers, 'being closed and shuffled up together, and being heavy and unwieldy withal they can never use save one, the same beaten side'. Best is a burden of a 'middle size', and no cannon larger than the demi-culverin.[44]

Boteler's 'Dialogue the Sixth, Touching the Order of Fleets of War in sailing, chases, boardings, battles' divides the fleet into three squadrons or if there are more than 100 ships, five squadrons, their formation controlled by signals. If single ship meets a single ship, and if the chaser is to leeward, she will attempt to meet the enemy at the nearest angle. If the enemy is to leeward, then the action to take is to run down on her. Boteler's wording is close to but not as lively as that of his predecessor, Captain John Smith, in *A Sea Grammar*. Like Smith, Boteler advises getting the weather gage. If the enemy has it, he says, shoot away his rigging so he must fall off, but do not shoot if the range is 'beyond the distance of musket shot at point blank', an order echoed by many others.

Even at this late date Boteler, like Smith, favours boarding, especially if the enemy ship is small. Otherwise, the instruction is to batter her with artillery so she will be forced 'either to yield or sink in the sea, and especially if your cannon be better than hers'. If boarding, lay the enemy's hawse, or even better, either in the bow, or her quarter, enter by her shrouds. If one has two vessels, writes Boteler, never flank the enemy, as one might fire on oneself. Be sure to stay upwind of the enemy until she is vanquished, and 'hold her under your lee until you be fully possessed of her'. If on the defence, get clear, outsail the enemy, or steal away in the night – not Grenville's way in 1591 off Flores, notes Boteler.[45]

Spanish, to Batter and Board

To concentrate firepower, whether on land or sea, it is essential to maintain formation. Early in the sixteenth century Alonso de Chaves, at the Court of Charles V and official lecturer at the Casa de Contratación, Seville, observes in *Espejo de Navigantes* (*Seaman's Glass*, 1530s) that 'ships at sea are as war-horses on land, since admitting they are not very nimble at turning at any pace, nevertheless a regular formation increases their power'. The Spanish Armada's crescent formation in 1588 was in essence a land battle line modified for defence at sea, and it worked.

Given a formation, where should a squadron position itself, relative to the wind and the enemy? Cesáreo Fernández Duro, nineteenth-century Spanish captain and historian, writes in *Armada Española* that in this period that before engaging the enemy it is essential to gain the windward gage.[46] A trumpet is to sound, and the fleet is to fall into order:

> and as they come into range they shall commence to play their most powerful artillery, taking care that the first shots do not miss, for, as I have said, when the first shots hit, inasmuch as they are the largest, they strike great dread and terror into the enemy ... Having so begun firing, they shall always first play the largest guns, which are on the side or board towards the enemy, and likewise they shall move over from the other side those guns which have wheeled carriages to run on the upper part of the deck and poop.

This last direction seems most unlikely.

Spanish naval practice in the Renaissance was the tried and true but medieval: maintaining a fixed formation, line abreast, preparatory to boarding. To the Spanish conquistador, indeed from the myrmidons of Agamemnon and Achilles on the plains of Troy to the battles of El Cid in Spain, true combat was seen as fighting man to man. Naval artillery was scorned as an 'ignoble arm' to be used only to soften the enemy prior to boarding.[47] The Spanish monarch Philip II much preferred winning by boarding the enemy and engaging man to man. But he cautioned the Duke of Medina Sidonia, reluctant yet loyal commander of his Armada fleet, about the English:

> In particular I must warn you that the enemy's intention will be to fight at long distance, on account of his advantage in artillery ... The aim of our men, on the contrary, must be to bring him to close quarters and grapple with the weapons they hold in their hands; and you will have to be very careful to carry this out. So that you will be well informed, I am sending you some reports from which you will see the way in which the enemy employs his artillery to fire low and sink his opponent's ships; and you will have to take such precautions as you consider necessary in this respect.[48]

These orders, dated 1 April 1588, are the same orders – verbatim – he had given to Sidonia's predecessor, the seasoned admiral, the Marques of Santa Cruz, just eleven months earlier, on 31 March 1587, before Cruz' fleet set out for the Americas.

Fernández Duro identifies Spanish practice in what Corbett calls the 'earliest known attempt to formulate a definite fighting formation and tactical system for sailing fleets'. Duro writes that as in a Renaissance army:

> so in a fleet, the captain-general ought to order the strongest and largest ships to form in one quarter to attack, grapple, board and break-up the enemy, and the lesser and weaker ships in another quarter apart, with their artillery and munitions to harass, pursue, and give chase to the enemy if he flies, and to come to the rescue wherever there is most need.

Smaller vessels should be stationed on either side of the main body. Was the enemy in close body or line ahead? Were the great ships in the centre or on the flanks? Where was the flagship? In order to see the enemy and to be able to fire on him, Duro writes, squadrons should do their best to gain the weather gage and stay upwind and should sail 'in line abreast' (not in single file, line ahead). If they sailed in file one behind the other only the leading ships could fight. If the enemy fleet formed a 'lance-head or triangle, then ours ought to form in two lines ... so as to take the enemy between them and engage them on both fronts'. If the enemy were to approach formed in two lines, then do the same. 'On no account must ours penetrate into the midst of the enemy's formation' as arms and smoke could envelope the fleet. Nelson was not yet on the horizon off Trafalgar, cutting through the line.

Once close in, what tactics are best? Duro writes that lesser weapons are to be employed: smaller artillery, missiles such as harpoons, stones, hand-guns, crossbows and then fireballs from the tops and from the castles, and at the same time 'calthrops, linstocks, stink-balls, grenades, and the scorpions for the sails and rigging'. The trumpets now sound. Men are to grapple and fight with scythes or shearhooks to cut the rigging. Others fire into the rigging and enemy crew. As the captain's voice cannot not be heard in the din, a trumpet, flag or topsail gives the signal. The flagship, he continues, should take 'great care not to grapple another, for then he could not see what is passing in the battle nor control it'. The Spanish view of boarding had changed little over the centuries. The accompanying armed boats are to close in once the ships have grappled. They should use their bases (culverin types) and harquebuses, or get close in and wedge the rudders or cut them and their gear away. Or they should leap aboard, or scuttle the ship with augers. [49]

English, Long-Range Fire

Board or batter with artillery? What led to using naval artillery as the primary weapon? The English knew of long-range bombardment from the example of the Portuguese armed merchantmen of the late fifteenth century. Since then they had been sailing the seas and to the ports of the pirate-infested Indian Ocean – for profit, not politics. This mercantilistic stance (English as well) is even reflected in the title of Don Manoel I (1495–1521), 'lord of the conquest, navigation and commerce of India, Ethiopia, Arabia and Persia'. [50] In 1500 Manoel issued orders to a fleet that:

> you are not to come to close quarter with them if you can avoid it, but only with your artillery are you to compel them to strike sail … so that this war be waged with greater safety, and so that less loss may result to the tople of your ships.

The Portuguese way was defensive and executed at long distance, an approach effective for decades against pirates in the Indian Ocean and the Red Sea. [51] It was not lost on Howard in 1588.

As the century drew on, the Portuguese continued to lead the way in 1555 by publishing what may be the first modern European manual of naval warfare. Fernão Oliveira, in *A Arte da Guerra do Mar* (*The Art of War at Sea*), [52] writes that 'at sea we fight at a distance', [53] seldom close enough for hand-to-hand combat. If attacking, the Portuguese would form a single straight line, as galleys did. The galleons would run down on the enemy in a line, turn, fire one battery, wear or gybe to fire the opposite battery, then fall off to let the rest of the line in turn attack and fire in similar fashion, with the squadron executing a series of figures of eight as they approached, fired and fell off – an early line-ahead formation.

Despite the Portuguese example, the early English tactics were similar to those of the Spanish. Take the first known English naval tactical instructions. Before November 1531, and probably written as orders for Henry VIII's attacks on French ports in 1512 and 1513, is Thomas Audley's *Book of Orders for the War both by Land and Sea*. It exemplifies late medieval practice: get the wind of the enemy, then board:

If they chase let them that chase shoot no ordnance till he be ready to board him[54] ... In case you board your enemy enter not till you see the smoke gone and then shoot off all your pieces, your port-pieces, the pieces of hail-shot, [and] cross-bow shot to beat his cage deck, and if you see his deck well ridden [cleared] then enter with your best men, but first win his tops in any wise if it be possible. In case you see there come rescue, bulge [scuttle] the enemy ship [but] first take heed your own men be retired, [and] take the captain with certain of the best with him, the rest [to be] committed to the sea, for else they will turn upon you to your confusion.[55]

Audley gives no specific formation, but he does direct the admiral to hoist a distinctive flag forward, and other vessels one aft, for recognition. Once having the wind, each captain is free to choose any enemy who is an equal match: 'Choose every man his bird.' The admiral is to keep a tender ready for escape if the enemy seizes his ship. Some additional pinnaces are kept in reserve to throw into battle as required.[56]

A century later, some were still ambivalent about boarding. To board a ship bristling with large-calibre cannon firing at short range was suicidal, Captain John Smith, a land soldier, admitted in 1627. He compares boarding a ship to charging trenches on land: 'He that hath tried himself as oft in the entering a resisting ship as I have done both them and the other, he would surely confess there is no such dangerous service ashore as a resolved, resolute fight at sea.' Nevertheless, Smith still prefers the old way, first firing on, then boarding the enemy, and he concludes that 'if a ship be open, presently to board her is the best way to take her'.[57] Smith's is the maxim of any foot soldier: to win, one must take and hold land. For Smith too, artillery bombardment alone is not sufficient for gaining victory.

I.A.A. Thompson sums up the difference between the English and Spanish fleets in 1588. The English tactic was to 'keep the action at long range, the Spanish to close, batter and board'.[58] The English long-range guns were superior to those of the Spanish, 'but also in heavy-shotted, medium- and short-range armament as well'. In fact, observes Thompson, 'the Spanish Armada was at such a decisive disadvantage in firepower, in both weight of shot and range, that it was probably incapable of winning the sea battle on whatever terms it was fought'.[59]

No closing, no grappling, no boarding – these were the express orders of Admiral, Charles, Lord Howard of Effingham, to the English fleet facing the Spanish Armada. The English were not to play to the Spaniard's strengths. Hawkyns and the other commanders realised that their only defence was in 'using stand-off gunnery to keep the enemy at bay until his ships were either disabled or driven away'.[60] Sir Walter Ralegh, one of the senior commanders, defended his admiral, pointing out that even without the Duke of Parma's troops, the Spanish had an army aboard, and the English did not. The Spanish had more tonnage, and it would have been folly for the English to engage close in. Observes Ralegh, Howard:

was better advised than many malignant fools were that found fault with his demeanor. The Spaniards had an army aboard them and he had none. They had more ships than he had, and of higher building and charging; so that had he entangled himself with these great and powerful vessels he had greatly endangered this Kingdom of England. But our Admiral knew his advantage and held it; which had he not done, he would not have been worthy to have held his head.[61]

The English, in smaller vessels and with fewer men, who had long faced the power of the Spanish in the West Indies, knew that without the numbers, sailing ability and superior gunnery would be decisive.

England's success against the Spanish Armada, summarises Parker, was from a combination of her race-built ships, a concentration of heavy guns on the principal ships, rapid rate of fire, and the Crown's sustained financial support over many years of the Royal Navy.[62] From 1577 until the Armada in 1588, and for nearly a decade after, the royal shipyards steadily modified older ships and built new ones along Hawkyns' race-built lines. By 1595, of the Navy's thirty-eight fighting ships, twenty-three exceeded 400 tons, with the fleet totalling nearly 20,000 tons. Parker notes that the 'ability to carry heavy artillery equivalent to almost 4.5 per cent of total displacement was unprecedented' in any navy at that time. As for ship design, to maintain stability and keep the centre of gravity low, particularly in race-built galleons, heavier artillery was located on the lower decks, close to the waterline. To keep the sea out when heeled, gunports were hinged. By the 1590s Hawkyns' programme to 'reform' the Elizabethan navy made it, writes Parker, 'the most powerful battle-fleet afloat anywhere in the world'.[63] But it was still not the world's largest battle-fleet. Spain's still was.

Naval Gunnery

Gunnery depended on accurate firing and rapid reloading. Tunstall writes:

> It is frequently asserted that, whereas the British fired at the French hulls, the French fired at the masts, rigging and sails of the British ships ... The hull was more difficult to hit but was the more decisive target ... British ships were often so crank that their seams leaked through the strain of their own guns being fired, so a few well placed enemy shots would soon have them hard at work at the pumps. Seen at a distance, the whole ship, rather than the hull alone, presented an easier target; in this case, damage aloft could stop a ship's advance or send her reeling out of the line ... With anything like a sea running, it was difficult to aim at the enemy's hull at any distance as it kept partially disappearing from view. There was also the difficulty of timing the fire; the French generally fired on the upward roll of the firing ship'.

The rigging was the larger and easier target to hit.

For British admirals, battles were determined by individual ships and squadrons. Only a few admirals fought major battles without having close tactical control.[64]

They preferred linear battles against the well-formed lines of the French, as splitting the fleet and attacking with separate squadrons dispersed the ships, risked piecemeal defeat, and did not concentrate firepower. Given the limited ability to signal orders with only flags, sail, cannon or lantern, organising and executing an elaborate attack just was not possible. An admiral would need to keep his plan simple: throw most of the fleet against some part of the enemy line and bring concentrated fire onto that part. If he were more ambitious he might try to break through the enemy's line.

Point-blank Range

While the English practiced long-range firing, they tried to make every shot count. Ralegh's instructions to his fleet of six vessels (later augmented to thirteen) on 3 May 1617, on the eve of sailing from Plymouth for Guiana, are illustrative. Ralegh took his instructions largely from William Gorges, written possibly as early as 1578. 'The gunners shall not shoot any great ordnance at other distance than point blank', writes Ralegh. An officer is to be appointed to see that no loose powder is carried between decks, or any powder near any linstock or match. Various hogsheads should be sawn in half and filled with water on the decks:

> You shall divide your carpenters, some in hold if any shot come between wind and water, and the rest between the decks, with plates of leads, plugs, and all things necessary laid by them. You shall also lay by your tubs of water certain wet blankets to cast upon and choke any fire.

The master and boatswain shall appoint sailors to every sail, and that the sailors must know their jobs and keep silent. No one is to board the enemy without order:

> because the loss of a ship to us is of more importance than the loss of ten ships to the enemy, as also by one man's boarding, all our fleet may be engaged; it being too great a dishonour to lose the least of our fleet. But every ship, if we be under the lee of any enemy, shall labour to recover the wind if the admiral endeavours it. But if we find any enemy to be leewards of us, the whole fleet shall follow the admiral, vice-admiral, or other leading ship within musket shot of the enemy [musket range was about 150 yards, effectively 80 yards]; giving so much liberty to the leading ship as after her broadside is delivered she may stay and trim her sails.

Like Oliveira, writing years earlier, Ralegh favoured a line-ahead formation employing the figure of eight:

> Then is the second ship to tack as the first ship and give the other side, keeping the enemy under a perpetual shot. This you must do upon the windermost ship or ships of an enemy, which you shall either batter in pieces, or force him or them to bear up and so entangle them, and drive them foul one of another to their utter confusion.

Musketeers shall shoot only at a distance ordered by their commanders:

> If the admiral give chase and be headmost man, the next ship shall take up his
> boat, if other order be not given. Or if any other ship be appointed to give
> chase, the next ship (if the chasing ship has a boat at her stern) shall take it.

If any make a ship strike her colours, that ship must hold back and not enter her
until the admiral arrives.

In a second set of orders Ralegh repeats that the fleet should get to windward
of the enemy and follow one of the flagships to within musket shot. The leading
ship is to fire broadside into the 'windermost' ships, then tack away. The rest of
the squadron follows in turn, notes Corbett, in line-ahead formation, each vessel
executing a similar figure of eight.[65]

Single Column Ahead

There is enough evidence to sketch out Tudor and Stuart battle practice, though
Brian Tunstall finds that except aboard galleys there is little on the interaction of
gunnery and tactics from 1500 to 1650.[66] At the start of our period, ships were
still using line-abreast formation, like an attacking infantry regiment. In galley
fashion, bow chasers provided firepower to soften the enemy before grappling
and boarding. With the demise of the galley the advantage of the line-ahead
firing broadsides over line abreast using bow ordnance was evident. Sir George
Biddlecombe, a mid-nineteenth-century captain, observes that as fleets are often
'promiscuously' scattered by the vagaries of wind and wave, 'it has been found
that there is no mode of preserving order in battles at sea'. He thus favours 'keeping on a line, not quite close hauled, ahead of each other, and under very moderate sail; the distance being according to circumstances'.[67]

The commander might approach line on, obliquely, or directly into the enemy
line, the quickest method. The aim was to minimise enemy fire. For all the attention to formations, British admirals observed that though battles were determined
by individual ships and squadrons, only a few major battles were won without
close tactical control. The line-ahead formation allows a squadron to close, turn
and bring most of its guns to bear on the target, concentrating the firepower of
the bronze culverins from a safe distance, in a word, '*Fernkampf*'.[68] Merrill Bartlett
writes:

> Whereas the Spanish, even with the Armada, sought close combat, trusting
> to the known superiority of their infantry on board these ships, English naval
> tactics, as if in continuation of insular tendency towards keeping the enemy
> at arms' length, adhered to a policy of distant combat, *Fernkampf*, relying on
> superior gunnery and sailing.[69]

This formation further allowed an admiral to gain the weather gage more easily,
and then, from upwind, fall off and attack or stand off and decline battle.[70]

The line-ahead formation had the further advantage that it brought fleets into action quickly with the least exposure to enemy fire By 1650 the single column ahead had been adopted as the standard attack formation.

Implied in these formations is that the admiral can control his fleet. But could he? During the Tudor and Stuart periods large English squadrons were rare for good reason. They usually failed because it was nearly impossible, once engaged, to maintain control. The few large ones include the English squadrons in the Channel against the Spanish crescent in 1588; Drake's 1585–86 West Indies voyage with some thirty-six vessels; Howard's fleet of some twenty-five, including Sir Richard Grenville's *Revenge*, in the Azores in 1591; Hawkyns' and Drake's 1595–96 West Indies voyage and Cumberland's to Puerto Rico in 1598, and Ralegh's smaller fleet of thirteen vessels to Guiana in 1617–18. Of these large fleets, only Drake's in 1585–86 achieved a clear victory.

From the seventeenth century on there was a split in thinking between the British and the French admirals on the matter of conducting a fleet in battle. British admirals preferred linear battles, the French (following the Spanish way), well-formed lines. The French felt that splitting the fleet and attacking with separate squadrons dispersed the ships and risked piecemeal defeat and, more important, it did not concentrate firepower. 'The main reason, however, for not adopting a more elaborate form of attack was the difficulty of organising and executing anything requiring sophistication and finesse, especially in view of the limited British signalling system', observes Tunstall.[71]

Clerk's 'cutting the line' and concentrating fire onto one part of the enemy to break the enemy's formation was Grenville's way in 1591 off Flores and Nelson's way against the French and Spanish in 1805 at Trafalgar. But the true character of the British sailor, censures Clerk, was 'so justly displayed in the obstinate resistance made by Sir Richard Greenville [sic], in a single ship, against a numerous Spanish fleet', when he attempted to escape by breaking through the Spanish line with the *Revenge* in 1591 off Flores, instead of falling off and running.[72] Spirit trumped discretion in Grenville's decision to run his single ship through the Spanish line, says Clerk 'in that he suffered the height of his spirit to transport him both beyond his discretion and charity'.[73] Best, he writes, is for the leading ship to fire a broadside into the 'windermost ship or ships of the enemy' then tack. Then the rest of the squadron is to follow in like fashion. Tunstall sees here 'a rudimentary line-ahead formation, moving in a succession of figures of eight'. The ship fires, comes about, fires again, one squadron following another in a figure of eight manoeuvre.[74] This line-ahead formation was truly tested in the Anglo-Dutch wars, if not earlier against the Armada. Gabriel Daniel in *Histoire de la Milice Françoise*, 1721, writes that line-ahead '*a été inventé par les Hollandois et les Anglais*' in their wars for commercial dominance, 1652–54 1665–67 and 1672–74 (but unlike the Anglo-French War, 1627–29, which was fought over religion). English tactics evolved when facing the Dutch for commercial dominance. Both favoured disabling but not destroying an enemy ship and her valuable cargo.[75]

Amphibious and Guerilla Operations

Amphibious operations were employed in the sixteenth and seventeenth centuries. Early on in the period soldiers, marines originally there for boarding ships, were now secretly landed ashore to take an objective, with their assault covered by fire from naval batteries.

These tactics were employed early on by the Portuguese in India. When Vasco da Gama attacked the Calicut fleet in 1503 the larger *naus* remained near the coastline, and small *caravelas* carrying thirty men, four heavy guns (two each side) six falconets and twelve smaller swivel guns secured a beachhead. These boats could also enter a harbour too shoal for deep-draught ocean-going ships. Nedwitt stresses 'how important the smaller boats were in the amphibious operations', while covered by artillery from the larger *naus* (Sp., *naos*). 'Virtually every action involved the Portuguese opening fire with their great ships [sic] guns and numerous accounts testify to the range, firepower and terrifying effect of this artillery'[76] when combined with the unexpected land attack.

Because their *naus* carried the supplies, the soldiers on land could move fast and be resupplied easily by the ships postioned close to shore. These large *naus* were also floating artillery batteries and fired their *bombardas grossas* at land targets. Sometimes ships' guns would be ferried ashore for use there:

> One great advantage of sea power was the capacity it gave the Portuguese to take their enemies by surprise. Ships could move troops and materiel quickly from one place to another. There were numerous occasions when an armed Portuguese fleet appeared unexpectedly before a town and was able to take full advantage of the unpreparedness of the enemy.[77]

In 1507, Afonso de Albuquerque, off the Arabian and Indian coasts found he needed provisions, supplies and water. These he could get either by means of tributes or by force.[78] The ports of Ormuz, Malacca and Goa were critical for servicing the Portuguese fleets and for administering Portugal's rule over the seas in the Orient. Albuquerque attacked the fort at Curiat by landing one contingent on a small island facing the fort and then 'went along the river to disembark at the other part ... and with all his people went on his way softly'.[79] He got his provisions. Though amphibious operations are notoriously difficult to execute because of the close co-ordination needed, the Portuguese were remarkably effective:

> This type of warfare enabled one of the smallest and poorest states in Europe to become a military power and to achieve military objectives in a way that would have been inconceivable had the Portuguese limited themselves to conventional land warfare or had they tried simply to use their ships to effect blockades.[80]

As part of this combined sea–land operation, Portuguese ships regularly carried soldiers. The purpose of these raids was plunder, and unlike the Spanish in the Americas, who were bent on empire and marched far inland for gold and glory, the mercantile Portuguese in the Orient stayed along the coast, close to the fleet, a practice repeated later in colonising Brazil. It was thought enough to establish trading posts in the port cities.

These lesssons the English learned well. Tudor England, in facing Europe's greatest power, Spain, adopted and adapted the earlier Portuguese amphibious tactics. The Portuguese also showed the English how to negotiate a surrender while at the same time pressing an attack on a port's shipping and simultaneously attacking with soldiers in two places at once, employing mobility and surprise.[81] Such was Drake's way in Callao harbour in Perú in 1579.[82] English ships engaged in amphibious raids first in the Caribbean and later on the Continent. Bartlett writes:

> Such operations, in particular landings, were more apt to be successful when undertaken by sailors with aid from armed men – more or less forerunners of marines. Indeed, the most successful actions were unofficial, like those of Drake in 1572–73 against Nombre de Dios and on the Isthmus of Panamá, and Spanish Pacific ports sacked during his circumnavigation of the globe (1577–80), most of which were small and poorly defended.[83]

Captain John Oxnam provides an example of an English guerilla operation. He built his 45ft pinnace secretly in the Panamanian forests. She had sail and some twenty oars, was armed with two cannon and was manned by a crew of sixty. Fifty English and about ten Cimarróns took her downriver to the Pacific. In January 1577 he made a surprise attack on the Archipiélago de las Perlas, looted its riches, and carried off slaves in a successful amphibious operation. From there he sailed out and took two unsuspecting barks and 160,000 pesos worth of treasure, the largest haul by an Englishman to that date.[84]

In attacking Santo Domingo during his 1585–86 voyage, Sir Francis Drake, similarly with local Cimarrón help, unnoticed, landed Christopher Carleill and a thousand men 10 miles down the coast from the city. At daybreak Drake made a show of attacking the fort from the sea side. The Spanish, in defending the coast, had left their rear exposed. The city was quickly overcome by Carleill's forces. Drake came away with 25,000 ducats in ransom and all the fort's cannon. Drake was next off to Cartagena. This time there was no surprise. He anchored in the outer harbour, and Carleill landed at dusk with six companies of troops. The English marched to the narrow neck at the edge of the city, defended by 300 Spanish soldiers, eleven cannon on two galleys, earthen bulwarks and rows of poisoned stakes driven into the beach by the Indians. But by timing the operation for low tide, Carleill's men simply marched into the surf around the defences as the ships fired on the town. Drake took the city. At Cartagena Drake used his usual amphibious raid: by working on two fronts, a frontal bombardment and a rear attack. The English never did take a single treasure convoy, even a single ship, from the *flota* from the Americas. Given such a poor record, writes Wernham, in 1595 'it was therefore natural that thoughts turned once again to Drake's old idea of catching that treasure at its dispatching end: at Panama, Nombre de Dios or

Havana' by means of a lightning-strike attack. But times had changed since the 1570s, when Drake had been successful. Spain's American colonies were not such easy pickings in 1595, not even for guerilla tactics.[85]

The 1588 engagements in the English Channel were all naval, undertaken to prevent the ambitious amphibious Spanish plan. It was to ferry the Duke of Parma's troops across from the Netherlands, land in England, establish a beach-head and march on London. But combined sea–land operations can be tricky. Untimely communication and co-ordination between Admiral Medina Sidonia and the Duke of Parma, as well as weather and the defensive tactics of the English fleet, combined to prevent the Spanish plan from working.

At one point in his life Sir James Lancaster had sailed under the Portuguese flag, and, as he says, from them he learned devious ways. Sailing under the English flag as a privateer he engaged in trading one day and raiding the next. It was what Goethe termed 'commerce, privateering and war, triune, inseparable'.[86] When his fleet arrived at Pernambuco in 1594 it was bent on plunder. In the vanguard of the attack was a galley-frigate (constructed on site). She carried eighty men and was propelled by oars. She had a single mast, sail, and in the bow, 'a good sacar and two murdering pieces' (smaller artillery pieces and mortars).[87] Lancaster first attacked with these small vessels at dawn, hoping for surprise, but the ships had been carried off by the tide away from the harbour entrance and out of range for artillery support. So Lancaster was forced to wait for the flood tide later in the day to make a second attack. Meanwhile, there was a Dutch fleet in the harbour. He got their support, and in a joint international operation, they took the fort and split the treasure. Here was a successful international amphibious force that resembled Drake's earlier unsuccessful joint raid with the Protestant French captain, Guillaume le Têtu, near Nombre de Dios in 1572.

Facing the greater numbers of Spanish soldiers, cannon and larger ships in the West Indies, the English commando-style raids made good sense. At home, amphibious raiding helped the English defend themselves against Spanish raids. The 'English riverine and lacustrine warfare' was successful, writes Mark Fissel, but it has been 'overshadowed by the more famous, but less effective, exploits of Elizabethan amphibious operations against Spain and in the Caribbean'.[88] It was at least profitable enough to encourage hundreds of privateers to sail for the Caribbean.

The Elizabethan war against Spain was foremost a land war, 'but an integral part of the war effort was a conscious assault on Spain's dominions in the New World', observes Wernham. 'One of the principal aims of English naval operations was to supplement the queen's income by plundering the Spaniards'. The very nature of such plunder was amphibious and guerilla. Amphibious operations require a 'balance between naval and military' components, Wernham adds. The Anglo-Spanish war was expanded by taking it to Spain's source of wealth in the Americas, and expanded in its form by using amphibious guerilla tactics. Unlike the Spanish, the English fought for gold and the flag. To get money for a cash-strapped queen, the immediate and practical way was 'by sacking or ransoming Spanish seaports and settlements in both the New World and the Old'. For that, the English had to balance different elements: 'Soldiers were needed as well as ships and mariners, and most English amphibious operations had such plundering as a principal purpose'. Such undertakings were mostly by private enterprise, supplemented by state investment, and were extensions of the privateering pre-1585 in which the queen contributed a few ships to an enterprise and raked in any profit. Wernham emphasises that 'Sir Francis Drake's 1585–86 expedition set the pattern.'[8]

But under lesser leadership amphibious operations did not always succeed. An example is when Essex attacked Cádiz in 1595. He launched his attack in broad daylight from the seaward side of Santa Catalina Bay while the Spanish watched from the hillside. The English regiments were transported in the ships' boats, formed in ranks abreast, with the lead boat flying the Cross of Saint George. A drum beat set the pace in an attack with pageantry, pomp and circumstance. It could have been Agincourt. The wind that day was onshore, and the Atlantic breakers steep and high. Several vessels were swamped, and many men drowned. Essex retreated. He tried again on the ebb tide, as the Spanish still looked on, amazed, in '*admiración*' at English ignorance. According to Sir Julian Corbett, 'these are the earliest known orders for landing troops from ships in the face of an enemy', something Drake would never have done.[90]

About the only success of Essex' operation was to carry off Bishop Osorius' library with books that would join Thomas Bodley's collection for a new library soon to be built at Oxford. The irony is that just ten days after Essex returned to England, the annual Spanish *flota* safely sailed into San Lucar with £4,000,000 in American treasure. Essex earlier had bragged that to harm Spain he would cut off 'his golden Indian stream, whereby we shall cut his life veins and let out the vital spirits of his estate'. His boastful words rang hollow.[91]

After Hawkyns' and Drake's failure to take San Juan in 1595, there was one notably successful English amphibious operation – that of Sir George Clifford, Earl of Cumberland. His 1598 attack on San Juan, Puerto Rico, followed Drake's practice of first landing troops some distance away, then approaching the enemy from the land, the attack covered by naval guns. But there was no surprise this time, and the Spanish defences held. It was only when the Spanish in Del Morro ran out of food and were decimated by illness that they surrendered. Cumberland took, but could not hold, the city. The Crown would not commit the resources to build on his victory, and his men, like the Spanish, were also dying from disease. Cumberland's was a private undertaking for profit, though the Crown found political satisfaction in the English finally having taken San Juan, a major gateway to the Caribbean. Wernham notes that strapped for cash, Elizabeth the realist was obliged to 'make a campaign pay for itself through plunder. Objectives could thus be dangerously diversified and hence unclear'.[92] His sack of the port could have served political ends, at no cost to the queen, but by then she was not interested. Cumberland withdrew after five months' occupation.

The English (like the Portuguese earlier) were scattered thin overseas. The queen could only further her aims with the aim of the merchant navy. Further, joint naval commands usually meant a split between an admiral and a land general. Sailors were loyal to one commander and soldiers to another. It was profit (before patriotism) that drove the engine of war and was the motive for both sailors and soldiers, and their officers. The soldiers were drawn from private resources, make them difficult for the Crown to command. It was a case of divided purposes writ large.[93]

Hostilities did not cease with the Treaty of London, 1604. Philip II's policy of attacking Britain continued under his son, Philip III. Three years earlier, in 1601, he had sent a fleet of forty-eight ships to the British Isles and successfully landed four thousand soldiers at Kinsale to aid Irish rebels and to establish a base from which to attack England. But English forces, as well as ague and dysentery, forced retreat after several months. The Spanish amphibious operations were failures in 1588, 1598 and 1601.[94]

Ralegh's 1617–18 Guiana expedition with a fleet of thirteen vessels can be read as a failed amphibious raid. First, the Spanish had been warned of the English fleet's plans. There was no surprise. Then Ralegh arrived in the Orinoco sick, and had to give over command to his friend Lawrence Keymis. Keymis was directed to row up the river to San Thomé to find gold (but without harming the Spanish). The English fleet anchored offshore, and boats went up the Rio Orinoco. For weeks there was no communication between ship and shore. The considerable firepower of Ralegh's fleet was useless. It was anchored leagues from the shore party, out of artillery range. For weeks there was no communcation with the landing party far upriver. At San Thomé, Ralegh's hotheaded son Wat led an attack on the Spanish and was killed, along with two English captains and others. The English lost some 250 men to disease or enemy fire. Keymis and the remainder staggered back to the fleet with only 600 *reales*, 150 quintals of tobacco, some church bells and other items. Once Ralegh was back in England this failure would cost him his life.[95]

In Spain, Cádiz was the target of another amphibious raid in 1625. English marines landed and marched into a nearby village where the wine for the West Indies *flota* was stored. The commander, Sir Edward Cecil, Lord Wimbledon reported that 'the whole army drank itself to madness' on empty stomachs. It seems that the English commanders had provided no food for the troops. All discipline fell into a stupor. An amphibious operation undone by wine.[96]

Seafaring Manuals

Many of the commanders in the first half of the seventeenth century went to sea as land generals knowing only army tactics. The regular standing fleet of warships was now commanded by military men who were soldiers first and only later seamen.[97] Robison observes that Cromwell's colonels now made Commonwealth captains, and generals of the sea 'may be said to have recast the navy and the strategy of Drake, Hawkins, and Raleigh', recast along the lines of the army. One rare exception was Sir William Penn, vice admiral, and a professional naval officer with extensive experience.[98] At the start of the Dutch Wars in 1652 these land generals were frustrated

Ark Royal, 551-ton race-built galleon, 1587. Built at Deptford for Sir Walter Ralegh as the *Ark Ralegh*, later sold to the Crown and renamed. English admiral (flagship) commanded by the Lord High Admiral Charles Howard against the Armada, 1588. Rebuilt as *Anne Royal* 1608 at Woolwich. Artist Claes Janszoon Visscher. (National Maritime Museum, Greenwich. Print Department, British Library)

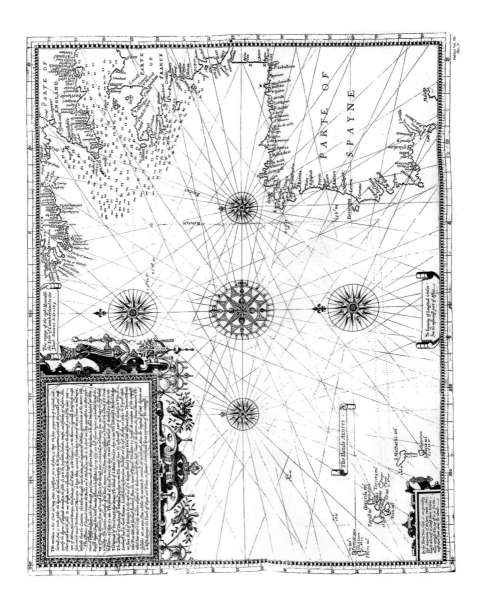

First map published in England to use Mercator–Wright projection, drawn by Edward Wright. Shows Sir George Clifford, 3rd Earl of Cumberland's 1589 voyage to the Azores. Published in *Wright's Certain Errors in Navigation*. (London: Valentine Sims, 1599)

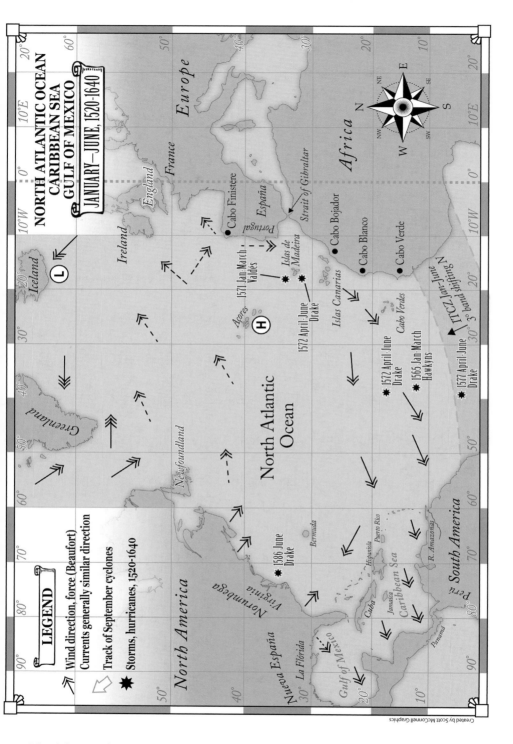

Pilot Atlas: North Atlantic Ocean, Caribbean Sea, Gulf of Mexico, January–June 1520–1640.
(Author's collection)

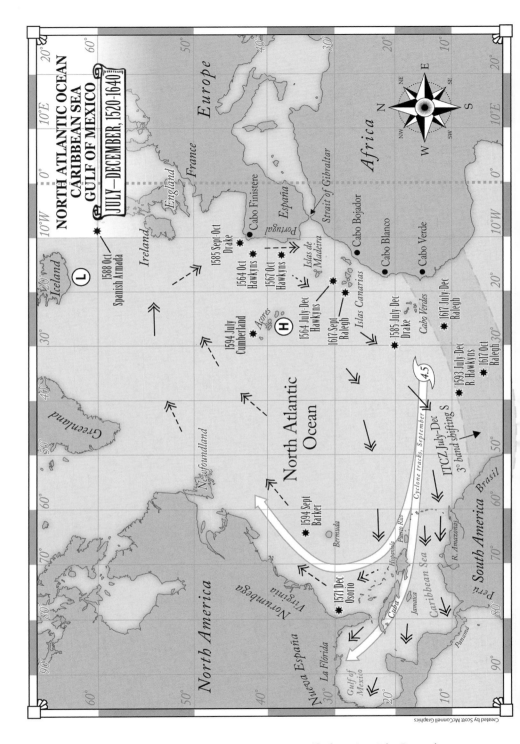

Pilot Atlas: North Atlantic Ocean, Caribbean Sea, Gulf of Mexico, July–December
1520–1640. (Author's collection)

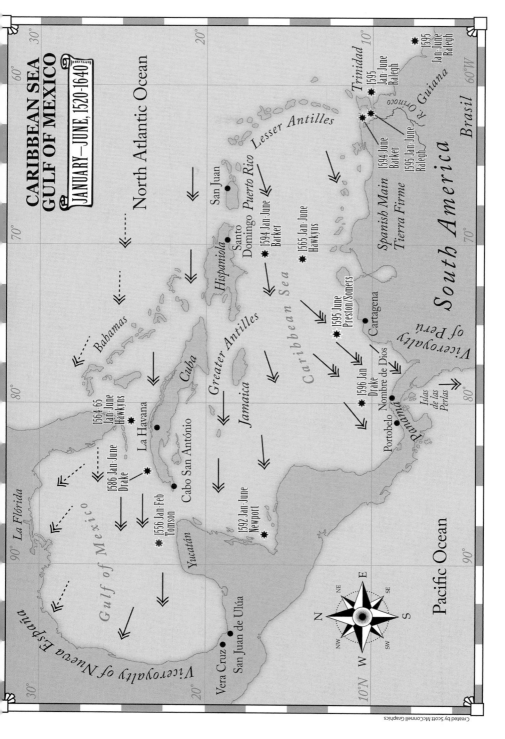

Pilot Atlas: Caribbean Sea, Gulf of Mexico, January–June 1520–1640. (Author's collection)

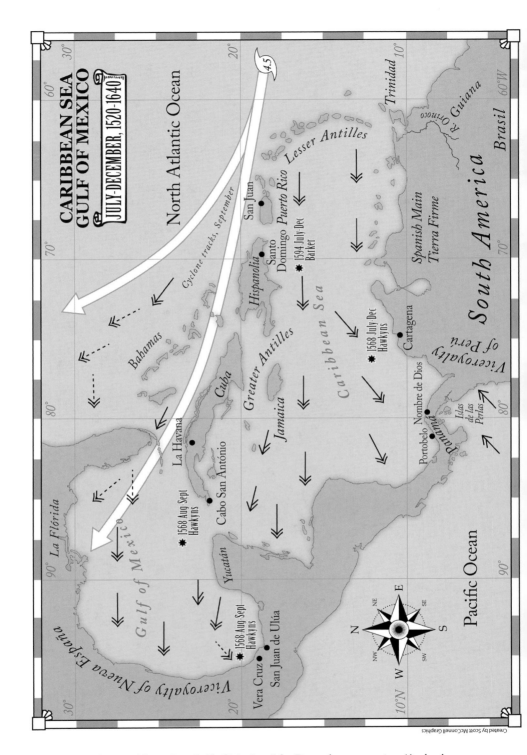

Pilot Atlas: Caribbean Sea, Gulf of Mexico, July–December 1520–1640. (Author's collection)

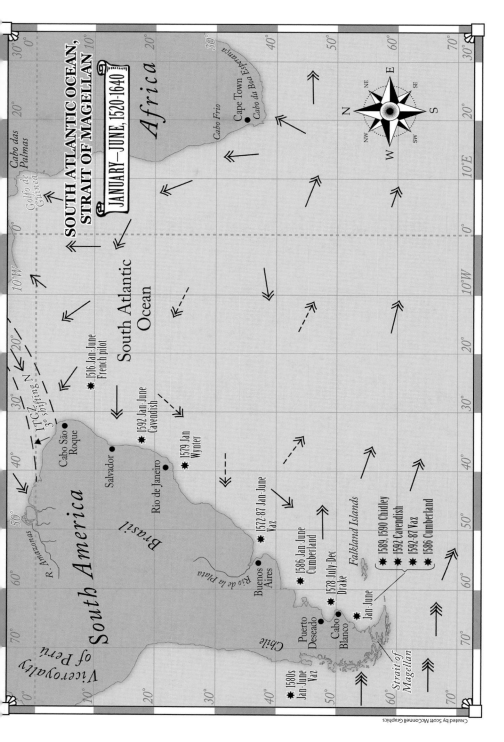

Pilot Atlas: South Atlantic Ocean, Strait of Magellan, January–June 1520–1640. (Author's collection)

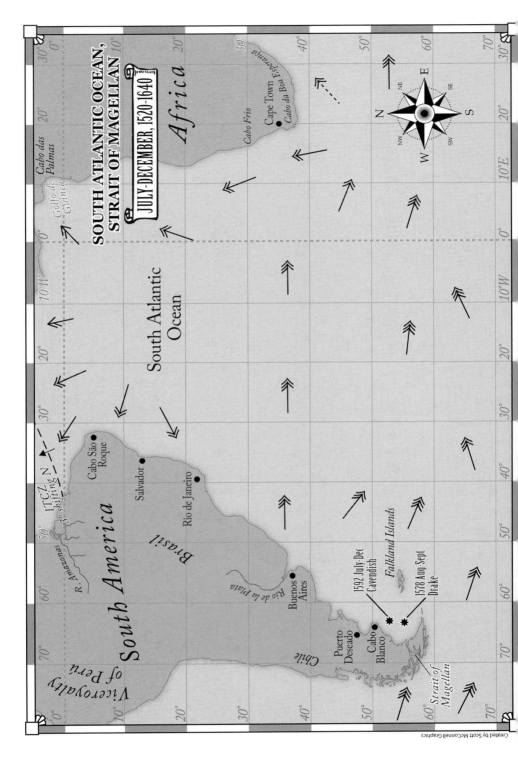

Pilot Atlas: South Atlantic Ocean, Strait of Magellan, July–December 1520–1640. (Author's collection)

Shipbuilding in the Americas. Hull under construction. Engraving in *Theodor de Bry, Grands Voyages*, Frankfurt, 1594. (Washington: Library of Congress)

Jesus of Lubeck, 700-ton carrack bought in Hamburg 1544, Hawkyns' admiral on two voyages in 1560s. Watercolour. (Anthony's Roll, Pepys Library, Magdalene College, Cambridge)

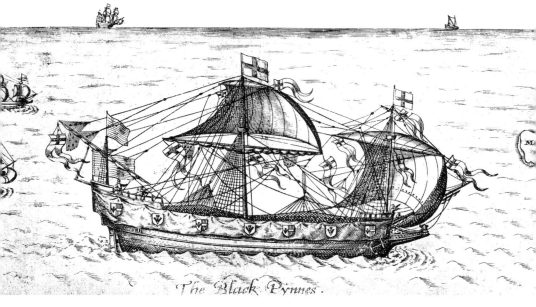

Black Pinnace. Engraving in The Procession at the Obsequies of Sir Philip Sidney, Knight, London, 1587. (Anthony's Roll, Pepys Library, Magdalene College, Cambridge)

Galley. Traditional Mediterranean warship, rowed and sailed. Engraving by Josef Furttenbach, *Architectura Navalis*, Ulm, 1629.

East Indiaman *Mauritius*, Early 1600s. Oil on canvas. Hendrik Cornelisz Vroom (1562/63–1640). Amsterdam: Rijksmuseum)

Dutch galleons ramming Spanish galleys off England, 3 October 1603. Oil on canvas, 1617. Hendrik Cornelisz Vroom (1562/63–1640). (Amsterdam: Rijksmuseum)

Culverins and cannon. Far two are culverins, closer two are demi-cannon. (Photo 2009. Portsmouth: Mary Rose Museum)

Queen Elizabeth I, 1592–95. Engraving by Crispijn van de Passe, after Isaac Oliver portrait, early seventeenth century.

King James I, 1604.
English School. Oil on
canvas.

King Philip II. Bust,
1550–1600. (Photo
Matthew G. Bizanz.
New York: Metropolitan
Museum of Art)

Above: Sir Walter Ralegh, 1598. Portrait attributed to William Segar or Fedrico Zuccaro (Zucchero). (National Portrait Gallery of Ireland, Dublin)

Left: Sir Francis Drake, age 42. Miniature painted 1581 by Nicholas Hilliard (1547–1619).

Sir John Hawkyns. Engraving by Henricus Hondius (Henry Holland), *Herwologia Anglica,* London, 1620.

Cross-staff. Figured in 'Allegory of Navigation', 1557. Oil on canvas, by Paolo Veronese. (Photo by Museum Associates, LACMA. Los Angleles: Los Angleles County Museum of Art)

Left: Traverse board. Pinnakompassi Forum Marinumissa. (Photo MKFI, 2012. Turku: Forum Marinum)

Below: James Seay Dean. (Author's collection)

by wind, weather and current. Any tactics were subject to the vagaries of the sea. Mahan quotes Napoleon, brilliant on land with his artillery, who observed that naval operations were too often *'fausse routes et moments perdus'*.[99]

To educate land generals and farmer-sailors, the decades from 1620 to 1640 saw bookstalls selling a new sort of book: popular manuals on seafaring. Quite different from the highly technical books of Bourne, Davis, Wright and others, these manuals defined sea terms and sketched situations for landsmen. They were not for the tarpaulin sailor, likely illiterate, who had no need for such books, as he learned the ropes at sea. These were written for gentleman captains in fine breeches and brass buckles who knew Charles I and his Court but not the quarterdeck of the *Sovereign of the Seas*. Such books also appealed to general readers who, in the uneasy times of Stuart England, looked back to the golden age when Hawkyns, Drake and Ralegh sailed for Good Queen Bess to singe the beard of the Spaniard. Mainwaring, in his preface to *Nomenclator Navalis*, or *The Seaman's Dictionary*, written in the early 1620s, states that 'few gentlemen (though they be called seamen) do fully and wholly understand what belongs to their profession; having only some scambling [slipshod] terms and names belonging to some parts of a ship'. He censures that many gentlemen set out on long voyages, 'and return, in a manner, as ignorant and as unable to do their country service as when they went out'.[100] For these gentleman captains, too, Captain John Smith in 1626 wrote *An Accidence or the Path-way to Experience*,[101] a word book largely based on Mainwaring's manuscript (not published until 1644) with examples and useful advice for all those who were called to or fancied the sea. It was timely, given England's resumption of hostilities with Spain in 1624 and England's current involvement in the Thirty Years' War, 1618–48.

George Villiers, Duke of Buckingham was such a case of a gentleman captain in velvet breeches, for whom Mainwaring had written his earlier manuscript. Villiers was in his twenties and had no knowledge of the sea when King James appointed him Lord High Admiral in January 1619. With commanders such as Villiers in mind, Smith, in 1627, published an expanded version of his 1626 book. More handbook than dictionary, *A Sea Grammar, with the Plaine Exposition of Smiths Accidence for young Sea-men, enlarged*[102] was intended to bring attention to warfare at sea. 'This little Pamphlet' was written, says Smith, by 'a miserable Practitioner in this Schoole of Warre by Sea and Land more than thirty years'. It proved popular with the public, and the first printing sold out quickly.

When the sometime privateer Boteler in 1634 wrote his 'Dialogues' (published only in 1685) he took parts from Smith's books. In a twist of mutual borrowings Smith, while writing his *Generall Historie of Virginia, New-England, and the Summer Isles*, 1624 (Bermuda), had likewise lifted parts from another manuscript attributed to Boteler, who had served as governor of Bermuda from 1619–22.[103] Smith's *Sea Grammar* has survived as the most popular word-books of the sea (though Mainwaring's has more authority), with editions published in 1653, 1691, 1692, 1699 and later. His *Sea Grammar* and *Accidence* have the distinction of being the first lexicographies published in English on the ways of the sea.

Notes

1 Geoffrey Parker, 'The Dreadnought Revolution of Tudor England', *Mariner's Mirror,* vol. 82, 269–300. Rpt. Jan Glete, ed. *Naval History 1000–1680* (Aldershot: Ashgate, 2005), 49–80.

2 Chapter 1, 'Ships Are But Boards', treats the construction of such new galleons in detail. On Hawkyns' 1568 defeat see TB, 36–42.

3 Quoted in Parker, 61.

4 Boteler, 197–8.

5 Nelson, *passim.* On the first armed pinnace built by the English in the Americas in 1576–77, see J.S. Dean, 'Bearding the Spaniard: Captain John Oxnam in the Pacific', *The Northern Mariner/Le Marin du Nord,* vol. 19, no. 4 (Oct. 2009), 379–92.

6 W.L. Rodgers, *Naval Warfare under Oars, 4th to 16th Centuries* (Annapolis: Naval Institute Press, 1939, 240–335.

7 See *TB,* 45–7.

8 John Clerk of Eldin, *An Essay on Naval Tactics, Systematical and Historical* (Edinburgh: Adam Black, 1782, 1827), 5.

9 Parker, 51.

10 Giles Milton graphically tells the tale in *White Gold: The Extraordinary Story of Thomas Pellow and North Africa's One Million European Slaves* (London: Hodder & Stoughton, 2004), 9–29. See also Alan G. Jamieson, *Lords of the Sea: A History of the Barbary Corsairs* (London: Redaktion Books, 2012).

11 Quoted in Milton, 59–61.

12 Sir Henry Mainwaring, 'Of the Beginnings, Practices, and Supression of Pirates', otherwise, as the 'Discourse of Pirates', ms c. 1617, pres. to king 1618, pub. 1644, rpt. and ed. G. E. Mainwaring and W. G. Perrin, in *The Life and Works of Sir Henry Mainwaring.* Publications of the Navy Records Society, vol.1: 54, 56, (London: Navy Records Society, 1920, 1922), vol. 2, 14–149.

13 Mainwaring, 15.

14 Mainwaring, 23–4.

15 Mainwaring, 43.

16 Mainwaring, 149.

17 Mainwaring, 47.

18 Chuck Meide, 'The Development and Design of Bronze Ordnance, Sixteenth through Nineteenth Centuries,' lecture (Williamsburg, Va.: College of William and Mary, Nov. 2002).

19 Spencer Tucker, *Arming the Fleet: U.S. Navy Ordnance in the Muzzle-Loading Era* (Annapolis: Naval Institute Press, 1989), 5–16.

20 Waters, 'Elizabethan Navy', 97.

21 Nelson, 36–7; Phillips, 51–7, 72–3.

22 For the armament of the Great Harry, and the types of ordnance generally, see Tucker, 5–16.

23 Nelson, 109–10.

24 Parker, 62.

25 Hughes, 41–7.

26 Robison, 42.

27 Nelson, 109–11.

28 Nelson, 112–13.

29 Rodgers, 240–335.

30 Quoted in Parker, 56.

31 Rodgers, 240.

32 Parker, 56.

33 Robison, 74.

34 Tucker, 14.

35 Brian Tunstall, *Naval Warfare in the Age of Sail: The Evolution of Fighting Tactics 1650–1815* (Annapolis: Naval Institute Press, 1990, and London: Conway Maritime Press, 1990), 1–11.

36 Tunstall, 1–11.

37 The first steam vessel was Marquis Claude de Jouffroy's *Le Palmipède*, 1776, followed in 1802 by the Scot William Symington's stern-paddlewheel tug, *Charlotte Dundas*, along the Forth and Clyde Canal. The first naval ship was the 90-gun *Le Napoléon*, a steam battleship, the term deriving from line-of-battle ship, launched 1850.

38 Kemp, s.v. 'line', and 'line of battle'.

39 Quoted in Robison, prefatory matter.

40 Quoted in Robison, 111.

41 One cable = 1/10th nautical mile, 100 fathoms (120 fathoms, US).

42 Quoted in Robison, 106–7. See Sir William Monson, *Naval Tracts*, in Michael Oppenheim (ed.), *The Naval Tracts of Sir William Monson*, Navy Records Society, vols 22 (1902), 23 (1902), 43 (1913), 45 (1914), 47 (1914) (London, 1902–14), passim.

43 Tunstall, 1–11.

44 Boteler, 252–3.

45 Boteler, 252–318.

46 Quoted in Corbett, *Fighting Instructions, 1530–1816* (1905), rpt. (Annapolis: Naval Institute Press, 1971 and London: Conway Maritime Press, Ltd, 1971), 4–5. See also Cesáreo Fernández Duro, *Armada Española desde la Union de los Reinos de Castilla y de Aragón*. (Madrid: El Progreso Editorial,1894).

47 Quoted in Robison, 72.

48 Philip's instructions, often reprinted. See Parker, 49–80.

49 Quoted in Corbett, *Fighting Instructions*, 4–5; Robison, 34; Duro, *Armada Española* .

50 Notice the similar emphasis on trade ('traffiques') in Hakluyt's title, 'navigations, voyages, traffiques & discoveries'. Navigation and trade went hand in hand. Similary, 'Trade Winds' derives from AS 'tredde wind' treading path, from 'tredan', to tread. See E. Cobham Brewer, *Dictionary of Phrase and Fable* (Philadelphia: Lippincott, and London: Cassell, 1894). Convention has linked 'trade' wrongly with commerce.

51 Quoted in Parker, 49–80.

52 Modern edn., Fernão Oliveira, *Arte da Guerra do Mar: Estratégia e Guerra Naval No Tempo dos Descobrimentos* (Lisboa: Edições 70, 2008).

53 Trans. Parker, 58.

54 To close with the ship. 'Enter' then meant the modern 'board'. Elizabethan mariners would say 'board and enter'.

55 Quoted in Corbett, *Fighting Instructions*, 1–77. Bracketed comment is Corbett's, except for my definitions of archaic words, also bracketed.

56 Robison, 28–30.

57 Captain John Smith, ed. Barbour, vol. 3, 100.

58 I.A.A. Thompson, 'Spanish Armada Guns', *Mariner's Mirror*, vol. 81, pp.148–55. Rpt. Glete 183–99.

59 Thompson, 183–99.

60 Parker, 66.

61 Quoted in Rodgers, 296.

62 Parker, 66.

63 Parker, 50, 53.

64 Tunstall, 1–11.

65 Quoted in Corbett, *Fighting Instructions*, 11, 41–3.

66 Tunstall, 11.

67 Captain Biddlecombe's diagrams and clear prose make this book a classic. Sir George Biddlecombe, *Naval Tactics and Trials of Sailing* (London: Charles Wilson, 1850), 16.

68 Merrill L. Bartlett, *Assault from the Sea: Essays on the History of Amphibious Warfare* (Annapolis: Naval Institute Press, 1983), 30.

69 Bartlett, 30.

70 Wayne P. Hughes, Jr., *Fleet Tactics: Theory and Practice* (Annapolis: Naval Institute Press, 1986), 41–7.

71 Tunstall, 1–11.

72 Clerk, 5.

73 Boteler, 303.

74 Tunstall, 1–11.

75 Tunstall, 82–9.

76 Malyn Nedwitt, 'Portuguese Amphibious Warfare in the East in the Sixteenth Century (1500–1520)', in D.J.B. Trim and Mark Charles Fissel (eds.), *Amphibious Warfare 1000–1700: Commerce, State Formation and European Expansion*. (Leiden, Boston: Brill, 2006), 112–18.

77 Nedwitt, 117.

78 Nedwitt, 103–21.

79 Quoted in Nedwitt, 118.

80 Nedwitt, 120.

81 Nedwitt, 119.

82 *TB*, 65–7.

83 Bartlett, 31.

84 *DE*, 115, 169–77, 230, 328; J.S. Dean, 'Bearding the Spaniard', 379–92.

85 Wernham, 'English amphibious warfare, 1587–1656: galleons, galleys, longboats, and cots', in Trim and Fissel, 200–03.

86 Quoted in Bartlett, 31.

87 Bartlett, 31.

88 Mark Charles Fissel, 'The King's Two Arms: French Amphibious Warfare in the Mediterranean under Louis XIV, 1664–1697', in Trim and Fissel, 217–61.

89 Wernham, in Trim and Fissel, 181–2, 202.

90 Quoted in Wernham, note 61, in Trim and Fissel, 205.

91 Quoted by Wernham, in Trim and Fissel, 208.

92 Wernham, in Trim and Fissel, 213.

93 Wernham, in Trim and Fissel, 213. See also also R.B. Wernham, *After the Armada: Elizabethan England and the Struggle for Western Europe 1588–1595* (London: Oxford University Press, 1984), and *The Return of the Armadas: The last Years of the Elizabethan War against Spain 1595–1603* (London: Oxford University Press, 1994).

94 Robison, 90.

95 *TB*, 189–96.

96 Robison, 84–90.

97 A.T. Mahan, *Naval Strategy Compared and Contrasted with the Principles and Practice of Military Operations on Land. Lectures given between 1887 and 1911* (Boston: Little, Brown, and Company, 1911), 64–5.

98 Robison, 92.

99 Quoted in Mahan, 113–14, 136.

100 Mainwaring, 83–4.

101 Captain John Smith, *An Accidence or the Path-way to Experience* (London: Jonas Man and Benjamin Fisher, 1626), rpt. Smith, vol. 3, 3–37.

102 Captain John Smith, *A Sea Grammar, with the Plaine Exposition of Smiths Accidence for young Sea-men, enlarged* (London: John Haviland, 1627), rpt. Smith, vol. 3, 39–121.

103 Nathaniel Boteler, 'A Dialogicall Discourse concerninge Marine Affaires', otherwise, *Six Dialogues about Sea Services. Between an High Admiral and a Captain at Sea* (London: Moses Pitt, 1685 (c. 1634), in Boteler, vol. 65.

6

'Plague of the Sea and Spoyle of Mariners'

'From lightning and tempest; from plague,
pestilence, and famine ... Good Lord, deliver us.'
The Litany, Book of Common Prayer, 1662

One particular voyage shows many of the vital – fatal – elements of passage-making in the Elizabethan age, an example of how difficult it could be for the sailor to remain healthy in tropical waters. By the summer of 1591 Thomas Cavendish had already successfully circumnavigated the globe when he set out on another voyage for the East Indies via Cape Horn. According to the account in Hakluyt's *Principal Navigations* written by one John Jane, 'a man of good observation, employed in the same, and many other voyages', it was a well-supported venture with a fleet of five well-found vessels, well provisioned, well manned and well commanded by a seasoned admiral who had three years earlier successfully rounded the earth.

This time, though, the infamous Strait of Magellan's weather proved the undoing of Cavendish and crew. The fleet's admiral was the *Galleon Leicester*. Jane, Cavendish's author, was aboard another vessel, the *Desire*, 120 tons, with the experienced John Davis as captain. 'The 26. of August 1591,' he recorded, 'we departed from Plymouth with 3. tall ships, and two barks', bound for the East Indies via Cape Horn. First, Cavendish was becalmed in the Doldrums near the equator for twenty-seven days, when most 'fell sick of the scurvy by reason of the extreme heat of the sun, and the vapours of the night'. Worse, at Cape Horn the crew 'endured extreme storms, with perpetual snow'.[1]

Once in the middle of the Strait off Cape Froward, a storm separated the fleet. Many men froze or starved to death. Thirty-nine crew of the *Desire* on 2 June 1592 petitioned the captain to give over the voyage and sail for home. Davis tried for the Strait again and again, but the ship was repeatedly driven back, until finally the *Desire* reached the South Sea on 13 September. The ship by then was a wreck. Two weeks later, on 2 October, it was hit by another Pacific storm that raged for more than a week. All aboard prepared for death, but this time the captain came about and returned through the Strait. Victuals were severely rationed for the passage home. Five months later, in early February 1592, of the seventy-six men who shipped out, there were only twenty-seven left alive. And still things worsened: as the drinking water grew fouler it brought on dysentery. When they reached Ireland, the crew numbered just sixteen, of whom only five could work the ship.

What of Cavendish in the *Galleon Leicester*, the other part of the expedition? Editor Samuel Purchas notes that the admiral experienced equally adverse weather and short supplies. Cavendish, like Davis, turned back, then missed both St Helena and Ascension Island in the South Atlantic because of poor navigation. By then Cavendish was gravely ill. Sometime in the second half of May 1592 he died and his body was committed to the waters of the South Atlantic.[2] Dysentery or scurvy may have been the cause of death. Of the other ship and the two barks, who knows their fate?

9

What was the state of medicine in this period? Any evidence of a disease is circumstantial at best, as the men afflicted are long gone, leaving no gums to examine for scurvy, no pitting oedema of the flesh to observe. Pathological examination of these mariners' bodies is not possible, though shipboard accounts of tropical diseases encountered aboard can at least flesh out the conditions. In this period, the empirical method of forensic study was new. Most still sought authority in Hippocrates and Galen. On board, there was likely to be a doctor of divinity, not a doctor of medicine. On a few larger ships there might be a surgeon. As surgeons used knives, they were classed with barbers. Such was medicine then. Furthermore, early medical descriptions illustrated symptoms, not the disease itself, a practice that in some instances still persists today. For instance, 'malaria', or 'bad air', does not even suggest the carrier of the disease, a particular mosquito, much less the cause of the disease itself. Yet, though conditions and some epidemiologies have changed, the essentials of the principal diseases are still the same, allowing us to study them. Malaria then is malaria now.[3]

What could the Elizabethan seaman off on a voyage from poxy Europe to an unknown Tropical America expect? At sea in the tropics, he would encounter a bagful of ills: dysentery (the flux), toxaemia, various intestinal infections, typhus, typhoid, paratyphoid fevers, scurvy, malaria (tertian and quartan agues), yellow fever, dengue fever, ergotism, pellagra, worms, hookworm anaemia, schistosomes (blood flukes), anaemia, ulcers, leishmaniasis, itchy skin lesions, heatstroke, poisonous fruits and fatal bites from snakes and spiders. Going to sea, bound for anywhere, was risky business. As Samuel Johnson was to write more than 200 years later: 'No man will be a sailor who has contrivance enough to get himself into a jail; for being in a ship is being in a jail, with the chance of being drowned ... A man in a jail has more room, better food and commonly better company'.[4] An invitation to such a voyage was likely to be to the next world, from whose bourn no traveller returns.

9

In time, early Tropical American discoveries would slowly but surely change Old World medicine, zoology and botany. Experience would supplant ancient authority.[5] Tracing the treatments for scurvy, to take just one disease during the period, illustrates the pace of advances in medical thinking. Scurvy was identified by the Egyptians as early as 1500 BC. About 400 BC Hippocrates accurately described a patient with scurvy as having 'foetid breath, lax gums and haemorrhage from the nose'. The Portuguese mariner Vasco da Gama on his East India voyage, 1497, carried citrus fruits for what the soldier-poet Luis de Camões called scurvy the 'dread disease', dread indeed, for during Magellan's 1519 circumnavigation half the crew died of it. As the number of long voyages in the sixteenth century increased, so did the need to deal with scurvy. Jacques Cartier, sailing to North America in 1536, sought remedy in spruce bark and leaves. In Holland in 1564 a Dutch physician prescribed Spanish citrus fruits, and in Mexico, *escorbuto* was treated with lemons, oranges and limes. Still, at the end of the sixteenth century and for two centuries later there was little true understanding in Europe and England about the causes of scurvy.

In some fleets, experimentation with remedies began to show benefit. The Dutch East Indies fleet that sailed in 1595 with a crew of 295 returned two years later with just 88 men. But the next year when the Dutch fleet provisioned for the East Indies it laid in lemon juice, brewed horseradish and scurvy cress. The voyage lost only fifteen men. In 1591–94 Sir James Lancaster sailed to Brazil and the East Indies. Many of his men died from scurvy. For his third voyage to the Far East in 1601–03, Lancaster's admiral, the *Red Dragon,* carried lemon juice. Of the 202 sailors, only a third of the men died, few enough to be considered a remarkable accomplishment.

The search for a cure continued in the seventeenth century. In 1617 Dr John Woodall (1556–1643), first Surgeon General of the East India Company, recommends in his *The Surgions Mate* oranges, limes and tamarinds, but especially lemons. Dr John Hall, Shakespeare's son-in-law and a renowned physician in Stratford-upon-Avon in the early seventeenth century, found help in brewing a beer or ale from scorbutic herbs such as scurvy grass, watercress and brook lime. Advances yes, but yet at about the same time, during the fifty-six-day crossing of the *Mayflower* to Massachussets in 1620, fifty of the 120 pilgrims, over a third, were lost to scurvy. There was clearly no unified aetiology of scurvy until well into the seventeenth century, just as there was not for most diseases contracted on long voyages.[6]

Like medicine (physic), knowledge of zoology and botany also advanced at a snail's pace. In 1552 Edward Wotton wrote *De Differentiis Animalium,* the first printed book by an Englishman on zoology, which Black observes was largely a dressing-up of Aristotle, Pliny and others.[7] What a breath of fresh air, then, is editor Samuel Purchas' translation of material by the French Calvinist captain John Lerius' (Jean de Léry). Lerius writes about much from his two years ashore living among the Brazilian Tupí-Guaraní, 1557–58. His account mentions plants, animals and the habits of the Indians, including how they treated tropical ills. His account was first published in France as *Historia navigationis in Brasiliam*, 1594. It reached English readers only thirty years later, in 1625, via Purchas' English translation in *Purchas his Pilgrims*.[8]

The study of botany illustrates the same point. Though botany was relatively advanced in England, English botanists still relied on ancient authorities such as Aristotle's *Historia Naturalis, Historia Animalium* and *De Plantis*. Such is John Maplet's *A Green Forest or a Natural History*, 1567, the work that introduces the phrase 'natural history' to England. It relies heavily on the ancients. Most of the leaders in botany were Continental. The father of English botany, William Turner, in *The Names of Herbs*, 1548, took the common names of plants and fitted them within the scheme followed in Europe used by the great naturalist Conrad Gesner and others. Turner's *The New Herball*, 1568, further names and classifies plants according to that system. What has been termed the greatest botanical study of the period is by Dutchman Matthias Lobel, a scientist who later was made James I's botanist. His *Adversaria*, London, 1571, classifies plants according to their characteristics, a large step towards modern thinking. Henry Lyte's *Nieuwe Herball*, 1578, is doubly derivative. It is a version of an earlier Dutch work published in 1564 that came to English via a French translation of 1577.

In terms of contributions of books on Tropical American sciences read in England, two works stand out beyond Lerius' account, one pharmacological, the other botanical. The first is a translation by John Frampton, an English merchant living in Seville, of Nicholas Monarde's *De las Drogas de las Indias*, 1565, rendered as *Joyful News out of the New World*, 1577. It introduces to English readers new tropical American vegetables and drugs. The second is the derivative work but still the most famous book, John Gerard's *The Herball, or Generall Historie of Plantes*, 1597, commonly known as *Gerards Herball*. It too is a compilation of the work of others, with illustrations, and was to become the standard botanical reference in England for many years. The Italian physician and botanist Andrea Cesalpino's pioneering *De Plantis XVI*, 1583, which Black calls 'the most significant investigation into plant physiology of the age' before the Swedish botanist Linnaeus' significant work in the eighteenth century, was unknown in England until the seventeenth century.[9] Despite advances, England was clearly behind Europe in all these sciences.

Amazingly, in the first voyages to the American Tropics we find no reports of death from acute toxaemia, scurvy or malaria. No sort of medical problem is mentioned. The lack of the mention of scurvy could mean the ships were well-enough supplied with fresh food for the relatively short periods at sea, too brief for scurvy and the other ills to develop. Or it was simply ignored. Sailing for the tropics was risky for sailor or colonist. When Charles Leigh sailed for the Amazon and Orinoco rivers on his second voyage to settle the area in 1604, Leigh, the surgeon John Burt and crew took a canoe some 90 miles up the River Aracawa, where Burt fell sick. When Leigh returned to the ship, he discovered most of the men were also ill, likely with malaria (the ague) or dysentery (the flux). Their local Indian hosts were also sick, and in any case had no food to give the English. Hospitality had worn thin. The author of Leigh's account adds that 'within three days after his return, shipwright Richard Haward died before he could make an end of his shallop'. And in September, the author writes that Leigh, 'himself began to droop, partly of grief to see the weak estate of his people, and the ill performance of the Indians' promises'. The cause was not the heat of the sun or the damp ground, and Leigh's remedies were ineffective:

> Before and after the sickness of our captain, many of our men fell sick, some of agues, some of fluxes, some of giddiness in their heads, whereby they would often fall down: which grew chiefly of the excessive heat of the sun in the day [sunstroke?], and of the extreme damp of the earth, which would so moisten our *hamackas* [hammocks], or cotton beds, wherein we lay a yard from the ground, that we were fain to imitate the Indians in making fires on both sides under them. And for all that we could do, some nine of our company were dead before our ship's arrival.'[10]

The English succumbed to new diseases, but they also brought their own European ones with them. At home, the main English diseases of the day were bubonic plague, chickenpox (the *varicella zoster* virus), smallpox (the variola virus), syphilis (the great pox), gonorrhea, scarlet fever (the A streptococcus bacterium, formerly known as scarlatina) and measles (a paramyxovirus of the genus *morbillivirus*, a highly infectious respiratory disease commonly called rubeola, not to be confused with Spanish rubella). After the plague, the worst was (and still is) malaria (mosquito-borne protists of the genus *plasmodium* that enter the blood stream and ultimately the liver).

With these summaries in mind, medical aspects of the early voyages will be given attention in greater detail below, then illustrated from voyagers' and sailors' accounts.

A. Tropical Diseases and Conditions

Classifications
Dion Bell, formerly Reader at the Liverpool School of Tropical Medicine, classifies the main categories of tropical diseases common to the Elizabethan sailor: 1. diseases presenting as fevers, including malaria, and typhoid and paratyphoid fevers (enteric fevers); 2. diseases presenting as diarrhoea, including amoebiasis (dysentery), and giardiasis; 3. those presenting as anaemia, including scurvy, and other various deficient diets producing ergotism and pellagra; and 4. various flukes, including blood flukes (schistosomes) and intestinal flukes.[11]

J.J. Keevil, Surgeon Commander of the Royal Navy and author of four volumes on the history of naval medicine, identifies three diseases or types of diseases usual on voyages to the tropics in the sixteenth and early seventeenth centuries. He categorises these in a slightly different way: 1. malaria, caused by the protosoon *Plasmodium* (*malariae* or *vivax*), transmitted by the female anopheles mosquito; 2. dysentery, resulting from rotten food, contaminated water and unsanitary shipboard conditions, food poisoning (toxaemia) and intestinal infections; and 3. scurvy (ascorbic acid or vitamin C deficiency), contracted on long voyages with a diet without limes, lemons, oranges or other foods with vitamin C.

Combining these two views, we can say that the Elizabethan sailor was subject to three major diseases – malaria, scurvy and dysentery – and some dozen other medical problems of the tropics. He may have cast off from the sceptred but plagued isle of England, but his tropical desert isle too often proved septic.

Shipboard accounts can suggest but rarely diagnose with certainty the diseases encountered. Yet it is instructive to read the descriptions of local remedies for the complex web of illnesses first encountered in the tropics.

1. Diseases that Present as Fevers: Malaria; Yellow Fever; Typhus, Typhoid Fever and Paratyphoid Fever; and Others

Malaria

Malaria, which comes from microorganisms called *plasmodia*, is by far the most important of all tropical diseases, followed in importance during our period by scurvy and dysentery. Malaria develops in three forms, then known as tertian, subtertian and quartan agues. In tertian malaria (tertian ague), *Plasmodium vivax, P. ovale*, fever recurs every three days – that is, on days 1, 3, 5. In quartan malaria (quartan ague), *P. malariae*, fever recurs every fourth day. In subtertian malaria (subtertian ague), *P. falciparum*, fever recurs more often than every third day. This ancient disease, known also as swamp fever or blackwater fever, was long thought to come from bad air (Ital., '*mal aria*'). The spleen enlarges and blood becomes infected. Abscesses develop, and toxaemia results in death.

The female anopheles mosquito is the carrier of the lethal *Plasmodium falciparum* variety. As the mosquito bites, the parasites enter the bloodstream, then lie dormant in the liver for varying periods, depending on the type of malaria, but never shorter than ten days and sometimes for more than a year. The fever is often irregular. Regular periodic fever usually does not occur until the disease manifests itself. Anaemia is most severe in *Plasmodium falciparum*. In acute cases of all forms of malaria, the spleen enlarges. As the parasite attacks the liver, jaundice occurs.

Typically the patient undergoes three stages: a cold stage, when he shivers and the temperature rises; a hot stage, when he is flushed, has a rapid, full pulse, and for a few hours a very high temperature; and a sweating stage, when he is drenched in sweat, and when the temperature drops rapidly. In the form *P. malariae*, a patient can experience recurring malaria attacks for longer than thirty years. Malaria affects the stomach and intestines and the nervous system (enteric) with vomiting and diarrhoea, and the brain with delirium, disorientation, stupor, coma, convulsions and focal neurological problems. The kidneys suffer renal failure, the liver becomes jaundiced, there is fever and the lungs develop pulmonary oedema.

Malaria is not just tropical. In the seventeenth-century temperate Europe it killed more people than any other disease. Cures attempted were purging, a starvation diet and bleeding. For years, malaria, a bacterial disease, was confused in the tropics with yellow fever, caused by a virus, as both are carried by mosquitoes and both are endemic to Africa. The voyages to the New World brought help. In 1631 the Spanish discovered the Peruvian bark *quina-quina*, from the myroxylon or cinchona tree. Its bark yielded quinine. Quinine worked.[12] One treatment today calls for chloroquine, a synthetic product, but the older quinine, a natural alkaloid derived from the bitter cinchona bark, is still used to treat non-severe *falciparum* malaria.[13]

Though he did not know it, the early English merchant Robert Tomson's observations in the 1550s on mosquitoes as a troublesome pest touched on the carrier of malaria. His is the earliest known English account of mosquitoes and hookworms in the American Tropics. He had sailed in the company of the Spanish to the Americas in 1555, arriving there in 1556.[14] In Santo Domingo he described mosquitoes and worms:[15]

> The country is most part of the year very hot, & very full of a kind of flies or gnats with long bills, which do prick & molest the people very much in the night when they are asleep, in pricking their faces and hands, and other parts of their bodies that lie uncovered, & make them to swell wonderfully.[16]

Tomson sailed westward, and in 1556 survived a Norther near the port of San Juan de Ulúa, the Gulf port for the Viceroyalty of Mexico. He made his way to nearby Vera Cruz, then a community of 300 households, a notoriously unhealthy place. Within two days of setting out from Vera Cruz for Mexico City, he came down with malaria, then commonly called an ague, probably the tertian or sub-tertian variety: 'And after we were entered two days journey into the country, I the said Robert Tomson fell so sick of an ague, that the next day I was not able to sit on my horse, but was fain to be carried upon Indians' backs, from thence to Mexico'.[17] The little annoyance turned out to be *P. falciparum*.

Drake, like others, found the cause of malaria in bad air, especially night airs at sea. He also mentions, correctly, that malaria is accompanied by a calentura or fever. In his 1585–86 voyage to the West Indies Drake writes that in Cartagena 'the calentura [fever] continued, killing some (being a pestilent spotted fever)[18] and spoiling others of their strength and memory for a long time'. In the murky diagnosis of the day, bad air was thought to be the source. Malaria was also confused with small pox:

> The *serena* or evening air is said to cause it to them which are then abroad, if not of that country: so that by holding their watch, the English were thus infected. This forced them to give over their intended voyage to Nombre de Dios, and Panama, sailing therefore alongst the coast of Florida.[19]

During that voyage, he writes that 'there died (most of the calentura) 700. persons'.

As had Tomson in the 1550s in Santo Domingo and Drake in 1580s Cartagena, so William Davies, barber and surgeon, found legions of mosquitoes in the Amazon in 1608. 'This country is full of muskitas [mosquitoes], which is a small fly, which much offends a stranger coming newly into the country… [the Indians] do use to anoint their bodies, both men and women, with a kind of red earth, because the muskitas, or flies shall not offend them.'[20] Not all mosquitoes, of course, are *P. falciparum*.

Yellow Fever

Mosquitoes, besides carrying malaria, can carry yellow fever, though by another sort of mosquito. In this period the cause of both malaria and yellow fever was thought to be night air. Yellow fever, an *arborvirus*, genus *flavivirus*, is endemic to Africa and spread to the Americas by about the mid-seventeenth century. It has no known cure, but vaccination is 95 per cent effective. Yellow fever brings on vomiting, diarrhoea, supression of urine and exhaustion. Its carrier is normally the *aëdes* mosquito but can be carried by other species as well. One case can spread and infect an entire crew. Elizabethan crews would contract it in coastal sub-Saharan Africa or in the Cabo Verdes islands where ships called before setting out west in the Trade Winds. On board, the *aëdes* mosquito thrives in ships' water butts. The immune systems of northern Europeans, such as those of Elizabethan sailors, were unprepared for yellow fever, contracted either before crossing the Atlantic or during the passage. Nor were they immune from it once ashore in the American tropics. West African slaves transported to the New World, though, had better natural immunity to many of the tropical illnesses that plagued Europeans.

Captain Lerius' two years with the Indians yields a detailed account of health, disease, the flora and fauna in Brazil, and the ways of the Indians.[21] In discussing one particular sort of monkey, he may unknowingly have provided us with the answer to why yellow fever took so long to reach tropical America, nearly a century and a half after the first European voyages to the Americas. It is the sagouin monkey, common to Guinea, Congo and Brazil, as he says:

> of the bigness of a squirrel, and of a red hair: but as touching the shape, in the snout, breast, neck, and almost all the other parts, being very like unto a Lion, and also hardy, it giveth place in beauty to none of the little beasts, which surely I saw there. And if were as easily brought over the sea as the rest, it would be of far greater price and estimation. But seeing it is of so weak a little body, that it cannot endure the working of the ship; for it is of that haughtiness of spirit, that if it be offended never so little, it would die through discontentment: yet some are here to be found.[22]

These 'haughty' little African monkeys suffered seasickness and would dehydrate and die during ocean crossings, thus for years did not transmit yellow fever to the New World. This held true until 1647, when it was first diagnosed in Barbados, carried there by a tough monkey that survived the ocean passage.[23]

Typhus and the Enteric Fevers: Typhoid and Paratyphoid

Like typhus, typhoid fever and paratyphoid fever are diseases of poor sanitation and are contracted by eating and drinking polluted water and spoiled food. Sixteenth-century ships were veritable sinks of contamination. Life aboard was generally far worse than ashore. Hundreds of men were crowded into a hull of a 150ft or so, far over the 'one ton of ship to one man' formula recommended. The lack of sanitation in such close quarters soon bred disease.

Typhus, known as 'ship's fever', was all too common and a case in point. It is neither a virus nor a bacterium but a *rickettsia*, a microorganism that lies somewhere between the two. Transmitted by lice that thrive in filthy conditions, it produces a high fever, a stupor and a rash that lasts for one to two weeks. Spanish sailors to Tropical America knew it as *modorra* (drowsiness). When it came ashore with the Spanish *marineros* in Mexico, it spread up into the highlands, where it killed off some two million Indians. The Aztecs believed it to be a punishment from the gods and was called *cocoliztli* (Nahuati, pestilence).[24]

Systemic septicaemic illnesses such as typhoid and paratyphoid fevers are caused by the *Salmonella typhi* and *Salmonella paratyphi* A, B and C. The A and B bacilli usually infect only humans, while the C bacillus can affect animals as well. These bacilli are spread by faecal pollution of water and food and are carried by flies, but not by lice. The symptoms are prolonged diarrhoea or constipation, abdominal pain, a high fever to 40°C (105°F), headaches, coughs, and exhaustion, often with red patches appearing on the abdomen. High fevers rise then fall for weeks at a time. Complications can be pneumonia, intestinal perforation, gastrointestinal haemorrhage and coma. The incubation period is about fourteen days, during which time the patient has headaches and a constant fever.[25]

2. Diseases that Present as Anaemia: Scurvy, Pellagra

With both tropic and arctic long-distance voyages becoming longer and more frequent in the sixteenth and early seventeenth centuries, the sailor could be at sea for months, even years. His diet did not promote good health: salted, dried or smoked meats and fish, cheese, hard tack, dried legumes, water and beer. Scurvy and pellagra from diet deficiency or imbalance were common.

Scurvy

Scurvy is a deficiency in ascorbic acid (vitamin C). Fresh fruits and vegetables were rare items in provisioning at home port or reprovisioning en route. In time, the dreaded symptoms appear. Within two months the skin becomes dry and rough; in three months the sailor is tired and listless; in six months, legs haemorrhage and wounds remain open; in seven and a half months the gums soften, swell and turn purple, and teeth become loose; between seven and nine months, cardiac and pulmonary difficulties develop. Stephen Beck estimates that between the years 1600 and 1800, scurvy alone killed over a million sailors.[26] As mentioned,

Cavendish and Hawkyns provisioned with oranges and lemons when sailing the tropics.[27] Hawkyns was a sailor's sailor, and was meticulously careful to keep his ship clean and his men healthy. En route to Brazil, Hawkyns presents a remarkably accurate description of this scourge of the sea:

> Being betwixt three and four degrees of the Equinoctial line, my company within a few days began to fall sick, of a disease which sea-men are wont to call the scurvy: and seemeth to be a kind of dropsy, and reigneth most in this climate of any that I have heard or read of in the world; though in all seas it is wont to help and increase the misery of man; it possesseth all those of which it taketh hold, with a loathsome sloathfulness, that even to eat they would be content to change with sleep and rest, which is the most pernicious enemy in this sickness that is known'.

Hawkyns writes that:

> it bringeth with a great desire to drink, and causeth a general swelling of all parts of the body, especially of the legs and gums, and many times the teeth fall out of the jaws without pain. The signs to know this disease in the beginning are diverse, by the swelling of the gums, by denting of the flesh of the legs with a man's finger, the pit remaining without filling up in a good space: others show it with their laziness, others complain of the crick of the back, &c. all which, are for the most part, certain tokens of infection.

Typical of his time, Hawkyns confuses cause with symptom:

> The cause is thought to be the stomach's feebleness, by change of air in untemperate climates, of diet in salt meats, boiled also in salt water and corrupted sometimes; the want of exercise also either in persons or elements, as in calms. And were it not for the moving of the sea by the force of winds, tides, and currents, it would corrupt all the world.

Commander Keevil comments that the marked oedema or 'denting flesh' suggests a lack of vitamin B as well as vitamin C, and that the crew had beri-beri as well as scurvy.[28]

The sixteenth-century saw the cause of scurvy in an excess of black bile, more than the spleen could regulate. The result was melancholia. From about 1500 to 1700 the usual treatment was *Cochlearia officinalis*, scurvy grass or spoonwort. But scurvy grass has only low quantities of vitamin C, and though it might ameliorate, it could not cure. Early on, Cavendish, Richard Hawkyns and Lancaster recognised that a better preventative and cure was in lemons and limes, with lemons being the more efficacious citric fruit.[29]

Pellagra

Another form of anaemia is pellagra, related to dermatitis, diarrhoea and dementia. It comes from a deficiency of niacin and other B vitamins and certain amino acids. Most hypochromic anaemia, the most important type, is due to iron deficiency. It is commonly found in diets based largely on maize (American corn) and little else, and maize has been a staple of native diets since pre-Columbian times. Consumption of alcohol and exposure to the sun can contribute to this sort of anaemia. The symptoms are tiredness, inability to sleep, loss of appetite, nausea, red skin, neck, lesions, gastrointestinal troubles, diarrhoea and psychotic and suicidal behaviour. A diet balanced with seafood, which contains iron, counters anaemia.[30]

3. Diseases that Present as Diarrhoea: Dysentery, Salmonella, Giardia

Contaminated water and rotten food, even if disease-free, can cause digestive distress or death. Water and food can also be carriers of diseases presenting as diarrhoea.

Dysentery

Dysentery, known to early sailors as bloody flux, can be amoebic or bacillary. It presents as and was sometimes confused with diarrhoea, with its frequent watery stools containing blood and mucus, and by painful attempts to defecate (tenesmus).

One type of dysentery is *amoebiasis*, an inflamation of the large intestine caused by the parasitic protozoan *Entamoeba histolytica*. It is spread faecally or orally, especially on crowded ships sailing in the tropics, with faecal contamination of water (water can also harbour typhoid and other bacilli). It flourishes in unsanitary conditions and where there is poor personal hygiene. Faecally fertilised fruits and vegetables may contain the protozoan. If it passes through the bowel it can enter the bloodstream and the liver, and pass through the diaphragm into the lungs. Amoebic dysentery is chronic, its onset gradual. Its incubation period is between twenty and ninety days (in contrast to bacillary dysentery, which incubates in under a week). The best prophylaxis for *amoebiasis* is to avoid hazardous foods such as salads, unwashed fruits and untreated water. Drugs such as clioquinol (Enterovioforme) treat the symptoms of diarrhoea but not its cause. This drug can have serious side effects.

Bacillary dysentery (bacillary *shigellosis*), the second type, also inhabits the large intestine. This form consists of several bacteria: *Campylobacter*, *Salmonella*, *Yersinia* and some forms of *Escherichia coli*. This last form is the most important single cause of diarrhoea, known colloquially in tropical climates as Montezuma's revenge, the Aztec two-step or Delhi belly. The bacteria of the genus *Shingella* are the most important agents, and *Shingella dysenteriae* is the most virulent of them. As in amoebic dysentery, the organisms are spread faecally and orally via contaminated food and water. Poor hygiene and sanitation, overcrowding, poor sewage conditions – all too common aboard early ships – contribute to bacillary dysentery.

Bacteria enter the mucosa of the large intestine, and cause mucus secretion, oedema, ulceration and bleeding. Incubation is between one and four days. At the start theere is nausea, abdominal pain, tenesmus and severe diarrhoea. Within three days stools exhibit blood, pus and mucus. The watery stools then produce dehydration, with death possible in as soon as twelve days. If there is to be recovery, it begins after two weeks, and cure takes about six weeks. Symptomatic relief can be had from loperamide (Imodium), but curing this sort of dysentery requires a quinolone antibiotic, though as it is an antibiotic it necessarily has side effects. The illness can be prevented by observing the adage, 'cook it, peel it, or leave it'.

All three of our principals and their crews – the Hawkynses, Drakes and Raleghs – contracted tropical diseases. It is likely that dysentery (though possibly malaria) struck Ralegh on his last voyage. It was the likely cause of the deaths of John Hawkyns and Francis Drake. Richard Hawkyns and Ralegh attempted to prevent it through better sanitation and personal hygiene, by having fresh water, and by avoiding unwashed local tropical fruits and vegetables.

Consider the last voyage of Hawkyns and Drake. In 1595 a cautious Sir John Hawkyns and choleric Sir Francis Drake set out as joint commanders of a large fleet for the Caribbean.[31] This English Armada was intended to break the flow of Peruvian and Mexican gold and silver back to Spain. The plan was to seize the treasure of a galleon lying at San Juan, Puerto Rico, then sail for the gold and silver coming from Perú through Panamá. But by the time the fleet reached the Virgin Islands, 'Sir John Hawkins was extreme sick'.[32] Gravely ill and unable to command, Hawkyns took to his bed. In the Virgins, Drake prepared for battle and drilled the soldiers. Purchas writes that:

> the last of this month Sir John Hawkins not able to bear his griefs out longer, sickened … The twelfth day we came to anchor afore the harbour at Porto Rico [San Juan], where died Sir Nicholas Clifford, by a shot from a platform, sitting at supper in the *Defiance*, with this shot was likewise Master Brewt Browne hurt, who lived but few days after, and this day also died Sir John Hawkins, whose death [by] many was much lamented.[33]

Hakluyt writes that as the fleet was anchoring at the eastern end of San Juan in preparation for taking the city, Hawkyns died aboard the *Garland* at three in the afternoon in his cabin.[34] Purchas notes in his account of the 1595 voyage of Hawkyns and Drake that 'November the twelfth, near the easternmost end of Saint Juan de Puerto Rico, Sir John Hawkins died'. Among sailors, the island of Puerto Rico was notorious for pestilence. Dysentery, the bloody flux, is the likely cause of Hawkyns' death.

Drake carried on with the attack. The Spanish troops on the ramparts of San Juan's El Morro easily beat back the English, who retreated to the western end of the island. Drake writes: 'We contented us with some refreshing of water, oranges and plantains, here were built four pinnaces more'.[35] Hoping for easier pickings, he set course across the Caribbean for Panamá's port of Nombre de Dios.

Like San Juan, Nombre de Dios was also known for being pestilent. Hakluyt tells us: 'The town was situated in a watery soil, and subject much to rain, very unhealthy as any place in the Indies, having great store of oranges, plantains, cassava roots, & such other fruits; but very dangerous to be eaten for breeding of diseases'. Though the water there was good, the climate was not. Drake finds Panamá a 'sickly climate also, and given to much rain',[36] and in particular, Nombre de Dios a 'town subject to rain, and very unhealthful'.[37]

The fleet anchored off Escudo, an island some 9 or 10 leagues off the coast. There, writes John Jane, was:

> great store of fresh water in every part of the island, and that is very good. It is a sickly climate also, and given to much rain: here we washed our ships, and set up the rest of our pinnaces. The 15 day Captain Plat died of sickness, and then Sir Francis Drake began to keep his cabin, and to complain of a scouring or flux.

The author continues: 'The 23 we set sail and stood up again for Portobelo, which is but 3 leagues to the westwards of Nombre de Dios.' Four days later 'died Captain Josias of the *Delight*, and Captain Egerton a Gentleman of the *Foresight*, and James Wood chief surgeon of the fleet out of the *Garland*'. On the night of:

> the 28 at 4 of the clock in the morning our general Sir Francis Drake departed this life, having been extremely sick of a flux, which began the night before to stop on him. He used some speeches at or a little before his death, rising and apparelling himself, but being brought to bed again within one hour died.[38]

On 28 January 1596, Purchas' author notes, 'this morning died our general Sir Francis Drake' of 'a flux'.[39] It was just under two weeks from when Drake took to his cabin to the night of his death. The signs point to bacillary dysentery as the likely cause.

That day, the fleet anchored in Portobelo, a small settlement of only eight or ten houses. The few inhabitants had fled:

> After our coming hither to anchor, and the solemn burial of our general Sir Francis in the sea: Sir Thomas Baskerville being aboard the *Defiance*, where M. Bride made a sermon, having to his audience all the captains in the fleet, Sir Thomas commanded all aboard the *Garland* with whom he held a council, & there showing his commission was accepted for general, & Captain Bodenham made captain of the *Defiance*, & M. Savill captain of the *Adventure*.[40]

Drake had wanted to be buried ashore, but instead was buried in a lead casket in the waters of the bay. In just six weeks, England had lost her two greatest admirals to diseases contracted in the tropics. What Spanish musket balls could not do, bugs did.

A 'cordon sanitaire' can isolate ships from each other and from the land, but once infection comes aboard, it can spread quickly. Such was the case with the

Hawkyns-Drake West Indian fleet. When it returned to Plymouth in early May 1596, its ranks were decimated, one fifth of the men who sailed out were lost to battle or disease. As Hakluyt's account of the deaths of Hawkyns and Drake was published when England and Spain were still at war, it is understandably brief, and leaves off details and answers to many questions.

Another piece written two years later, 1598, in the same waters that took Hawkyns – Puerto Rico – adds more. Dr Layfield, chaplain to George Clifford, Third Earl of Cumberland, describes symptoms that point to dysentery (it and malaria were well known in Puerto Rico). As Cumberland was attacking San Juan:

> many of our men fell sick, and at the very first not very many died. The Spanish as well as the English were both sick and died of the sickness, as besides seralta was seen in divers others.[41] Others suspected their bodily labours to have procured it, and both seem to have concurred. In July and August is their winter, so called for their great rains at those times, which to bodies already rarified by the heat of the sun then over them, and yet rather where vehement exercise hath more opened the pores whereby inward heat is exhaled, must needs be very dangerous.

The theory of humours, then accepted, has it that pestilent vapours could enter the body through open pores in the skin.

Layfield continues with a full description:

> It was an extreme looseness of the body, which within few days would grow into a flux of blood, sometimes in the beginning accompanied with a hot ague, but always in the end attended by an extreme debility and waste of spirits: so that some two days before death, the arms and legs of the sick would be wonderful cold. And that was held for a certain sign of near departure. This sickness usually within few days (for it was very extreme to the number of sixty, eighty, and an hundred stools in an artificial day) brought a languishing weakness over all the body, so that one man's sickness (if he were of any note) commonly kept two from doing duties. And this was it, which rather then the number already dead, made his Lordship first think of quitting the place. For though towards the beginning of July, there were not much above two hundred dead, yet was there twice as many sick, and there was no great hope to recover the most of them. The ships were left weakly manned, for when we landed we landed about a thousand men, of which the greater part was dead or made unserviceable for the present. There were above 400 reported dead when his Lordship left the town, and surely as many so sick, that most of them could not bring themselves aboard, before his Lordship left the place.[42]

The description suggests bacillary dysentery.

Salmonella, Common Diarrhoea, Giardia

Diarrhoea can be present in several other diseases besides those above. When it is acute and accompanied by fever and blood, the causes can be bacillary dysentery or *Salmonella* enterocolitis, especially when there is unsanitary food handling, notably in meat. If the diarrhoea is accompanied by fever but no blood, then the causes can be, among others, *Salmonella* enteritis and malaria (especially *Plasmodium falciparum*). Salmonella is found in contaminated food (but not water), and brings on fever and chills, followed by vomiting and diarrhoea. It has an incubation period of twelve to forty-eight hours, and has over 100 forms. If the diarrhoea is without fever but with blood, the most important cause is amoebiasis. This acute diarrhoea comes from food poisoning, one cause being enterotoxigenic strains of *Escherichia coli*, the travellers' malady common in the tropics.

Ralegh's sailing orders for his 1617–18 voyage warned sailors not to eat raw fruit and vegetables or acute diarrhoea would result. If the diarrhoea were to persistent over a period of months, one cause could be another organism, giardia, that natural phenomenon that is hard to detect and still harder to treat.[43] The giardia protosoan appears after two to six weeks of contact. It is almost always spread by the oral-faecal route from human to human, though animals can also be infected with it. It ranges far and wide, from low to high latitudes. Beavers in the wilds of North America have been found infected with it. The accompanying diarrhoea occurs usually three to eight times a day, with a pale, offensive, bulky stool accompanied by much flatus. The sailor burps and farts a sulphurous gas. Epidemics can occur when water contaminated with the cysts is taken aboard. Caution dictates avoiding raw vegetables and ordinary tap water, especially in the tropics, just as Ralegh advises. Boiling or filtering is used to destroy the cysts, though such ways are not fully effective for killing this highly resistant organism.[44]

4. Other Conditions and Ills

Besides the three principal diseases – malaria, scurvy and dysentery – the sailor encountered other ills: leishmaniasis, a protozoan parasite transmitted by sand flies; trypanosomiasis, a flagellate protozoan parasite (Chagas' disease); and dengue fever, a virus carried by the mosquito *aëdes aegyptyi* (which also carries yellow fever). Some diseases are found in contaminated water and in mosquito bites by helminths, the parasitic worms that inhabit the intestines and feed off the human host – tapeworms, roundworms and flukes such as blood flukes (schistosomes), hence schistosomiasis or snail fever, a freshwater parasitic disease. Sexually transmitted conditions can be bacterial (as are gonorrhoea and syphilis) but there are others that are viral, fungal, parasitic and protozoal. Other conditions and remedies figure in the early accounts: haemorrhoids; menses and mothers' back pains; psychiatric ills (caused by an imbalance of humours); poxes (greatpox or syphilis, and small pox; respiratory ills such as rheum (a cold) with watery discharge from eyes and nose, coughs; poisoning from fruits, vegetables or snake bites; dizziness, burns and sunstroke.[45]

Poisons

Lerius, in the 1550s, warned of poisonous Brazilian apples. He writes:

> Especially on the shore there are many small shrubs, the apples whereof being
> very like unto our country [France] medlars, are dangerously eaten. Therefore,
> when the Barbarians see the French men, and other strangers coming to gather
> those apples, often using the word *ypochi*, in their country language, they
> admonish them to abstain from them.[46]

This Brazil was clearly a post-lapsarian garden.

Layfield from Puerto Rico warns in 1598 of the dangers of eating the raw cassava root:

> This root is very full of liquor, which must be carefully pressed forth, before the
> dryer part be fit to make bread. For the root eaten with the juice, or the juice by
> it self, bringeth a painful swelling in the belly, whereof death doth often follow.
> Wherefore the Spaniards generally hold it for a kind of poison. Yet our men (I
> am told) meeting with the roots unpressed, and mistaking them for potatoes
> (whereby you may conjecture their shape) have eaten them without after feeling
> any mortal distemper. And to a body whose natural heat is able to overcome their
> crudity and rawness, there is happily no present danger, for they tell me that of
> this juice sodden, there is made a pretty kind of drink somewhat like small ale.[47]

Charles Leigh in Guiana in 1604 warns against cassava. 'The juice thereof they
crush out most carefully being rank poison raw'.[48] Poisonous if eaten raw, but
when cooked this starch was (and still is) the staple of the Tropical American diet.

Contaminated Water, Dews

When Ralegh departed from Guiana in 1595, he left behind Francis Sparrey and
a cabin boy, Hugh Godwin, to reconnoitre and to keep an English presence there
By 1602, after seven years in the Guiana jungle, Sparrey had a rather different view
of disease from his master's about the Orinoco. It was not the Eden that Ralegh
painted to the expedition's investors in 1595. Sparrey writes: 'To the Westward of
Capuri in the Province of Amapaia, is most vile, unwholesome, and bad water
to drink: It is of a bad tawny colour; it hath killed many a man, both Indians and
others. They say this water commeth from Anebas.' To the north of the River
Orinoco is the River Drano. 'The danger for entering this River is nothing, but
the doubt is only of the bad water, and most terrible dews which fall from the
moors, which are unhealthful, and kill the Indians daily; for that continually when
they travel they lie in the open air'.[49] Guiana like Brazil was no paradise.

Parasites

Merchant-traveller Tomson was in Santo Domingo in the 1550s. He provides the
first known description in English of the Caribbean hookworm:

There is another kind of small worm which creepeth into the soles of men's feet & especially of the black Moors and children which use to go barefoot, & maketh their feet to grow as big as a man's head, & doth so ache that it would make one run mad. They have no remedy for the same, but to open the flesh sometimes 3. or 4. inches & so dig them out.[50]

Removing worms and parasites made for more misery. Charles Leigh writes from the River Orinoco in 1604:

We were mightily vexed with a kind of worm, which at first was like to a flea, and would creep into the feet especially, and under the nails, and would exceedingly torment us, the time it was in, and more in the pulling out with a pin or needle, if they were few. But one of our men having his feet over-grown with them, for want of hose and shoes, was fain to submit himself to the Indians' cure, who tying one of his legs first with his feet upward, poured hot melted wax which is black upon it, and letting it lie upon it till it was thoroughly cold, they forcibly pulled it off; and therewithal the worms came out sticking in the same, seven or eight hundred in number. This man was named John Nettleton a dyer of London, which afterward was drowned.

Tropical parasites, including hookworm (ancyclostomiasis), entering via the soles of feet, were some of many problems for the English. The solution? From the Orinoco Charles wrote to his brother Sir Olave Leigh back in England: send out more colonists.[51]

Sexually Transmitted Diseases: Bacterial and Viral

Gonorrhoea (caused by *Neisseria gonorrhoeae* bacterium), syphilis (caused by *Treponema pallidum* bacterium), chlamydia (caused by bacterium *Treponema pallidum*, and a fourth, prichamoniasis (caused by the protozoan parasite *Trichomones vaginalis*) are bacterial and now can be treated by antibiotics. Other venereal diseases are viral – HIV, genital warts, herpes and hepatitis – and have no known cure.

Both San Juan de Ulúa and Vera Cruz (now not two ports but one city) were then hot, humid and teeming with venereal disease. Tomson's is the first known English account of heatstroke and (likely) gonorrhoea contracted in Vera Cruz in the 1550s:

This town also is subject to great sickness, and in my time many of the mariners & officers of the ships did die with those diseases, there accustomed, & especially those that were not used to the country, nor knew the danger thereof, but would commonly go in the sun in the heat of the day, & did eat fruit of the country with much disorder, and especially gave themselves to women's company at their first coming: whereupon they were cast into a burning ague, of the which few escaped.

The sexual habits of the locals also drew the attention of Lerius, while living with them. He writes that the Tupí-Guaraní:

> hate adulterous women, that it lieth in the husband's power either to kill the adulteress, or at the least, to put her away with great ignominy and reproach. This surely is true, so that (as I have already said) I have seen very many in diverse villages deflowered by the Neustrian interpreters [French Huguenots, from Aquitaine to the English Channel], who yet were not reproachfully disgraced for the same.

The Brazilian 'savages', he says, are generally chaste, though the Indians:

> are not very careful of preserving the chastity of unmarried women: nay, they easily prostitute them to any man … I have observed that the younger sort both men and women are not very much given to lust: and I would our country people [French] could moderate themselves as well in this behalf.

But when it comes to buggery, he adds, 'that heinous and abominable wickedness reigneth among them.'[52]

Lerius says of those with venereal diseases:

> they are sometimes sick of fevers, and other common diseases; but, not so often, as we use to be. Moreover, they are troubled with a certain incurable disease, which they call *pians* [likely syphilis]. This, for the most part proceedeth of lust: yet, I have seen the little children infected therewith, not unlike the manner of our country measles. This contagion breaketh out into pustles, broader then a thumb, which overspread the whole body, and also the face itself.[53]

Alligators, Snakes, Cannibals

William Davies, Barber Surgeon of London, in 1608 found the Amazon a:

> place of continual tempests, as lightning, thunder, and rain, and so extreme, that it continues most commonly sixteen or eighteen hours in four and twenty. There are so many standing waters in this country, which be full of alligators, guianes, with many other several water serpents, and great store of fresh fish, of strange fashions.[54]

Ralegh's cabin boy, Hugh Godwin, left in Guiana in 1595 to learn the language and customs of the Indians, was eaten by an alligator.

John Nicol was sent out by Sir Olave Leigh in 1605–06 to augment the numbers at Guiana. Storms, contrary winds and no food on that passage out forced the ship to leave sixty-seven colonists on St Lucia, where the Caribes killed and ate some, while other colonists starved:

For we continued fifteen days having no kind of meat but wilks [welks], salt
water, and tobacco; which did nothing at all nourish us, yet nevertheless it took
away the desire of hunger, and saved us from eating one another. In those fifteen
days five of our company pined to death, because they could not take tobacco:
John Parkins, Edward Greene, Thomas Stubbes, Andrew Swash, and an old man
called John. By noting two or three of our men to die, we knew by those tokens
when we drew near our death: which were these, first they would swell very
big, and shortly after fall to the very bones, and wanting strength to hold up
their heads, they would fall down, and droop into their bosoms, and in twelve
hours after yield up the ghost.[55]

Nicol was lucky to find help among the Spaniards:

My lot fell out to be entertained by one whose name was Señor Francisco Lopez:
and being extremely sick of a calenture, or hot fever, one Captain Peroso which
had married his daughter having good skill in physic, came daily to my chamber,
and there let my blood, dieted me, and purged me, giving his own wife in charge.[56]

Master John Wilson, 'of Wansted in Essex, one of the last ten that returned
into England from Wiapoco in Guiana 1606' reports that on arriving, he found
Captain Charles Leigh and the rest of the company sick and mutinous. 'The general himself was very weak and much changed, which partly proceeded by reason
of their great want of victuals', and by reason of 'discontent and sickness'. Wilson
soon experienced these things himself. He went with others inland:

And after our journey by reason of such rain and foul weather as we had in
the same, most of our company fell sick, and for that they had no comfortable
drinks, nor any comforts that sick persons do want, diverse of them died of the
flux; which the Indians (as also the disease called the calenture) know right
well for to cure, yet concealed it ... But unto us after his death they did reveal,
which sickness amongst the company caused no small grief unto our general,
and chiefly to see such wants amongst them.

Leigh's plans for more aid from England were in vain:

Presently after he had shipped his provision, and such commodities as he had
gathered together in the country, and was in a readiness to depart for England,
he sickened of the flux, and died aboard his ship, and was by Captain Huntly
secretly buried on the Land, the twentieth of March, whose death was so secretly
kept by the captain, and the master of the ship, that most of the company knew
not thereof. The reason was, because there was provision too little for them
which were shipped.

Huntly set sail on 2 April 1605, and promised to return within seven months with aid for the thirty-five colonists left behind. These remaining colonists planted some twenty acres of flax and tobacco, and waited for harvest. They hoped these commodities would fetch a good profit in London. The ship never returned.[57]

In 1606, William Turner, son of a London doctor, was one of those who were landed on St Lucia. Rumour had it, he writes, that Captain Charles Leigh died in the pinnace while returning to England, or that he was killed in his hammock at Wiapoco. As for the thirty-five men left in the colony, they 'were in great misery and extremity, both for lack of health and scarcity of victuals'.[58]

B. Treatments in the Tropics

Some treatments already familiar to the early voyagers could ease or help to ward off shipboard illness or those contracted ashore. Some treatments were Old World ones, some from the New World.

Clean Clothes, a Draught of Drink

Hawkyns writes that for scurvy:

> the best prevention for this disease (in my judgement) is to keep clean the ship, to besprinkle her ordinarily with vinegar, or to burn tar, and some sweet savours, to feed upon as few salt meats in the hot country as may be, and especially to shun all kinds of salt fish, and to reserve them for the cold climates, and not to dress any meat with salt water, nor to suffer the company to wash their shirts nor clothes in it, nor to sleep in their clothes when they are wet.

The ship must also carry extra clothes for the sailors:

> Being a common calamity amongst the ordinary sort of mariners, to spend their thrift on the shore, and to bring to sea no more clothes than they have backs; for the body of man is not refreshed with any thing more, then with shifting clean clothes: a great preservative of health in hot countries.

The crew is healthiest when engaged in physical activity, 'in some bodily exercise of work, of agility, of pastimes, of dancing, of use of arms: these help much to banish this infirmity'. The third preventative is for the captain:

> in the morning at discharge of the watch, to give every man a bit of bread, and a draught of drink, either beer, or wine mingled with water (at the least, the one half) or a quantity mingled with beer, that the pores of the body may be full, when the vapours of the sea ascend up. The morning draught should be ever of the best, and choicest of that in the ship. Pure wine I hold to be more hurtful, than the other is profitable. In this, others will be of a contrary opinion, but

I think partial. If not, then leave I the remedies thereof to those physicians and surgeons who have experience.[59]

Clean Ballast, Hammocks

Cleanliness helped to prevent dysentery and contaminated food and water. During the sixteenth and early seventeenth centuries, some captains issued orders for cleanliness. Sebastian Cabot, who on 9 May 1553 as governor of the Merchant Adventurers, drew up rules for a voyage to China. Once a week the captain was to read this to the crew:'No liquor to be spilt in the ballast, nor filthiness to left with[in] board; the cook room, and all other places, to be kept clean for the better health of the company.'[60] Cabins bred filth, sedition and fires, so cut away the partitions. Later, Sir John Hawkyns had the cookroom of his flagship *Mary Rose* (a later ship of the same name as the celebrated one) moved from the hold to the upper deck, 'as well for the better stowing of her victuals as also for better preserving her whole company in health during that voyage being bound to the southwards'.[61] The *Instructions Issued to the Royal Navy*, 1596, contains the directive that 'you shall give order that your ship may be kept clean daily and sometimes washed; what with God's favour, shall preserve from sickness and avoid many inconveniences'.[62]

As a measure toward better health, hammocks were officially adopted in 1597, when Sir Edmund Carey paid Roger Langford £300 for 300 bolts of canvas 'to make hanging cabones [cabins] or beds' for the Earl of Essex' fleet. Men commonly slept on the deck. Hammocks, long used throughout the Americas by peoples ranging from the Mayans to the Brazilian Indians, had early on been adopted by Portuguese and Spanish vessels. At his host Indians' suggestion, Jean Lerius in 1557 took up sleeping in a hammock ashore. He enthusiastically recommended them to others. On his 1595 voyage to Guiana, Sir Walter Ralegh found them to be excellent bedding for the tropics, at sea and ashore: 'Those beds which they call Hamacas or Brazil beds, wherein in hot countries all the Spaniards use to lie commonly, and in no other, neither did we ourselves while we were there.'[63] Hammocks were not only comfortable, but they kept the sailor off a damp deck or piece of ground.[64] A hammock is still commonly carried by travellers in the northeast of Brazil. Lodgings provide hooks in the walls from which to hang them.

Fresh Water

Foul drinking water can bring on diarrhoea. Sir Richard Hawkyns in 1593–94 describes one solution for obtaining fresh water:

> And although our fresh water had failed us many days (before we saw the shore) by reason of our long navigation, without touching any land, and the excessive drinking of the sick and diseased (which could not be excused) yet with an invention I had in my ship, I easily drew out of the water of the sea sufficient quantity of fresh water to sustain my people, with little expense of fuel, for with four billets I stilled a hogshead of water, and therewith dressed the meat for the sick and whole. The water so distilled, we found to be wholesome and nourishing.[65]

Hawkyns was the first known English mariner to distill salt water while at sea to make fresh, though the process was known to the ancient Greeks, and likely practised by the Spanish mariners by the early sixteenth century.

Toward the end of his three years in Guiana, Robert Harcourt's time was shortened, he writes, when the ship's captain:

> came unto me, and told me plainly, that if I made any longer abode in that country, I would never in those ships return into England: or if I did adventure it, my self, and all my company would starve at sea for want of beer, cider, and water, for all my cask was spoiled, because it was not iron-bound; the wooden hoops flew off, by reason of the heat of the climate; and our beer, and cider, (whereof we had good store) did leak about the ship, that we could hardly save sufficient to relieve us, if we made a longer stay upon the coast; which was the master's fault, having had a special charge to be careful of that only point.[66]

In the tropics, the Shakespearean song 'Fear No More the Heat of the Sun' was not so. In the heat, the lack of water, cider and beer was a serious matter.

Dr Stevens Water, Oranges and Lemons
Richard Hawkyns' antidote for scurvy?

> That which I have seen most fruitful for this sickness, is sour oranges and lemons, and a water which amongst others (for my particular provision) I carried to the sea, called Dr Stevens water, of which, for that his virtue was not then well known unto me, I carried but little, and it took end quickly, but gave health to those that used it. The oil of vitry [vitriolic acid?] is beneficial for this disease; taking two drops of it, and mingled in a draught of water, with a little sugar. It taketh away the thirst, and helpeth to cleanse and comfort the stomach: But the principal of all is the air of the land; for the sea is natural for fishes, and the land for men. And the oftener a man can have his people to land (not hindering his voyage), the better it is, and the profitablest course that he can take to refresh them.

As did others of his time in following the ancients, Richard Hawkyns attributes scurvy to the air, but his recommendation that sailors eat lemons was right on the mark. Richard Hawkyns further directed that salty foods be avoided and that sailors be issued a daily ration of beer or wine cut with water. This was to keep the pores of the skin full and prevent sea vapours from entering the body and infecting it with scurvy. He wishes that:

> some learned man would write of it, for it is the plague of the sea, and the spoil of mariners; doubtless, it would be a work worthy of a worthy man, and most beneficial for our country, for in twenty years (since I have used the sea) I dare take upon me, to give account of ten thousand men consumed with this disease.[67]

Spirits

As for alcohol, Dr Layfield in 1598 observes that heat and liquor do not mix well in hot climates. 'For drinks, the Spaniard doth here, as in Spain he doth, use water for most of his drink, which in so hot a climate, would well agree with the English after some acquaintance'.[68]

All that glisters is not Guianan gold. In February 1595 Sir Walter Ralegh set out with five ships for Guiana and the Orinoco River to plant a colony and to seek riches. It was rare for a member of Queen Elizabeth's court to sail to the Americas, even one out of favour. In his *Discoverie of the Large, Rich, and Beautifull Empire of Guiana*, 1595, he addresses his dedicatees Charles Howard, Lord Admiral, and Robert Cecil, Privy Councillor: 'I have been accompanied with many sorrows, with labour, hunger, heat, sickness, & peril: It appeareth notwithstanding that I made no other bravado of going to the sea.' His *Discoverie* has little of illness in his report and much of perfection. Still, on ascending the River Orinoco, a passage of hundreds of miles upstream, Ralegh writes that 'the further we went on (our victual decreasing and the air breeding great faintness) we grew weaker and weaker, when we had most need of strength and ability'.[69]

C. Simples Discovered

The voyagers' accounts include descriptions of remedies learned in the tropics. Some treatments proved effective, others not so. Still others remain as medical mythology.

Ships returned from the American Tropics, and Europe's pharmacopia grew larger with exotic simples. New drugs and treatments from the tropics, all outside European medicine, were offered up to treat the old problems of flux, the pox, colic, toothaches, liver problems and more. Purchas, with guarded enthusiasm, includes the extensive and anonymous 'Treatise of Brazil', 1601, possibly written by the Portuguese, Manoel Tristão, in *Purchas His Pilgrims*, 1625. 'It seemeth that this climate doth flow in poison, as well for the many snakes there are, as for the multitude of scorpions, spiders, and other unclean creatures, and the lizards are so many that they cover the walls of the house, and the holes are full of them'. Yet, he adds, the country provides remedies. Here are a few:

For Wounds, Take Cupayba

The oil from the *cupayba*, a fig tree, writes Tristão, is good for wounds, 'and taketh away all the scar', just as the *ambaya* fig trees, whose bark, once scraped and crushed to a juice, serves to heal wounds in a short time. Another fig tree, the *ambaygtinga*, 'which they call of Hell, ambaigtina, is found in Taperas' [Tapera]. Its 'leaves are much esteemed for them that do vomit, and cannot retain that which they eat, anointing the stomach with the oil, it taketh away the oppilations, and the colic'. For the bloody flux: 'Of the trees *igbacamuci* there are many in Saint Vincent [São Vicente]: They bear a certain fruit as good as quinces, fashioned like a pan or a pot, they have within certain small seeds, they are the only remedy for the bloody flux.' The *igcigca* produces a 'white liquor that doth congeal; it serveth for plasters in cold diseases'.[70]

For the Flux, Take Guava

During the return passage from Puerto Rico to England in 1598, Chaplain Layfield addressed cures for the flux and other ills. He notes that Puerto Rico has a remedy for flux – *guava*:

> Their guavas are a lesser fruit, as big as a peach, and without not much unlike, but within not solid as the mammeis [Port. *mamão* or papaya] or as an apple is, but full of such little seeds as a goose-berry hath, not so greenish, but inclining to a sanguine colour, the taste of this is (me thought) like to a very ripe great white plum: this fruit is (which a man would not think) a remedy against the flux, and so are their papaes, a fruit like an apple of a waterish Welsh taste. They have plums black and white, their stones much bigger, and their meat much less then in England, and these also stay the flux. And so doe their wild grapes, which are a fruit growing in clusters, and therein only (methinks) like grapes, they are round, and as great as a good musket-bullet.[71]

For Flux and Worms, Difficult Menses, Cankers, Take Tyroqui, Embeguacu, Cobaura

Brazil provided remedies for parasites and dysentery:

> The herb tyroqui or tareroqui is a principal remedy for the bloody flux ... The Indians perfume themselves with this herb when they are sick, that they may not die, and for a certain sickness that is common in the country, and it is called the sickness of the worm.

Purchas' marginalia: 'Perhaps the worm in the fundament mentioned by Sir R. Hawkyns'. [Ancyclostomiasis resulting in anaemia.] Purchas:

> It is a great remedy; it serveth to kill the worm in the oxen and swine, and for empostumes [secretions from a man's cod]. This herb is as withered all night, and as asleep, and as soon as the sun riseth, it openeth again, and shutteth again when it is set.

To ease a woman's menses, there is the herb *embeguaçu*, which:

> serveth much for the flux of blood, especially in women ... This being taken, to wit, the bark of it, and perfuming the party in the place of the flux, it ceaseth presently.

Further comment is that *caa obetinga* 'being laid to the wound cleaveth fast, and healeth it'. Then another simple: 'Cobaura serveth for old sores that have already no other remedy, it is laid beaten and burnt in the wound, and eateth presently all the canker, and bringeth a new skin'.[72]

For Flux, Take Kellette

Robert Harcourt noted other treatments used in Guiana:

> There is a berry in those parts very excellent against the bloody-flux, by the Indians it is called kellette. The juice of the leaf called uppee, cureth the wounds of the poisoned arrows. The juice of the leaf called icari, is good against the headache. Many other drugs and simples are there found of singular properties both in physic and chirurgerie [surgery], which if they should be severally described according to their value and worthiness, would contain a large volume.[73]

For Wounds from Poisoned Arrows, Take Tupara

With his characteristic curiosity in scientific matters, Ralegh in 1595 learned from the Arawaks of a remedy for their poisoned arrows, taken from:

> the juice of a root called tupara: the same also quencheth marvellously the heat of burning fevers, and healeth inward wounds, and broken veins, that bleed within the body … Some of the Spaniards have been cured in ordinary wounds, of the common poisoned arrows with the juice of garlic: but this a general rule for all men that shall hereafter travel the Indies where poisoned arrows are used, that they must abstain from drink, for if they take any liquor into their body, as they shall be marvellously provoked thereunto by drought, I say, if they drink before the wound be dressed, or soon upon it, there is no way with them but present death.

Ralegh found Guiana healthier than other parts of the Caribbean: 'The rest of the Indies for calms and diseases very troublesome.'[74]

For Haemorrhoids, Take Yri

Frequently, these maritime accounts express the common Renaissance idea that when God inflicts pain, he benevolently provides a cure. The seafarers brought back to Europe some of these cures from Tropical America. Lerius in the 1550s notes the American palm tree *yri*. Its round fruit is 'like damsons in the shape of a large cluster of so great weight, that it may hardly be lifted up with one hand, but the kernel only is of the bigness of a cherry, and may be eaten'.[75] The leaves of the *yri* can treat haemorrhoids. 'In the top of these palms, there is a certain white young tendril or branch, which we cut off, to eat the same: Philippus who was troubled with the haemorrhoids, affirmed, that it was a remedy for that disease, the warrantable truth whereof I leave to the physicians'.[76] Brazil, it seems, might yet be a Garden of Eden.

For Menses, Purge Blood

Part of the medical theory of humours found that blood–letting, particularly when done in springtime, was efficacious in re-establishing the balance within the black and yellow bile, phlegm and blood. Lerius tells us that the Brazilian Tupí Indians took such purgation further:

> For the space of an whole year, while we lived in those countries, we never saw any woman having the flowres [flowers, flows, menses]. I think that they divert that flux by some means unknown to us. For I saw maidens of twelve years old, whose sides were cut by their mothers, from the arm-hole down to the knee, with a very sharp tusk of a certain beast. And the young girls gnashing with their teeth through extremity of pain, bleed very much: I conjecture that they prevented their monthly flux by this remedy.[77]

For Palsy, a Moist Head, or a Rheumatic Brain, Take Colliman

From Guiana Robert Harcourt wrote a detailed account back to Prince Charles and observes that he met the Indian chief Leonard Ragapo, who had returned with Ralegh to England after the voyage to Guiana in 1595. Ragapo recommends that the English should move their settlement along the Orinoco to higher ground as where they were was unhealthy, and that the men at the low ground at Wiapoco:

> would there be subject to sickness and die: and for an instance he named Captain Leigh, and his company, who formerly were planted there, and almost all died by sickness in the same place: But he assured me that his own country Cooshebery [inland] was of a good air, pleasant, and healthful.

Like Tristão, Harcourt also commends Guiana, and says that for all its many ills, its herbs can work marvellous cures. Various gums have 'been proved by Master Cary of Wictham [Wycombe] in Buckinghamshire (a Gentleman of great judgement and practice in physic)', and he recommends *colliman* or *carriman*:

> If you put a little of it upon burning coals, it filleth all the room with a most sweet and pleasant savour. He further reporteth of it, that certainly if you hold your head over the fume thereof three or four times a day, it cureth the giddiness of the head, and is also a most excellent comfort and remedy for a cold, moist, and rheumatic brain: it is also good against the resolution (or as the common sort call it) the dead palsy, whereof the giddiness of the head is often a messenger, and the fore-teller of that most pernicious grief.

For Female Back Pains, Take Colliman

Gum of that same *colliman*, reports Harcourt, helps women who have had children and are suffering lower back pains:

For remedy whereof, it is to be melted in a pewter vessel with a gentle fire, then with a knife it must be spread lightly upon a piece of leather, and laid warm to the place grieved, until it come off of it self. This plaster is also very good for aches, and doth greatly comfort and strengthen the sinews. Thus much hath Master Cary written and reported of it, and hath proved by his own experience.

It is a veritable cure-all. 'This gum is also approved to be an excellent remedy against the gout; and of singular virtue in the cure of wounds.' Similarly, 'barratta is a balm good for wounds'.

But watch out for:

a little green apple, by the Indians called in their language, the sleeping apple; which in operation is so violent, that one little bit thereof doth cause a man to sleep to death: the least drop of the juice of it, will purge in vehement and excessive manner, as dangerously was proved by my cousin Unton Fisher, who first found it: for biting a little of it for a taste, and finding it to burn his mouth in some extremity, did suddenly spit it out again, but some small quantity of the juice (against his will) went down into his stomach, which for two or three days space did provoke in him an extraordinary sleepiness, and purged him with sixty seats. This apple, for the purging virtue in so small a quantity, is like to be of good price, and great estimation in the practice of physic; for the learned physicians do well know how to correct the sleeping quality thereof wherein the danger resteth.[78]

For the Pox, Take Curupicaiba and Caarobmocorandiba

Curupicaiba 'is the only remedy for wounds both green and old, and for the pox, and it taketh away all the scar from the wounds'. The pox here is smallpox, chickenpox or syphillis (great pox). The wood *caarobmocorandiba* 'healeth the looseness, the pox, and other diseases of cold, it is grey, and hath the pith very hard as the wood of China'. Abundant is the tree *iaaburandiba*, whose leaves 'are the only remedy for the sicknesses of the liver, and many in this Brazil have already been cured of most grievous diseases of the liver, with the eating of them'. The *betele*'s roots are 'an excellent remedy for the tooth-ache'. The *caaroba* [*caroba*] tree provides a cure for the pox:

There is a great abundance of the trees caaroba, the leaves of these chewed and laid to the pock-sore dry and heal it in such a manner, that it never cometh again, and it seemeth that the wood hath the same effect that the China wood, and that of the Antilles have for the same disease. Of the flower they make a conserve for those that are sick of the pox.[79]

For Coughs, Burns, the Hot Baths at Nevis

On the return passage, Harcourt's ship called at the island of Neves, where there were more cures. Writes Harcourt:

In this island there an hot bath, which as well for the reports that I have heard, as also for that I have seen and found by experience, I do hold for one of the best and most sovereign in the world. I have heard that divers of our nation have there been cured of the leprosy, and that one of the same persons now, or lately dwelt at Woolwich near the River of Thames, by whom the truth may be known, if any man desire to be further satisfied therein … For at my coming thither, I was grievously vexed with an extreme cough, which I much feared would turn me to great harm, but by bathing in the bath, and drinking of the water, I was speedily cured: and ever since that time, I have found the state of my body (I give God thanks for it) far exceeding what it was before, in strength and health. Moreover, one of my company, named John Huntbatch (servant to my brother) as he was making a fire, burned his hand with gunpowder, and was in doubt thereby to lose the use of one or two of his fingers, which were shrunk up with the fire, but he went presently to the bath, and washed and bathed his hand a good space therein, which soopled [made supple] his fingers in such a manner, that with great ease he could stir and stretch them out, and the fire was so washed out of his hand that within the space of twenty four hours, by twice or thrice washing and bathing it, the soreness thereof was cured, only the eye-sore for the time remained. Furthermore, two or three other of my company having swellings in their legs, were by the bath cured in a day.

Harcourt concludes by noting that unlike other voyages, his was unusually healthy:

During the time of my voyage, we lost but one land-man, who died in Guiana; and one sailor, and an Indian boy, who died at sea in our return: and during the space of these three years last past since the voyage, of all the men which I left in the country, being in number about thirty, there died but six, whereof one was drowned, another was an old man of threescore years of age, and another took his death by his own disorder; the rest died of sickness, as pleased God the giver of life: for such small loss, his holy name be blessed now and ever.[80]

For Ague, Take Jetigeuçu, for Snake Bites, Cayapia

Tristão found still more simples for the drug chest. *Jetigeuçu* has:

certain roots, long like radice [radish], but of a good bigness, they serve for a purge, this root is taken beaten in wine or water for the ague: it is taken preserved in sugar like marmalade, it is boiled with a hen, causeth great thirst, but is profitable and of great operation. Igpecaya, or pigaya is profitable for the bloody flux … but the smell is strong and terrible. A new miracle herb of the time was the herb cayapia, 'an only remedy for whatsoever poison, especially of snakes, and so it is called the snake's herb, and it is as good a remedy as the unicorn and bada, bezar [bezoar] stone, or coco of Maldiva … It is also a great remedy for the wounds with the arrows that are poisoned, when any is hurt he remaineth fearless and secure, drinking the water of this root, it is also a great remedy for the fever, continuing it and drinking of it some mornings, this herb smelleth like the fig-tree leaves of Spain.[81]

For humours and Rheum, Take Petum or Tobacco, the Holy Herb

Lerius in the 1550s reports that the Caribes would aid their dancing with the smoke from the psychotropic herb *petum*. It was used it to heighten the effect of rituals, used as a cure for ills, and to increase strength. 'I observed that with a very long cane, wherein they put the herb petum', then smoke it. Purchas adds a marginal comment: 'Petum by the author is thought to differ from tobacco, because it hath a pleasing scent, &c. I think it the same.' The Indians lit the leaves, then 'turned themselves hither and thither, and blew out the fume of that herb upon them that stood round about them, with these words: Receive the spirit of fortitude, whereby you may all overcome your enemies. And this was often done by these Caribes.'[82] Despite Purchas, Lerius may be making the earliest French-English reference to New World marijuana (Lat., *Cannabis sativa*; Port., *maconha*) likely imported from Angola by slaves, and planted by them between the rows of sugar cane in the fields of the *engenhos de açúcar* of Brazil's *nordeste*. The slaves smoked it for hallucinogenic, medical and ritualistic purposes. Earlier still, the Portuguese had imported *maconha* from India for the pleasure of the Portuguese court. It was also used generally as a physic: in poultices and drunk as a tonic to alleviate rheumatism, 'female problems', colic, toothaches, constipation, gonorrhoea and lassitude. Marijuana and tobacco were both valued for treating many of the same ills. In the 1540s *maconha* first arrived in Brazil, at the time tobacco was starting to be exported. Early on in colonial Brazil both leaves were valued for their psychotropic properties.[83]

Tobacco (Port., *tobaco, fume*), was also known as the 'Holy Herb, valued as a cure-all for sundry conditions,' as Purchas' note puts it. The miracle drug tobacco:

> serveth for divers diseases, as wounds, and coughs, the rheum, &c. and principally it serveth for the sick of the head, the stomach, and for the shortness of breath, or the chin-cough. In this country they make certain coffins of palm-tree leaves, and being full of this herb dried and setting it on fire at the one end, they put the other in the mouth and drink the smoke, it is one of the delicates and dainties of this country; and all the countrymen, and even the Portugals are even lost for it, and it is their great vice, to be all day and all night laid in their nets, to drink this smoke, and are drunk with it as if it were with wine.

Homeward bound on Drake's 1586 voyage while calling at Ralegh's Virginia colony, Drake (or Purchas, his editor), recalls in the 1620s that according to the historian William Camden, these colonists were 'the first bringers in of the use of tobacco, since so frequently abused by our nation'.[84] The author notes two other herbs:

> Guaraquimiya is the myrtle tree of Portugal, and besides other good properties that it hath, like the broom-rape, the seed of it is the only remedie for the body-worms, and ordinarily they that eat it do void them presently. Camaracatimbae

is like to the silvas of Portugal, it is boiled in water, and the said water is the only remedy for scabbews [scabes?], the pox, and new wounds.[85]

In 1595, the first book in English on sotweed was published anonymously (with illustrations) as *Tobacco*. In the year of his accession, 1603, King James, who detested the plant, wrote *A Counterblaste to Tobacco* and comments the next year that those who use this expensive 'precious stink' are unbaptised barbarians. He taxed tobacco heavily, then losing substantial revenue from the tobacco, soon remitted most of the tax. Tobacco for a time served as legal tender in America. Records show that in 1619 the first shipment of women for wives arrived in Jamestown at a cost per woman of 120 lb of tobacco. Two years later, when sixty women were shipped to the colony, the rate had increased to 150 lb per woman.[86]

Manoel Tristão had praised the efficacy of Brazilian tobacco in 1601. Less than ten years later in neighbouring Guiana, Harcourt observed that tobacco, 'which albeit some dislike, yet the generality of men in this kingdom doth with great affection entertain it'. Sotweed was hated by James I (Virginians noted that its users were soon besotted.), but tobacco and sugar were destined to be the principal cash crops that made the American colonies profitable, and some 175 years later tobacco would fund a revolution:

> The tobacco that was brought into this kindgom in the year of our Lord 1610 was at the least worth 60. thousand pounds. And since that time the store that yearly hath come in, was little less. It is planted, gathered, seasoned, and made up fit for the merchant in short time, and with easy labour.

A small field of tobacco with minimal labour yielded great profit, whereas sugar required much greater acreage and labour for the same result.[87]

For Other Ills, Consult the Sea Captain's Book

In the 1590s English books for the well-being of mariners began to appear in some number. *The Cures of the Diseased in Remote Regions Preventing Mortality Incident in Forraine Attempts of the English Nation*, 1598, is the first English book on tropical medicine. It was written by the sea captain George Wateson, Joseph Singer and one G.W. (George Whetstone, playwright and soldier who had suffered yellow fever while a prisoner in Spain?). *Cures of the Diseased* is based on Wateson's first-hand experience in voyaging to the West Indies, and Central and South America. Here is knowledge based on observed fact, not ancient second-hand authority. Hakluyt had planned to include Wateson's work in *Principal Navigations*, but William Gilbert, physician to Elizabeth and James I, dissuaded him, saying he himself would write something along the same lines. Gilbert had no knowledge of the tropics, and never did write (nor could he write) such a book. Wateson's valuable book contains chapters on typhus, yellow fever, dysentery and other diseases, and was to become the trusted English authority on tropical medicine for the next 100 years.[88]

Decline of the Fleet and Tropical Physic

As the Elizabethan age was followed by the Jacobean, the quality of health aboard ships declined. After the Treaty of London in 1604 the Navy was viewed as superfluous, and not surprisingly fell into neglect. The treaty maintained Spain's hegemony in the Americas, and caused the overseas trade to drop. The standards of health slipped. Mortality rates on voyages once again rose alarmingly. In just over a decade, the hard-gained knowledge of tropical medicine gained over a century was quickly lost.

An exception was Ralegh. Twenty-two years after he first set foot in Guiana in 1595 to plant a colony, he returned, in 1617. Ralegh made meticulous preparations and fitted out of the *Destiny* from his experience from over twenty years earlier. Health was a major concern. His instructions for the voyage are specific: 'You shall take especial care of keeping of our ships clean between decks'; 'Every man [shall] put his apparel in canvas cloak bags'; 'You shall take especial care when God shall send us to land in the Indies, not to eat any fruit unknown, which fruit you do not find eaten with worms or beasts under the tree'; and 'You shall avoid sleeping on the ground, and eating of new fish until it be salted two or three hours, which will otherwise breed a most dangerous flux; so will the eating of over-fat hogs or fat turtles'.

Despite the guidance, Ralegh's men took ill even before reaching the Canaries. Once there, fruit helped the crew by staving off scurvy, but two weeks later, they were presenting as what Ralegh calls a fever or 'calenture', which Keevil thinks may have been yellow fever added to the scurvy but which might also have been malaria. On the passage, many crew in the fleet fell ill, Ralegh seriously so. When the *Destiny* dropped anchor in the Orinoco River, Ralegh was far too sick to lead the shore party inland and was carried ashore to recover. He was forced to delegate his authority to others, a fatal move, it turned out.

What besides scurvy killed off so many mariners over the years? Dysentery, the blood flux, was the usual likely cause, though malaria was also a major disease of the time. Keevil suggests that Hawkyns and Drake likely died from dysentery. Aboard ship, food was rotten and the water foul, causing poisoning. Once ashore in the American tropics, more than a dozen diseases awaited the sailor. By sea or land, along with dysentry, three diseases stand out: acute toxaemia from contaminated food and water, coupled with dysentery; scurvy, a vitamin C deficiency; and malaria, the tertian and quartan agues.

What Spanish muskets did not do, filth, mosquitoes, bugs and worms did. In 1595, before the task force attacked San Juan, Puerto Rico, Hawkyns was hastily buried at sea full fathom five somewhere deep in the shadows of San Juan's fort, El Morro. Drake, with more ceremony, was sealed in a lead coffin and lies still at the bottom of the bay of Nombre de Dios, Panamá. Only his drum came home to Buckland Abbey in Devon. Disease killed Hawkyns and Drake, and led to Ralegh's death. What is remarkable is that the Elizabethans and early Jacobeans could voyage out to the American tropics and return home at all.

Notes

1 *PN*, 11:389–416.

2 *PN*, 11:389–416; *PP*, 16:146–78; *TB*, 111–16.

3 Andrew Wear, *Knowledge and Practice in English Medicine, 1550–1680* (Cambridge: Cambridge Univ. Press, 2000), 37–45; Frederick F. Cartwright and Michael Biddiss, *Disease & History* (Stroud: Sutton Publishing Ltd, 2000), esp. Chapter 8, 'Mosquitoes, Flies, Travel and Exploration', 148–67; also Kenneth F. Kiple (ed.), *Plague, Pox & Pestilence* (London: George Weidenfeld & Nicholson Ltd, 1997), and (ed.), and his *The Cambridge Historical Dictionary of Disease* (Cambridge: Cambridge University Press, 2003), passim.

4 James Boswell, *Life of Johnson*, 1759, quoted in *The Oxford Dictionary of Quotations* (London: Oxford University Press, 1949).

5 J.B. Black, *The Reign of Elizabeth, 1558–1603*, 2nd edn, Oxford History of England series (Oxford: Clarendon Press, 1969), 314.

6 Jeremy Hugh Barron, 'Sailors' scurvy before and after James Lind – a reassessment', *Nutritional Reviews, International Life Sciences Institute*, vol. 67, no 6, pp.315–32.

7 Black, 315.

8 *PP*, 16:518–79.

9 Black, 317.

10 *PP*, 16:309–23.

11 Dion R. Bell, *Lecture Notes on Tropical Medicine*, 4th edn. (Oxford: Blackwell Science Ltd, 1995), *passim*.

12 Kiple, *Plague*, 98, *Disease*, 203–7.

13 Bell, 3–37.

14 *PN*, 9: 338–58.

15 Not Henry Hawks in 1572, despite Keevil, 122.

16 *PN*, 9:342.

17 *PN*, 9:354–5.

18 Probably smallpox.

19 *PP*, 16:106–35.

20 *PP*, 16:413–16.

21 *PP*, 16:518–79.

22 *PP*, 16:526.

23 Cartwright, 148; J.J. Keevil, *Medicine and the Navy, 1200–1900*. Vol. 1:1200–1649 (Edinburgh and London: E. & S. Livingstone, Ltd, 1957), 60–255.

24 Kiple, *Plague*, 106. Coincidental with the arrival of the Spanish. The epidemic of 1545 had a mortality rate of 80 per cent.

25 Kiple, *Plague*, 14.

26 Kiple, *Plague*, 68–73.

27 *PP*, 17:57–199.

28 *PP*, 17:75–6; Keevil, 101.

29 Kiple, *Plague*, 69, *Disease*, 295–8.

30 Kiple, *Plague*, 12-13, 118, *Disease*, 242–4; Bell, 279–90.

31 *PP*, 16:130–33.

32 *PN*, 10:229.

33 *PP*, 16:128.

34 *PN*, 10:230.

35 *PP*, 16:106–35.

36 *PN*, 10: 237–9.

37 *PP*, 16:125.

38 *PN*, 10:239.

39 *PP*, 16:126, 130.
40 *PN*, 10:240.
41 The term Layfield uses is 'seralta', possibly the fever *serena*, mosquito-borne malaria contracted in the evening sereno, the moist night air.
42 *PP*, 16:27–106.
43 Bell, 169–78.
44 Bell, 156–60.
45 Bell, *passim*.
46 *PP*, 16:538.
47 *PP*, 16:96–7.
48 *PP*, 16:309–23.
49 *PP*, 16:304–8.
50 *PN*, 9:342.
51 *PP*, 16:309–23.
52 *PP*, 16:563.
53 *PP*, 16:576–7.
54 *PP*, 16:413–16.
55 *PP*, 16: 324–37.
56 *PP*, 16:333.
57 *PP*, 16:338–51.
58 *PP*, 16:35–57.
59 *PP*, 17:57–199.
60 Quoted in Keevil, p. 113.
61 Quoted in Keevil, 115–6.
62 Quoted in Keevil, 114.
63 *PN*, 10:376; quoted in Keevil, 115.
64 See Chapter 1, 'Ships Are But Boards'.
65 *PP*, 17: 90.
66 *PP*, 16:358–402.
67 *PP*, 17:75–6.
68 *PP*, 16:98,417–517.
69 *PN*, 10:338–433.
70 *PP*, 16:417–517.
71 *PP*, 16:94.
72 *PP*, 16:417–517.
73 *PP*, 16:358–402.
74 *PN*, 10:338–433.
75 *PP*, 16:557.
76 *PP*, 16:537.
77 *PP*, 16:565.
78 *PP*, 16:358–402.
79 *PP*, 16:417–517.
80 *PP*, 16:358–402.
81 *PP*, 16:417–517.
82 *PP*, 16:555.
83 Harry William Hutchinson, 'Patterns of Marihuana Use in Brazil', in Vera Rubin (ed.), *Cannabis and Culture* (The Hage: Mouton & Co., 1975), 173–83. See also from Rubin's anthology: Lambos Comitas, 'The Social Nexus of Ganja in Jamaica', 119–32; Roberto Williams-Garcia, 'The Ritual Use of Cannabis in Mexico', 133–46; William L. Partridge, 'Cannabis and Cultural Groups in a Colombian Municipio, 147–72; Vera Rubin, 'The "Ganja Vision" in Jamaica', 257–68; Alvaro de Rubim de Pinho, 'Social and Medical

Aspects of the Use of Cannabis in Brazil', 293–302; B.R. Elejalde, 'Marihuana and Genetic Studies in Colombia: The Problem in the City and in the Country', 327–44; Joseph Shaeffer, 'The Significance of Marihuana in a Small Agricultural Community in Jamaica', 355–88; W.E. Carter and W.J. Coggins, 'Chronic Cannabis Use in Costa Rica: A Description of Research Objectives', 389–400; Johannes Wilbert, 'Magico-Religious Use of Tobacco among South American Indians', 439–62; Michael H. Beaubrun, 'Cannabis or Alcohol: The Jamaican Experience', 485–96.

84 *PP*, 16:121.

85 *PP*, 16:417–517.

86 George Arents, *Books, Manuscripts and Drawings Relating to Tobacco* (Washington: Library of Congress, Government Printing Office, 1938); see www.tobacco.org.; www.historian.org.

87 *PP*, 16:358–402.

88 Keevil, 119–20.

7

Traffiques and Booty

> 'Whosoever commands the sea commands the trade; whosoever commands the trade of the world commands the riches of the world, and consequently the world itself.'
> *Sir Walter Ralegh,* History of the World, 1614

Trade in the period 1520–1640 took five forms, largely following each other, though with some overlap. First was open trade, such as the centuries of trade between England and Portugal. The elder William Hawkyns' various voyages in the 1530s to Africa and Portuguese Brazil, for instance, can be seen as a continuation of the Anglo-Luso trading in place since medieval times. It was such open and legitimate activity that his son, Sir John Hawkyns, wished to expand with his three slaving voyages of the 1560s by supplying labour – African slaves – to Spanish America. The Treaty of Tordesillas, 1494, had restricted commerce in the New World to only Portugal and Spain. But the Spanish colonists needed slaves, and lesser officials at first allowed trade, if it was covert. This second form was carried out under the counter, around in the next bay, on the quiet. Such was English trade in the Caribbean in the first part of the 1560s as practised by John Hawkyns. When even that trade was denied the English by the end of the 1560s, they resorted to a third means, profit by piracy. This was Drake's way. At times it was carried out under the tissue of legality covered by letters of marque, as with Cumberland, or by letters of redress, as with Christopher Newport. 'Privateering' as a term appeared only in the latter part of the seventeenth century. The fourth sort of trade was profit from the spoils of war, as with when the *Nuestra Señora del Rosario* with a pay-chest of 50,000 ducats was captured by the English in 1588.[1] The fifth form of trade was intranational, as trade between a colony and the home country, usually in an exchange of raw resources for finished goods. In most cases the colony's raw materials were traded for the finished products of the home country. In a few cases the manufacture was supplied by the colonies, as in the case of Mexican and Cuban shipbuilding. Whether raw or finished product, this fifth form could happen only after there was substantial settlement. For the Spanish, this was after the 1520s, for the English, a full century and more later, when tobacco began to be exported to England. Consider these five forms in turn.

9

As Quinn and Ryan observe, the business of going to sea was, for the English, not primarily politics, but commerce. Profit was realised various ways. Waging war, wages for labour, goods for services rendered — most trading was a meshing of gunpowder, tobacco and sugar. The Hawkynses, for one, went to sea not for flag or cross but for profit, and had learned from their trading partners, the Portuguese, that trading ultramarine was best done in heavily armed merchantmen, especially when sailing the dangerous waters of piracy or politics of a hostile Spanish America. England's growth from a perhiperal coastal trading nation into the dominant transatlantic mercantile power was challenged in the sixteenth century by the Spanish, and in the seventeenth by the Dutch and French. Spanish hostility towards the English was evident before 1520, long before the Anglo-Spanish War, 1585–1604. The primarily issue was trade, but it was in some cases coloured by religion and politics. Profit depended on control of the seas, as Ralegh observed.

The Treaty of London, 1604, between Spain and England acknowledged the right of religious freedom for the English, that is, the Church of England. But more important, it reaffirmed Spain's exclusive trading rights in her American colonies.[2] The English had long argued (first with the Portuguese in Africa, later the Spanish in the Americas) that paper treaties were worthless unless backed by the power of commerce or conquest by force. England was too weak to destroy Spanish seapower by force, leaving only commerce. She could at least bloody Spain's nose at the marketplace. Hence there was a century of skirmishes and raids in the West Indies, and a fortnight of open war in summer 1588, in the Enterprise of England. After a century, English trade would be able to export cloth, woollens and manufactured goods to Spanish America. Preying on shipping and attacking Spanish ports were two ways to exchange goods. 'Privateering made a large contribution to the resources of capital, shipping and seamanship that made possible the oceanic successes of the seventeenth century, successes which grew directly and immediately out of privateering', writes Kenneth Andrews.[3] Here, then, was the start of England's 'blue water strategy' of empire founded on worldwide trade.

The English profited from their depredations. Without a large Royal Navy, Drake and others engaged in a 'reversion of the nation's sea forces to individualism and a welter of petty plunder' observes Andrews.[4] It was far cheaper to arm private merchantmen than to maintain two dozen royal warships. One merchantman could carry both powder and shot, and goods to trade. Privateering was a logical development from individual maritime enterprise that had begun centuries earlier in Bristol, then moved to Plymouth, Southampton and London. The privateering voyages were non-royal, individual, or syndicate ventures. As Andrews writes, 'the characteristic form of Elizabethan maritime warfare was privateering … and the management and conduct of the queen's ships was the responsibility of men who had grown up in the school of oceanic trade and plunder and remained promoters and leaders of the privateering war'.[5]

Three outstanding seafaring West Country merchant mariner families stand out. First were three generations of Hawkynses, whose ships were armed for both commerce and profit. Quite different were the Drakes, the second family, especially Sir Francis Drake, whose idea of trade was trading not bales of woollens for ox hides, tobacco or sugar but gunfire for gold. 'We must have gold', were nearly his last words before his death off Panamá in 1596. It was primarily Drake's cannon, as Andrews writes, that secured the 'freedom if not the mastery of the ocean. This freedom they exploited in a campaign of plunder which developed their capital, shipping and experienced manpower to a new level, laying the foundations of oceanic trade and empire in the new century.'[6] The third family was embodied in Sir Walter Ralegh. He disdained open piracy under the bloody flag, calling it 'mere picory', but even he turned a blind eye to nefarious activity by his captains when it furthered his grand imperial theme, colonisation for his queen. Not the least, as with other courtier-privateers such as Cumberland, it might repair his fortunes, and as well put money in the purse.

What drove England to shift from coastal to oceanic sailing? From the time of the Middle Ages, England's traditional export had been raw wool. English raw woollens were bought and finished in the Lowlands, but much of the Lowlands came under Spanish rule early in the sixteenth century and co-operation with the Catholics was unrealistic. Supplying raw wool for Flemish weavers to manufacture as finished cloth no longer worked. Now, Protestant England had to provide finished cloth, to develop the industry vertically. English shortcloth (undyed and unfinished woollen cloth), had been commonly sold through Antwerp, but there was a growing demand in Germany for not just English shortcloth but also heavier dyed and finished woollen cloths, expanding the trade for finished goods. England sought to meet that demand by producing and exporting them.

A second change was one of taste. American cane sugar overtook England's traditional beet root sugar. The new sweet-tooth craving led John Watts and others to initiate voyages to the Americas for the London sugar refining industry, voyages that also lined the pockets through some incidental privateering on the side. A third item was American tobacco, first Trinidadian, later Virginian. It was an easily grown cash crop and in great demand for its heady buzz. Some thought the weed infernal; others saw it as a holy herb, a miracle drug that could cure a host of ills. These two, tobacco and sugar, became the two most profitable cargoes from the Americas.[7] Spain viewed these commercial developments with alarm, and by about 1612 had effectively shut down England's sources for Caribbean tobacco. In response, England transplanted Trinidadian tobacco to Virginia and Bermuda, outside Spanish reach. Sugar too would expand into the Caribbean, out of Spanish control.

At home in England, other major industries were shipbuilding and metal industries, including arms manufacture. These two were interconnected. According to Quinn and Ryan, 'the contribution of the availability of cheaply produced ordnance to the rise of English seapower in the sixteenth century can hardly be overrated'.[8] Expansion overseas, then, was largely a drive to gain new markets for England's exports, made necessary after Spain restricted England's trade with the Lowlands. The New World became an outlet for finished products in exchange for raw goods using the triangular route: England–Africa–Americas. Such were the elder Hawkyns' voyages to Africa and Brazil, and his son Sir John Hawkyns' three slaving voyages to Sierra Leone and then the Caribbean in the 1560s, early instances of supplying finished products or ready slave labour for gold, silver, jewels and hides.

The full faith and credit of the English pound also figures here. What made such international trade possible was the emergence of mobile capital, helped significantly when Elizabeth reformed the coinage system in 1560. A reliable currency made England a more reliable international trading partner with Europe. As for Drake's voyages in the 1570s, Quinn and Ryan suggest that they were not undertaken simply as a vendetta to revenge San Juan de Ulúa but as a display of 'individual opportunism, coloured by hostile sentiments, in pursuit of self-advancement and self-enrichment'.[9]

No Peace Beyond the Line

What goods were traded? Since the Middle Ages, wool, tin and copper had long been the bulk of cargoes carried in English hulls. John Hawkyns' slaving voyages in the '60s were different. Hawkyns traded labour – slaves – for anything considered valuable once back in England, from gold to hides. He shrewdly capitalised on the Spanish colonists' increasing need for labour to work the fields of the sugar plantations. Given the official restrictions, Hawkyns resorted to devious means, 'trade by force of arms', as Quinn and Ryan put it. Hawkyns was a master at such trade, though some of his captains were less adroit.[10] But even this dubious commerce was cut off after 1568. As Quinn and Ryan observe, that battle in Mexico's small Gulf port of San Juan de Ulúa 'brought to an end all hope of peaceful access to the Caribbean but nearly brought about a war with Spain'. The Spanish empire was, indeed, vulnerable, but it was also very powerful, and could concentrate its force on intruders, in battle or by diplomacy.

Quinn and Ryan observe:

> The Hawkins voyages, however, displayed an altogether new level and type of transatlantic activity on the part of the English. Philip II learned, moreover, that his power to stop or at least impede the English cloth trade by closing the port of Antwerp would be met by a show of aggressive reprisals at home and abroad. The queen's part in the enterprise, though it ended in an English defeat, indicated that she wished Spain to understand that she was by no means helpless at sea.[11]

There was no certainly no peace beyond the line nor any pretence of legitimate trade as England challenged Spain.[12] Following in the wake of some highly successful French corsairs, the English turned to profit by privateering or piracy.

St George, St Andrew

Trading goods gave way to trading broadsides. English corsairs flew a red flag –
the *Joli Rouge*, anglicised as the Jolly Roger (the devil). The flag signalled that no
quarter would be given. Privateers might hoist a red cross on a white ground,
England's cross of St George. This flag would challenge the Spanish naval ensign, a
red saltire on a white ground – the cross of St Andrew, similar to the *crux decussata*,
Cruz de Borgoña, the Burgundy Cross, used by the Spanish since 1516 because of
Philip's familial connection to Burgundy, but reversed for the Armada ships to a
yellow cross on a red field.[13]

The second stage in Anglo-Spanish relations grew into the third, warfare at sea.
In the 1550s French corsairs in American and Azorean waters had regularly pil-
laged and plundered the Spanish. The French early on attacked Spain's sources of
wealth in the Americas, especially the flow from the silver mines at Perú's Potosí
(now within Bolivia), as a way to cut her power in Europe. Quinn and Ryan
observe that King Henry II and Gaspard de Coligny, the Huguenot admiral of
France, proposed as early as 1558 that a:

> squadron of twelve warships and a force of 1,200 troops should sail to the
> Caribbean in the spring of the year, sack Santo Domingo and Puerto Rico and
> proceed to Nombre de Dios where troops should seize Panamá's storehouse of
> the bullion shipped from Perú. The object of the proposed raid was to divert a
> year's supply of treasure for the Escorial into the coffers of France. The one raid
> would create such lack of confidence in Spain's capacity to police the Caribbean
> that Philip's revenue from the Indies would be cut off for two years.[14]

The Treaty of Cateau-Cambrésis, 1559, stopped this plan from being carried
out. But the idea of a peremptory raid on Spanish-American wealth was not
lost on French corsairs or on Drake from the 1570s onward. For both France
and England, any form of colonisation, from planting fields to building harbours, can be seen as an extension of the attempt to contain Spain.

When advantageous, the English would join with the French in the Americas
to attack Spanish ships and ports, and take bronze cannon, gold, silver, pearls,
jewels – all rare cargoes. In the early 1570s Drake retaliated for the San Juan
de Ulúa massacre with pillage in the Caribbean. His voyages of 1570, 1571
and 1572-73, were acts of revenge sweetened by profit. The the last two were
jointly carried out with French corsairs, who saw eye to eye with Drake when
it came to the Spanish. In 1573 Drake and French corsair Guillaume le Têtu
together attacked the mule trains from Panamá to Nombre de Dios. Though
in the skirmish Le Têtu was captured and killed, Drake struck it rich, netting
a haul worth at least £20,000.[15] Such privateering and piracy were backed by
capital investment from London merchants and courtiers. Most of these ventures lost money, but a few, such as Drake's circumnavigation and most of his
Caribbean voyages, were highly profitable. The risk was high, but occasionally
so was the return.

There were, of course, many failures. The most conspicuous examples from the 1570s were Sir Martin Frobisher's three voyages in 1576, 1577 and 1578. The allure was easy access to Oriental riches via the Northwest Passage through a new area, what the queen called Meta Incognita. Besides a new route, the voyagers also hoped for gold. These unknown shores would later become part of northern Canada. Ice and geography stopped Frobisher's way to the Orient, but he did return with ore. Once home, though, Frobisher's rocks proved to be pyrite, fool's gold. The investors lost heavily. The worthless rocks, mined at with great effort, were now used to repair roads around London. In similar venture, Ralegh's attempt to find gold in Guiana in 1595 proved equally fruitless, though rich deposits were indeed discovered there three centuries later.

Drake's 1577–80 circumnavigation was different. Mining for gold was no part of his plan. Word was put about that Drake was seeking out unoccupied lands south of the Rio de la Plata and up the coast of Chile, but his real object was to seize Spanish bullion from unsuspecting ships and ports along the Pacific coast. Drake plundered his way north from Valparaiso to Guatulco in Mexico. Near the equator he caught the ship he had long been stalking. The *Nuestra Señora de la Concepción* (nicknamed *Cacafuego*) was carrying a treasure of 362,000 pesos' worth of bullion. Quinn and Ryan underscore: 'This was something altogether outside the range of previous piracy, an empire's ransom.' The queen was greatly enriched, and investors got large returns on their initial outlay. 'The economic importance of the great plundering expedition was scarcely less considerable than the remarkable seamanship displayed by the commander', comment the authors. Such success led to the queen's tacit approval of Drake's attack on Spanish shipping.

The privateer Christopher Newport, later captain of the 120-ton *Susan Constant*, one of two ships that brought colonists to Jamestown in 1607, like many saw waging war not so much as patriotic but as a mercantalistic extension of trade and piracy. Waging war was seen as a chance to seize a fortune. The queen more than once complained bitterly that her mariners sailed more for profit than service to her.[16] Global extension into the Atlantic and beyond, observe Quinn and Ryan, 'owed more to the efforts of individuals whose objectives were short-term, personal and financial than to any systematic policy of state'.[17]

The merchant-captain seeking profit usually had to settle for cargoes of less glitz and little gold but of greater bulk: hides, brazilwood, dyes, highly profitable Trinidadian tobacco and sugar from Brazil and Pernambuco and later from the Caribbean islands. Next in value came sarsaparilla, guiacum and cochineal. This was the bulk of the booty taken during the Anglo-Spanish War, 1585–1604, when piracy was at its height. In the 1590s, piracy accounted for fifty-six expeditions and 137 separate voyages.[18] The great numbers suggest that there was potential profit to be made. Elizabeth's naval muscle came primarily from her merchant captains, whatever flag they flew, the Jolly Roger or the Cross of St George. John Masefield, editor of *Hakluyt's Voyages* in 1907, wrote in his poem 'Cargoes' of Spanish galleons from Panamá laden with diamonds, cinnamon and gold.[19]

Cargoes were the point. What cargoes, then, filled the holds of English galleons from the American Tropics?

Fair Winds, Prosperous Voyages

In 1517 Sir Thomas Pert voyaged to the Caribbean and the port of San Domingo, sailing 'with merchandise to traffique', but he was promptly repulsed and trade was denied him. On the island of St John he and his men complained that they had come only 'to trade and traffique for their money and merchandise'. Was his voyage a cover, a challenge, or was it in fact for honest trade? Hakluyt continues: 'In this place they had certain victuals, and for recompense they gave and paid them with certain vessel of wrought tin and other things. And afterward they departed toward Europe.' Hakluyt's marginal note sees it as a commercial voyage: 'It cannot be denied but that they were furnished with wares for honest traffique and exchange.'[20] The Spanish saw it otherwise. They cited the Treaty of Tordesillas and subsequent treaties that gave rule of America to either the Portuguese or Spanish, and under that, a monopoly on trade. The English countered, citing precedence and centuries-old trading treaties with Spain and Portugal. They argued that only effective occupation determined dominion, and that in any case Spanish hegemony in the New World could not prohibit trade as it was and had long been allowed in European waters. Here was the rub for well over the next 100 years, in one place and another. That rub often chaffed into open sores. The issue was trade, not religion. Henry VIII's break with Rome came later, in 1532 and 1533.

Ox Hides, *Cana Fistula*, Pearls

Before the Spanish hardened their trade embargo in the 1560s, English merchants traded openly in the Americas. In the 1530s William Hawkyns the Elder made several voyages to Brazil, an extension overseas of the long-standing English–Portuguese commerce. It was the elder Hawkyns who initiated the triangular route from Africa, to Brazil, to England. His son John Hawkyns, as noted, expanded the triangle to Spanish America through his slaving voyages.

Some English merchant activity took place under the Spanish flag. In the 1550s Robert Tomson sailed from England on a three-year voyage, first to Lisbon, then Cádiz and Seville, where:

> having seen the fleets of ships come out of the Indies to that city, with such great quantity of gold & silver, pearls, precious stones, sugar, hides, ginger, and divers other rich commodities, he did determine with himself to seek means and opportunity to pass over to see that rich country from whence such great quantity of rich commodities came.[21]

Tomson and other English merchants sailed in a Spanish fleet for Hispaniola (then known also as Santo Domingo), which, writes Hakluyt, yields:

great store of sugar, hides of oxen, bulls and kine, ginger, cana fistula & salsa perillia: mines of silver & gold there are none, but in some rivers there is found some small quantity of gold. The principal coin that they do traffique withal in that place, is black money made of copper & brass: and this they say they do use not for that they lack money of gold and silver to trade withal out of the other parts of India, but because if they should have good money, the merchants that deal with them in trade, would carry away their gold and silver, and let the country commodities lie still.

Merchant Tomson landed in Mexico and contracted malaria. Still, ague-eyed he watched for profitable cargoes. Mexico, besides its gold and silver, had 'balm, salsa perilla, cana fistula, sugar, ox hides' and other goods sought by European markets.[22] His mentions of '*cana fistula*' are some of the earliest English references to sugar cane, the crop that became the chief export of Brazil and the Caribbean islands. So important would sugar become in the next 200 years that in the Treaty of Paris, 1763, France traded all of Canada for five small Caribbean islands – St Lucia, Guadeloupe, Marie-Galante, Desirade, Martinique – for their sugar.

Lerius writes in the 1550s about the wood *araboutan* or brazilwood, Brazil's first export to Europe, not for timber, but as a dye. 'The Brazil tree is the most famous of all that soil (from whence also that country hath taken the name) especially for the colour which our dyers make therewith.' The Indians carried the timber to load in European ships, amazed that Europeans would go to such trouble to ship wood to Europe. One of the elders questioned Captain Lerius:

What meaneth it, that you Mair and Peros (that is French men and Portugals) come so far to fetch wood? Doth your country yield you no wood for the fire? Then said I, it yieldeth fuel surely, and that in great plenty, but not of those kinds of trees, such as yours are; especially brazil, which our men carry from hence, not to burn, as you suppose, but for to dye. Here he presently excepting; but have you, said he, need of so great plenty of that wood? Yea surely, said I, for seeing even one merchant with us possesseth more scarlet clothes, more knives and scissors, and more looking-glasses (allegingly known and familiar examples unto him) then all those which were ever brought hither unto you; he only will buy all the brazil, to the end that many ships might return laden from hence. Ah (saith the Barbarian) you tell me strange and wonderful things.

Lerius writes that he and other travellers:

never travelled far from home without a satchel full of merchandises, which might serve us in stead of money … Departing therefore thence, we gave our hosts, what we thought good: to wit, knives, scissors, pinsers, to the men: combs, looking-glasses, bracelets, and glass beads, to the women: and fish-hooks to the children.[23]

Such bobbles were similar to those sent from England to colonists in Brazil in exchange for sugar, as John Whitehall found in the 1570s.[24]

Black Gold as Labour

Hawkyns' three slaving voyages to the Caribbean of the 1560s illustrate the difficulties in trading with the Spanish. On his first voyage, 1562–63, Hawkyns bartered his African slaves for Caribbean hides, ginger, sugar and pearls with relatively minor resistance. In the 1550s in the West Indies the Spanish usually paid 100 ducats per slave, 120 ducats in Mexico. As Hawkyns was operating outside Spanish law, he charged less or paid large bribes to get a profit.[25] Hawkyns chose small ports on Hispaniola – La Isabela, Puerto de Plata and Monte Christi – instead of going to Santo Domingo, then the administrative centre for the Spanish Caribbean, where he would have met stiff official resistance. He quietly traded his slaves for gold, silver, pearls, hides and sugar. He was happy to discover that this first voyage gave him more business than he could handle. As the bulk of the hides and sugar were beyond the 260 tons he could carry in his own ships, Hawkyns had to charter two Spanish *caravelas* to carry these extra cargoes back. One vessel, the *Sancto Amarco* sailed for Lisbon, and the other San Lucar. The goods of the first were promptly impounded by the Portuguese authorities, the second by the Spanish. Hawkyns' own three ships left the West Indies and arrived back in England in August 1563. Despite the loss of the two chartered ships and their cargoes (about 500 hides and two chests of sugar in each ship, not a comparatively valuable cargo), that first voyage was still a great financial success, with promise of more. Hawkyns had shrewdly traded in the face of official Spanish resistance. Licentiate Echegoyan wrote to the Crown on 4 November that Hawkyns' ships, laden with slaves and other stolen merchandise, sold their cargo in exchange for silver, gold, jewels and hides. The whole affair, says Echegoyan, 'is a huge jest. This colony will shortly become England, unless a remedy is applied'.[26]

Hawkyns' second voyage, 1564–65, was similar to the first, but this time with seven ships.[27] Once in the Indies and at La Margarita, Hawkyns was entertained by the *Alcalde* and supplied with 'beeves' and sheep. But though the mayor was cordial, he refused to give Hawkyns a license to trade. The viceroy, writes Hawkyns, had ordered that 'no man should traffic with us, but should resist us with all the force they could'. Hawkyns left for Cumaná. He demanded traffic, but 'they made him answer, they were but soldiers newly come thither, and were not able to buy one Negro'. Hawkyns' arrival at Borburata in April 1565 initiated a flurry of Spanish correspondence. The governor's lieutenant and deputy treasurer at Borburata, António de Bárrios, wrote to Licentiate Alonso Bernaldez, governor of Venezuela and resident of Coro, that on 3 April 'there appeared off this town seven sails, one of which vessels is very powerful. The fleet is English and so rich in slaves and merchandise that they affirm it to be worth more than 100,000 *pesos*.' He said the commander, Hawkyns, intended 'to sell with authorization and unless this license is given him he threatens with great oaths to do what harm and damage he may be able'. The province at the time was poor and the colonists sickly, a state in which matter:

> neither God, Our Lord, nor his majesty is well served. The royal revenues would be augmented and the country benefitted, for this captain promises to please everybody. He brings more than four hundred negroes ... I beg your honour to deign to extend the license and open the way, for in addition to the benefit and relief this would mean to all, and increase of the royal revenue, to do so will obviate the great damage and hardship we anticipate ... I see no better remedy than to let this fellow sell, for in addition to the duties he will pay, a quantity of gold will be smelted.

If not, he adds, 'greater evil is ahead of us, for if the town is burned it will mean its abandonment, in addition to which we will be turned into the woods in weather bad enough to kill us even were we strong, as we are not, but very sickly'.[28]

Hawkyns points out to the governor that he once had offered his services to the Spanish king to rid the seas of corsairs, and argues that on this voyage he was:

> by contrary weather driven to these coasts where, since I have found a convenient harbour, it behoves me to repair and refurnish my ships to continue said voyage; And whereas to do this I have need to sell the slaves and merchandise I carry; And whom I served when he was king of England; I therefore petition your honour to grant me license to sell my cargo.

Hawkyns says he will pay the usual duties but counters that if his petition is not granted:

> I shall seek my own solution, for I cannot leave this port, nor will I leave, without supplying my said necessities, for even were I willing to do so, yet am I unable, for I cannot prevail with my people. Therefore, since between England and Spain there is no enmity nor war, and this fleet belongs to the queen, my mistress, of which and of all else herein stated I am ready to furnish depositions, let your honour not anger me nor move me to aught that I should not do, as will be inevitable if your honour refuse me the license I ask. I protest that if from its refusal harm and damage follow, the fault and responsibility will be your honour's. I ask for witnesses to this petition and a certificate. John Hawkins.

No one came to buy Hawkyns' slaves. He showed the local officials what he paid for the slaves, his expenses in feeding them, the wages for his sailors. He said he must thus sell them at a price higher than what the Spanish had set. The Spanish agreed to ignore the license and bought a few slaves. The governor issued Hawkyns a license, but would not budge on assessing custom of 30 ducats per head for the king. Hawkyns protested that either he must 'be a great loser by his wares' or the officers must lower such unreasonable duty, for he could not charge the buyers any more. 'Therefore the sixteenth of April he prepared 100 men well armed with bows, arrows, harquebuses and pikes, with the which he marched to the townwards, and being perceived by the governor, he straight with all expedition sent messengers to know his request.' Hawkyns' author continues:

> So our captain declaring how unreasonable a thing the King's custom was, requested to have the same abated, and to pay seven and a half per centum, which is the ordinary custom for wares through his dominions there, and unto this if they would not grant, he would displease them. And this word being carried to the governor, answer was returned that all things should be to his content.[29]

For two weeks they traded with the poor folk of Borburata. The rich still held back and would not trade.

Three days later, on 19 April 1565, Governor Bernáldez covered his actions in a deposition to the Crown. He had been forced to grant Hawkyns permission to trade, but, he writes, he allowed only the specifics of Hawkyns' petition and no more. He had decided just in time, for Hawkyns was ready to attack: 'The main body of English troops was very near, the flag in sight, and the weapons, and the drum beating, and the men also were seen, marching all in good order, who seemed in number to be as many as three hundred soldiers.' The governor quickly sent the licence to Hawkyns. The English troops kept advancing. Mistrustful, Hawkyns demanded two hostages. The Spanish complied. Wrote Bernáldez, 'they were Sebastian Davila, burgher of Coro, and Vicente Roberos, burgher of Trujillo. With their arrival the English forces were tranquillized and returned into their ships'.[30] Trade now took place.

Hawkyns hoped to relieve himself of the rest of his slaves and cargo. But just as he was concluding his business in Borburata a large war party of 200 Caribes arrived in canoes to burn the port and capture the Spanish as prisoners. The Spanish beat them back, and caught one Caribe guide, who had 'for his travail a stake thrust through his fundament, and so out at his neck'.[31] After the interruption Hawkyns concluded his trading, and before saiing off, obtained a certificate of good conduct from the treasurer. At Rio de la Hacha he sold the remaining 300 slaves and much merchandise, including wine, flour, biscuit, cloth, linens and clothing – all things the Spanish colonists desperately needed and paid for in Spanish gold and silver. Though Hawkyns left without payment for a debt owed him, he did take orders for more slaves and goods to be brought out on his next voyage. The *Jesus of Lubeck* and the other six ships set sail on 31 May on a course north-east for Hispaniola, then home. The prospects for Anglo-Spanish trade were promising.

This 1564–65 voyage built on the success of Hawkyns' first one in 1562–63. Despite strong official Spanish resistance all along the Spanish Main, substantial profit, it seemed, could be had from selling slaves and goods to Spanish colonists. But it took finesse, patience and determination. From England, the Spanish

Ambassador Guzman de Silva reported with grave concern to King Philip that Hawkyns' voyage had yielded a lucrative 60 per cent return.[32] In Spain, Philip in response ordered his navy to catch and punish this English heretic trader. In England, Queen Elizabeth was delighted, and granted Hawkyns a coat of arms, one that appropriately emblazons as its crest a demi-Moor bound in a cord.

Hawkyns' third voyage, 'troublesome', left Plymouth in October 1567, once more with six ships, bound again for Guinea and the West Indies.[33] Once at Guinea he took on between four and 500 slaves, and in February 1568 set his course westward. He made his Caribbean landfall at Dominica on 27 March. From there he trafficked with the Spanish 'somewhat hardly, because the king had straightly commanded all his governors in those parts, by no means to suffer any trade to be made with us'.[34] To be allowed to trade Hawkyns gave 'great gifts' to the royal treasurer, Miguel de Castellanos, who justified the bribes to the Crown: 'If I would not he made great threats'. Hawkyns landed his forces, and so overwhelming were they that Castellanos wrote that 'it seemed to me to be madness to attempt to oppose the attack of such superior force'.[35]

But there was no trading. Hawkyns burned half the town, then took 400 men and field artillery inland to torch the *ingenios de azúcar*. But ahead of the English the Spanish had burned their haciendas and began shooting back. The Englishman returned to town 'in very desperate humour and burned the government house and another large portion of the town'.[36] Castellanos recounts that two of his slaves had gone over to Hawkyns. They were happy to take the English to where the Spanish had hidden their valuables. Hawkyns took the loot, and further demanded ransom for the colonists held as prisoners. The treasurer writes that 'I paid over the 4000 *pesos* and the enemy released the prisoners. Although they promised to restore the property they had taken from them, they did not fulfil this promise. On the contrary, they stole it and carried it off'. As for the slaves? 'I handed them over to your majesty's royal law that they might be punished and made an example to all the rest on this coast, and so the mulatto was hung and the negro quartered'.[37]

The Spanish letter continues: As the English could not feed some of the slaves, they set them ashore. Some of these were children not six years old, and some were 'old males and old females (over 100 years)', left as recompense for the damage to the town. Castellanos, acting for the Crown, took these slaves to be fattened for selling. Proceeds from their sale would of course be deposited in the royal treasury. 'I entreat your majesty to advise what is to be done'. As for the government house, if the king wished, it would be rebuilt, which would be in the royal interest, 'because of the great danger of fire and also for the safety of your majesty's royal treasury'.[38] This third voyage was a sign of things to come.

Hawkyns' fleet was soon caught in a hurricane in the Gulf of Mexico. Hawkyns put into San Juan de Ulúa, and caught by the Spanish, lost his cargo, the queen's carrack and her brass cannon, and nearly his life. Profit? All lost. After 1568, with few exceptions, trade with Spain or her Americas was clearly out of the question. Raiding, with or without licence, was to be the new way to profit.

English under Spanish Ensign

Other English merchants residing in Spain also decided to seek their fortunes in Spanish America. One was John Chilton, living in Spain since 1561.[39] He sailed to the West Indies in spring 1568 in a Spanish fleet and under Spanish law and for two years traded in Mexico. In the port of Navidad, Xalisco, he notes that the Manila galleons were laden with 'mantles made of cotton wool, wax, and fine platters gilded, made of earth, and much gold'. In Guatemala and Honduras he sold 'fannile [aniline] … which is a kind of thing to dye blue withal', in exchange for 'Spanish annile and cochineal [red-scarlet dye] (inferior to that from Nova Hispania), silver and gold, hides, and salsa perilla [sarsaparilla].'[40] Carmine and cochineal produced dyes much prized in Europe, and these, after silver, were counted precious commodities. He writes that Cuba exported mostly hides, used salt as currency, and that the coinage was copper. At the town of Mérida, in the Yucatán, the 'chiefest merchandise' was 'a certain wood called campeche' (*palo tinto*) named for the gulf of that name, used to make pink, blue, green and black dyes. Frigates at the port of San Juan de Ulúa laded wax, cacao, honey and, as in Navidad, mantles of cotton wool.

Those goods and the yearly tribute taken from the Indies to Spain brought 'between nine and ten millions of gold and silver'.[41] Englishman Chilton writes about Spanish colonial rule:

> And the king to keep the country always in subjection, and to his own use, hath straightly provided by law, upon pain of death, and loss of goods, that none of these countries should traffique with any other nation, although the people themselves do much now desire to trade with any other then with them, and would undoubtedly do, if they feared not the peril ensuing thereupon.[42]

Chilton well understood Hawkyns' problem.

For some five years prior to 1572, at about the time of Hawkyns' disaster, another English merchant, Henry Hawks, had turned his eye towards profit in México and had taken passage under the Spanish *crux decussata*, like Chilton. Five leagues north of the port of San Juan de Ulúa is Vera Cruz. Barks or frigates, writes Hawks, 'carry all their merchandise which commeth out of Spain, to the said town: and in like manner bring all the gold, silver, cochinilla, hides, and other things that the ships carry into Spain unto them. Nova Hispania yields buffalo and salt.' As for cacao, 'a berry like unto an almond', he says with enthusiasm, 'it is the best merchandise that is in all the Indies. The Indians make drink of it, and in like manner meat to eat. It goeth currently for money in any market or faire, and may buy any flesh, fish, bread or cheese, or other things.' There is 'great abundance of sugar'.

The Indians are 'much given to drink', quaffing *pulco*, a 'certain kind of wine which they make with honey of magueiz [*maguey* or *agave*, source of *pulque* and *mezcal*], and roots, and other things which they use to put into the same … They are soon drunk, and given to much beastliness, and void of all goodness.'

The drink provoked lechery, and induced the Indians to sodomise their mothers and daughters, says Hawks, 'whereupon they are defended from drinking of wines, upon pains of money, as well he that selleth the wines as the Indian that drinketh the same. And if this commandment were not, all the wine in Spain and France were not sufficient for the West Indies only.' Commodities for sale are cotton, copper, lead and cattle. 'You may have a great steer that hath an hundred weight of tallow in his belly for sixteen shillings; and some one man hath 20000 head of cattle of his own. They sell the hides unto the merchants, who lade into Spain as many as may be well spared.'

In Cuba and Puerto Rico, there is much sugar (*sacharum officinarum*) and *caña fistula* (or *cassia fistula*, the golden shower tree prized as a purgative), 'which daily they send into Spain'. The wool of the Indies is 'as good as the wool of Spain'. He writes:

> I have seen cloth made in the city of Mexico, which hath been sold for ten pesos a vare [*vara*, three *pies* or feet, about a yard in length], which is almost four pounds English, and the vare is less then our yard. They have woad [for its blue dye] growing in the country, and alum, and brazil [for red dyes], and divers other things to dye withal, so that they make all colours … They make hats, as many as do serve the country, very fine and good, and sell them better cheap, then they can be brought out of Spain, and in like manner send them into Peru … They make no kersies [kersey, the coarse woollen cloth], but they make much cloth, which is coarse, and sell it for less then 12. pence the vare. It is called sayal [sisal, from the *agave* plant]. They have much silk, and make all manner of sorts thereof, as taffetas, satins, velvets of all colours, and they are as good as the silks of Spain, saving that the colours are not so perfect: but the blacks are better then the blacks that come out of Spain.[43]

Given his close attention to wools and various cloths, Hawks indeed might have been a member of the venerable Drapers' Company.

Piracy in Hides and Sugar

Beginning in the 1570s, any pretence of legitimate trade soon gave way to open piracy, the third way to turn a profit. Whatever gained by fair or foul means, a cargo was expected to bring reward. Privateers commonly raided cattle farms and sugar mills. To sweeten the booty, occasionally there was more: 'Silver, gold, money, pearls and other precious stones and similar valuables were the most important item in some half a dozen cargoes and often figured in others', writes Andrews. 'Wines, indigo, ginger, sarsparilla, logwood, balsam, *cassia fistula* and cochineal are all mentioned several times; tobacco only once.' Tobacco would come later:

> These commodities commanded a good market in England, and on the whole prizes taken in the West Indies were more valuable than those taken in

European waters. Cargoes of varied European manufactures were occasionally captured in the Caribbean, but were not so highly prized. Foodstuffs – cassava bread, hogs, turtles, and the like – were frequently captured, and were useful for revictualling, but were not brought home'.[44]

Reprisal, besides profit, was in many cases another motive. As a merchant mariner, Andrew Barker had business in Tenerife, where he traded in cloth, wines and sugar. But in 1575 he and his goods were seized by the Spanish, he was imprisoned, interrogated by the Inquisition and fined. On release, Barker furnished two barks in 1576 and sailed for the bay of Tolú, on the Spanish Main. In revenge, he took a frigate with a treasure of gold, silver, coin and 'certain green stones called emeralds, whereof one very great, being set in gold, was found tied secretly about the thigh of a friar', one of the passengers. During his voyage he also seized four cast ordnance, three harquebuses, sixteen Spanish 'calivers' and 'a book of Navigation', as well as 'certain Spaniards, whereof one was the Scrivano or secretary of Carthagena, who (being a man of some note) was put to his ransom, which was paid in gold'. Satisfaction received for the wrongs, Barker was homeward bound when the frigate carrying the treasure, 'overset with sail, with a flaw of wind was overthrown, and all the goods therein perished. Therein also were 14 persons drowned, and nine saved.' Violence begat more violence. Captain Barker's crew mutinied and killed him. On reaching Plymouth, the mutineers were tried, convicted and imprisoned.[45]

Drake's circumnavigation, 1577–80, was an extraordinarily profitable voyage of reprisal for Drake, the City's adventurers and for the queen. Off the coast of Perú the treasure from the *Nuestra Senora de la Concepcion*, (the *Cacafuego*) yielded more than 400,000 pesos of gold, silver and coin. The sum included 80 pounds of gold, 1,300 bars of silver and 14 chests of silver *reales*, and further 'uncustomed' treasure. It took them five days to transfer it all to the *Pelican* (earlier renamed the *Golden Hinde* at the Strait).

That expedition was followed by a West Indian voyage, 1585–86, in which Drake sacked Santo Domingo and Cartagena. Santo Domingo (the venerable capital was by then in decay) yielded only 25,000 ducats in ransom. Worse yet for Spanish pride, Drake made off with a prized silk escutcheon on which was emblazoned the Spanish king's motto: *Orbis Non Sufficit* – the world is not enough. Drake also took hides, sugar, ordnance, church bells, three ships and eighty slaves. The Spanish reckoned the total loss at about 200,000 ducats, no doubt an inflated figure. Next, at Cartagena, Drake demanded 400,000 ducats but could get only 107,000 ducats, paid in gold and jewels and silver wedges. Elsewhere he took 50,000 ducats from the royal treasury. The proceeds of the voyage were estimated at £64,900: plate and bullion, £42,000; pearls, £3,500; ordnance, £5,500; ships, £12,500; hides, £1,800; iron and lead, £600. Net valuation was £47,900 (less sailors' pay). The Royal Commission in June 1587 recommended that adventurers who put up money be paid 15s for each pound invested, with the possibility of at most 12d per pound more. The queen's dividend was set at 15s for each pound ventured, and added to her portion, an additional £350 16s 4d.[46] Privateering could sometimes pay exceptionally well.

Letters of Reprisal

The English voyages to the West Indies during the years 1588 to 1595 were, as far as we know, almost all privateering voyages. From 1589 to 1591 at least 235 English ships made privateering voyages to the Cabo Verdes and the Americas, records Andrews. Most of those engaged in privateering in the West Indies were from London. Such ships required great capital expenditure, and that required substantial London money. Privateers were usually equipped, armed, victualled and supplied with powder and shot for a six-month cruise. Crews usually got no wages, but shared among them a one-third share of the prizes, besides any pillage. A joint-stock system of investment was usual. 'There is no doubt what the attractions were – the promise of plunder and the looser discipline', writes Andrews. 'Drunkeness and disorder were very common in ships of reprisal. The taking of a prize often led to quarrels, insults and stabbings, or, if there were wines aboard, to orgies of drinking.' Not without reason, the governor of La Havana, Juan de Texeda, called English corsairs 'a lot of drunkards … a low lot'.[47]

It was such ships that supplied crews for the Royal Navy. With the sailors came their tactics. 'The characteristic form of Elizabethan maritime warfare was privateering … The management and conduct of the queen's ships was the responsibility of men who had grown up in the school of oceanic trade and plunder and remained promoters and leaders of the privateering war.' Drake was instrumental in securing the 'freedom if not the mastery of the ocean. This freedom they exploited in a campaign of plunder which developed their capital, shipping and experienced manpower to a new level, laying the foundations of oceanic trade and empire in the new century', writes Irene Wright.[48]

Privateering voyages could be profitable. Leading merchants in England, especially in London, invested regularly in such voyages, and a profitable return was expected. These were the same careful investors, adventurers and promoters who later were to form the Virginia and East India companies. 'The more routine venture, with limited aims and an experienced leader, could with reasonable luck make a saving voyage. It was unusual for an expedition to fail to pick up a few prizes', observes Andrews. He calculates that of twenty-five privateering expeditions he examined (well over 200 took place within just three years), fifteen of those were financially successful and three or four were highly profitable. No doubt there were other voyages that made money. West Indian privateering was thus not quite the gamble as it may have seemed. Captains generally took the least risky course, and would settle for small but steady gain. If lucky, they might also seize a treasure ship.[49]

Whereas the French and Dutch concentrated on trade rather than plunder, the English approach was to engage in both in the same voyage. In 1591 at least eleven English privateers were cruising the West Indies. Five of these were sent

out by John Watts and his partners, two others by a group of London merchants,
three by Sir George Carey, plus one other privateer:

> Financially the voyage was undoubtedly a great success for Watts and his
> partners, in spite of the embezzlement of some of the prize goods. Watts himself
> officially admitted the value of the goods (after pillage) at nearly £32,000.
> The *Trinity* alone was worth about £20,000 and the first prize taken near
> Spain was substantial. Altogether the eight prizes probably made up some
> £40,000, after the crews had seized what they could by way of pillage and
> straightforward theft.[50]

Andrews sums up the voyage: 'A profit of 100 per cent would not have been
"a small return" for a privateering venture, but in this case the profit probably
amounted to over 200 per cent.'[51]

Jars of Copper Money, the *Madre De Dios*

Christopher Newport's voyage of 1592 sailed as a fleet of four heavily armed
ships, supported in paper by letters of reprisal.[52] This powerful privateering fleet
was financed by eleven shareholders, seven London merchants and two ship-
owning masters from London. At Dominica in the West Indies, Newport reports,
'making stay a day or two, we bartered with the savages for certain commodities
of theirs, viz. tobacco, hens, potato roots, &c.'. From a Portuguese ship (Portugal,
England's old ally, had been under Spanish rule since 1580) Newport took 300
slaves, 'young and old'. Off Hispaniola's south coast, he boarded a frigate, 'wherein
were 22 jars of copper-money, being bound for S. Juan de Puerto Rico, to buy
wine there'. Elsewhere, a night attack yielded sugar, chickens and cattle. In the
Bay of Honduras his fleet took two valuable prizes, and at Puerto de Cabalos,
much quicksilver and iron. Passing the gulf of Florida he came onto another prize
that yielded fifty-five hogs, and some 2 hundredweight of 'excellent tobacco
rolled up in seines [fishing nets]. We lightened them of their hogs and tobacco,
and sent the men away with their frigate.'

On the return passage, off Flores in the Azores, Newport and other on 3 August
1592 took one of the most famous prizes in Elizabethan maritime history, the
Portuguese carrack *Mãe de Deus* (*Madre de Dios*), returning from the East Indies
and bound for Lisbon. This 1,600-ton prize, with seven decks, thirty-two cannon,
over 600 crew, alone made the expedition profitable for the mariners and shareholders. Her hold was filled with jewels, gold, silver, pearls, ambergris, silks, cochineal, ebony and exotic oriental spices – 900 tons of the spoils of war. Newport
sums up the voyage:

> We took and sacked four towns, seventeen frigates, and two ships, whereof
> eight were taken in the bay of Honduras; of all which we brought but two into
> England: the rest we sunk, burnt, and one of them we sent away with their men.

And to make up the full number of twenty, the Spaniards themselves set one on fire in the bay of Honduras, lest we should be masters of it.[53]

Newport stands as an example of a talented merchant, privateer and passenger ship captain. Fifteen years later, in a more peaceful capacity, he would be carrying colonists to Virginia.

Other less spectacular privateers could also turn a profit. William King's *Salomon* was a powerful ship, with twenty-six pieces of ordinance and ninety men. She provisioned for a year and sailed for the West Indies. There, King chased a prize from Honduras into a harbour north-west of La Havana and took her, 'laden with tanned hides, salsa perilla, indico, raw hides, and good store of balsamum: and she had four chests of gold, which they got on land before we could come to them'.[54] John Ridlesden, a London gentleman, sailed to the West Indies in 1595 in the barks *Bond* and *Violet*, both vessels of about 60 tons, and the *Scorpion*. Near the Canaries he seized a much larger Spanish ship bound for La Havana 'of the burthen of six score tons or there abouts ... being laden with cordage, some forty or fifty tons of Canary, some wines, some oil, some iron works, and sundry other things'.[55]

Another privateer was the powerful merchantman *Rose Lion*. In late September and early October 1594 she was fitted out by her captain, Thomas West, for four leading London merchants to engage in privateering. Her 1594 voyage was backed by Thomas Myddelton, chief partner in 'one of the two leading sugar refineries in London, trading on a large scale in sugar in Antwerp', writes Andrews. Myddelton was well-established in the sugar industry. The Mincing Lane sugar house in London had been his since 1583. 'He traded to Spain and to the Azores, and, at the end of the war, to the West Indies.' After 1585 Myddelton became interested in privateering as a business venture. This captain of industry owned or partly owned a number of ships, lying in London and Weymouth:

> Above all, he was a sugar merchant, and sugar figured more largely than any other commodity in the prize goods of the Spanish war. Much of Myddelton's profit came from the purchase of the numerous cargoes of sugar taken by other privateers, but he also sent out his own expeditions and invested in others' ventures.[56]

Seizing cargoes of sugar by privateering certainly cut down his costs in sugar production and increased his profit.

Worm-Eaten Ginger

Not all voyages were lucrative. Near Santo Domingo in March 1595 Captain West took 'with small fight' a prize called the *Fortune*, laden with ginger, sugar, and other goods, some of it worthless. The ginger was 'very ill conditioned, ungarbled, full of dust, worm eaten and rotten wet and dry'. The powdered sugar was 'very moist and packed of diverse sorts', the moscavados (unrefined dark brown sugar) was mixed with coarse whites. The *cassia fistula* was 'ungarbled much broken and dry'.

A libel (charge) against Thomas West notes the *Fortune*'s cargo: 'In the said ship called the *Fortune* at St Domingo 1350 kintalls [the quintal, early a hundredweight of fresh or dried fish] of ginger, 82 chests of sugar 24 hogsheads of cassia fistula & 400 kintalls of guacum wood' (guaiac wood, lignum vitae).[57] Little profit indeed.

Plantations, Flax, Cotton, Tobacco

The first voyages by the English to the American tropics were primarily for exploration and trade, but, significantly and equally important was another aim, colonisation, especially along the north coast of South America, particularly along the banks of the Amazon and Orinoco rivers. At this point trade was moving to the fourth stage, that of intracolonial trading among the colonies and England. Between these two rivers the English found an area larger than France and Spain combined. And, the Portuguese or Spanish in the 1590s were hardly there. It was a golden chance to establish a tropical England presence, as well as a naval base from which to attack the Spanish. With the end of the Anglo-Spanish War in 1604, over a dozen fledgling English colonies along the South American coast for a decade or two traded the few raw materials for finished ones. 'Planting' and 'plantation' in the American tropics, Hakluyt's watchwords in the 1580s, gained promise in Ralegh's Guiana in the 1590s, and achieved reality in English settlements along the Amazon and Orinoco in the 1610s.

Captain Charles Leigh set sail from Woolwich in March 1604 in a small 50-ton bark, with a crew of forty-six, bound for Guiana. On 22 May 1604 he anchored in the River Caroleigh, 'heretofore called Wyapoco'. He took possession of the land, and in a letter to his brother, Sir Olave Leigh, he writes that he finds Guiana a viable site for colonisation. Already, he writes, Dutch ships regularly call there for flax. Bring out English weavers, he urges. He says that besides the flax, he has found that cotton and sugar cane grew well and that more should be planted. He hopes that in a year he can fill an English ship's hold with flax.[58]

Two years later, 1606, though, things were quite different. John Wilson of Wansted, Essex, described his time in Guiana at that same colony of Wiapoco.[59] He says that Captain Charles Leigh and his brother, Sir Olave, had sent out the *Phoenix* in 1604 with fifty settlers and provisions. Once ashore, the settlers were soon discontented, and 'cried to their captain, home, home'.[60] Despite some grumbling, Guiana was hardly a port of last resort. For some years it would attract yet more English adventurers. In 1606 William Turner, the son of a London physician, sailed to Guiana,[61] only to find that Captain Charles Leigh had died on board the ship that was about to take him back to England. He finds the Caribbean islands promising. St Lucia is fertile, and St Vincent, Grenada, and La Margarita were growing tobacco.[62] But during Wilson's two years in Guiana, he saw starvation and increasingly melancholy colonists. Still optimistic, he wrote back to England of the prospects of gold and silver, flax and tobacco. Wilson returned to England in 1606.[63] Many of the colonists, like Wilson, came for a time, then returned home.

Robert Harcourt, another colonist, writes that sugar and tobacco were presently the major crops in Guiana. Tobacco, he writes, holds its price and is lucrative for both farmers and merchants. In sweet words worthy of Ralegh, he writes that tobacco 'will bring as great a benefit and profit to the undertakers, as ever the Spaniards gained by the best and richest silver mine in all their Indies'. Harcourt reports that though gold is not abundant, the presence of white spar indicates that 'there was gold and silver to be mined'.[64]

Nine years later, 1617, when Ralegh was at last released from the Tower of London, it is not surprising that he chose Guiana over Virginia for his salvation. He needed to clear his name of treason, and he needed money. Guiana promised gold, Virginia was barely surviving, and certainly had no gold. But the reality? Once there, Keymis' sacking of San Thomé yielded just 150 quintals of tobacco, 600 Spanish *reales*, a single gold bar, an ingot, a heavy gold chain, a large silver handbasin, guns, some church bells and church ornaments. According to the Spanish sources the loot amounted to about 40,000 *reales*. Once back in England, Ralegh, feverish with ague, was arrested for violating the terms of his parole (not antagonising the Spanish, but returning with much gold). His few personal effects were inventoried: 'a Guiana idol of God', 'one plot [map] of Guiana and Nova (R—) [Reyno de Granada] and another of the river of Orenoque', a 'plot of Panama', a 'trial of Guiana ore with a description thereof', a 'sprig jewel', and 'five assays of the silver mine'. This haul was too little, not enough to buy Ralegh a reprieve from the the headsman's axe that autumn.

Notes

1 N.A.M. Rodger, *The Safeguard of the Sea, A Naval History of Britain, 660–1649* (New York: W.W. Norton & Company (1997), 1998), 266.

2 David B. Quinn and A.N. Ryan, *England's Sea Empire, 1550–1642* (London: George Allen & Unwin, 1983), 125. Abbr. *ES*. This chapter owes much to Quinn and Ryan's careful research, and especially to a summer working with Ryan.

3 Kenneth R. Andrews, *Drake's Voyages: A Re-Assessment of Their Place in Elizabethan Maritime Expansion* (London: Weidenfeld and Nicholson, 1967), 156. Abbr. *DV*.

4 *DV*, 156–7.

5 *DV*, 185.

6 *DV*, 186.

7 *ES*, 14–24.

8 *ES*, 60.

9 *ES*, 81.

10 *ES*, 31.

11 *ES*, 29.

12 The phrase should read 'lines', the lines of amity agreed to by the French and Spanish at the Peace of Cateau-Cambrésis, 1559. The lines were the Tropic of Cancer, at 23° 26' N Lat. and the traditional prime meridian on El Hierro (Meridiano), now 18° W Long. in the Canarias. On the European side of these lines the treaty was binding, to the west and south it was not.

13 The British Union Flag dates from 1606 (Scotland and England had united in 1603 on James I's accession), and thus for the period of this study, a vessel sailing in the Jacobean

period might fly that flag. To stop merchant vessels from flying the Union Flag to avoid paying harbour dues, Charles I decreed in 1634 (a law still in force) that only Royal vessels were permitted to fly the Union Flag as an ensign. The union was ratified by Parliament only in 1707, the flag modified slightly when Ireland was included in 1801. The mergers of the three crosses of St George, St Andrew and St Patrick brought further modifications resulting in the current Union Flag. Royal Navy vessels fly the white ensign (Cross of St George, with the Union Flag in the upper left canton); Royal Navy officers and some others, the blue ensign (a blue ground with the Union Flag in that canton); civilian (and merchant) vessels, the red ensign (a red ground with the Union Flag in the canton).

14 *ES*, 79–80.
15 Harry Kelsey, *Sir Francis Drake, the Queen's Pirate* (New Haven: Yale University Press, 1998), 40–67.
16 *ES*, 41, 69.
17 *ES*, 79.
18 *ES*, 123.
19 From 'Cargoes', 1902, written by Masefield. Masefield also edited a popular Everyman eight volume edition of *Principal Navigations* in 1907, just after the Hakluyt Society's authoritative *Principal Navigations*, 12 vols, 1903–05. He writes: 'Stately Spanish galleon coming from the Isthmus, / Dipping through the Tropics by the palm-green shores, / With a cargo of diamonds, / Emeralds, amythysts, / Topazes, and cinnamon, and gold moidores.'
20 *PN*, 10:3.
21 *PN*, 9:338–58.
22 *PN*, 9:358.
23 *PP*, 16:518–79.
24 Williamson, *HP*, 56–67; see also his earlier *Sir John Hawkins: The Time and the Man* (Oxford: Clarendon Press, 1927). Abbr. *JH*.
25 See *TB*, 63–5: From England bring out knives, hats lined with taffeta, tools, guitar strings and kersies to be sold in the Canarias. At the Canarias take on Canary wine and cordovan hides for Brazil. On the return, lade sugar for England.
26 *SD*, 72–5.
27 *PN*, 10: 9–63; *SD*, 76–108; *HP*, 70, note 1.
28 *SD*, 76–7.
29 *PN*, 10:32–4.
30 *SD*, 85–6.
31 *PN*, 10:35–6.
32 *HP*, 87.
33 *PN*, 10:64–74.
34 *SD*, 120–3.
35 *SD*, 120.
36 *SD*, 121.
37 *SD*, 122.
38 *SD*, 122–3.
39 *PN*, 9:360–77.
40 *PN*, 9:366–7.
41 *PN*, 9: 375.
42 *PN*, 9:377.
43 *PN*, 9:390.
44 *EP*, 31.
45 *PN*, 10:82–8; *DE*, 335–8.

46 *DW*, 59–60.
47 *EP*, 24–5.
48 *DE*, 185–6.
49 *EP*, 33–4.
50 *EP*, 104.
51 *EP*, 38–9, 104.
52 *PN*, 10:184–90; *EP*, 184–208.
53 *EP*, 187–95.
54 *PN*, 10:190–3; *EP*, 209–18.
55 *EP*, 326–29.
56 *EP*, 338–76.
57 *EP*, 340–9.
58 *PP*, 16: 309–23.
59 *PP*, 16:338–51.
60 *PP*, 16:338.
61 *PP*, 16:352–57.
62 *PP*, 16:352–7.
63 *PP*, 16:338–51.
64 *PP*, 16:358–402.

8

Epilogue

'O my America, my new found land,
My kingdom … my mine of precious stones, my empery.'
John Donne, 'To His Mistress Going to Bed', 1669

The Elizabethan and Jacobean sea voyages to the American tropics, 1520s to the 1640s, vividly illustrate the extraordinary growth from medieval to modern times. England at first lagged behind Portugal and Spain in maritime expansion to both the East and West Indies, then came to surpass them. In just over 100 years, the world changed radically. Discoveries from the Americas aided progress at home in especially five areas, following the scheme of this book: ship design and construction; mathematics and navigation; ship handling and naval tactics; medicine; and transoceanic commerce.

Ship Design, Construction

Transoceanic sailing to the tropics or arctics tested ships rigorously. One English captain, after escaping first a hurricane then Spanish attack, returned to England and ripped away his ships' medieval design in favour of a building a new sort of ship. Gone was the giant carrack he had to leave behind. Profile, sail plan, draught and length-to-beam ratio would change. The new race-built galleons proved to be sea-kindly, fast and responsive. Armed with new bronze demi-culverins, they proved their worth against the power of the Spanish Armada and against the power of the Roaring Forties at Cape Horn. The same decade, the 1570s, saw the end of an era in the last fight off Lepanto between fleets of galleys, venerable vessels that had ruled the Mediterranean for nearly two thousand years, warships designed to ram and board. Another vessel had taken the galley's place: the small but seaworthy pinnace or frigate. Like galleys, these too were self-propelled, sail-driven with auxiliary oars, but were built more stoutly for the open ocean. They could explore, resupply and take on coastal or ocean prey in the Barbary Coast, the Caribbean or the Strait of Magellan. As for ordnance, the older iron cannon, with brittle barrels that would explode, gave way to bronze culverins that were safer, more accurate and more powerful. Their rapid and deadly fire at long range changed naval tactics. Shipwrights had steadily improved ship design, and foundries cast better cannon, factors that worked hand in hand to change naval tactics and strategy.

England's old ally Portugal capitulated to Spanish rule in 1580, and English vessels sailing the American Tropics found they were now in enemy waters: outnumbered, outgunned, out-provisioned, very far from home, with no bases for repair or resupply. An English ship had to be self-sufficient and heavily armed. Self-sufficiency also meant building pinnaces in the Panamá jungle, and in surprise attacks, raiding coastal islands and Spanish ships for gold, food and drink. Spanish shipyards in the Caribbean came to design and build ships equal to those from Spain. It was a Mexican naval architect, not a Spaniard, who wrote the world's first shipbuilding manual. From Cuban yards, where skilled labour and timber from nearby forests were plentiful and cheap, Spain ordered frigates in the 1590s be built for another Armada against England.

Mathematics, Navigation

At the start, the English did not have the skilled mariners, charts and instruments for oceanic sailing. A captain on an ocean voyage would often kidnap an Iberian pilot and steal his charts and instruments. English navigation first translated and corrected Portuguese and Spanish texts. Only after a quarter century did the English began to write their own texts. Mathematician and navigator next came together to meet the demands of oceanic sailing. These mathematician-mariners corrected errors here and there, adopted the decimal point and the equal, plus, minus and times signs, corrected parallax error in the cross-staff, and figured a course in degrees on a magnetic compass rather than in rhumb lines of wind. And thanks to a Scottish laird, towards the end of the period, a sea pilot now could calculate using logarithms and had a slide rule to aid in solving the problem of the navigational triangle. A Flemish mathematician had earlier projected a sphere onto a planar surface with minimal distortion, and by the turn of the century an English innkeeper, mathematician and gunner had corrected and advanced that projection to make it practical for use at sea. An Italian and two Englishmen figured out how to calculate angular distance between heavenly bodies, though the instruments of the day were still too crude to make fine measurements. At sea, one English merchant-captain happened onto currents in the Caribbean and Gulf of Mexico. His observations advanced maritime cartography. While sailing westward, another found magnetic anomolies in his compass readings, adding incrementally to the data needed for improving charts by noting patterns of compass variation.

Ship Handling, Naval Tactics

Technology and strategy drive tactics. Throughout most of the period, the Spanish fought using yesteryear's technology. They disdained naval artillery as being non-chivalric, and insisted that boarding was necessary for victory. The English were outnumbered by the Spanish in tonnage, short-range firepower and manpower, and realised that grappling and boarding were suicidal. Long-range gunnery, long tested in the Caribbean, was the answer. The new bronze demi-culverin proved to be the best weapon. It was more accurate than the older iron cannon, and when loaded with a more powerful charge, had a longer range and effective force. These new guns brought on new formations and tactics. Ordering vessels line abreast, the formation used by galleys or by infantry regiments ashore, no longer made sense. The single column ahead, figure of eight and crossing the T, with minimal risk of exposure to gunfire, were better. Firing at a long range also lessened risk. Disable the enemy, then later take her, her cargo and cannon. These were the ways that the privateer, the pirate and the armed merchantman brought to the Royal Navy.

On a strategic level, the English, following the French lead, realised that to contain Spain in Europe, it was necessary to attack her American source of gold that filled the Escorial's war chest. Against a powerful Spain, the English had to adopt the tactics of the guerilla fighter or pirate with or without papers. From runaway slaves, the *cimarrónes*, the English seadogs learned how the underdog fights. English captains and crews like Drake ambushed mule trains loaded with treasure and kidnapped resident governors for ransom, made surprise attacks on coastal *fragatas*, taking food and loot. Midnight raids on ports such as San Agustín, Santo Domingo or Cartagena were carried out commando style by secretly landing soldiers a distance away while ships' cannon, close inshore, battered fort and town. Approaching from behind, the soldiers attacked, took the treasury's gold and silver ingots, and sent the inhabitants in their cotton nightshirts running.

The queen, lacking a large navy, was happy for her armed merchant navy to sack and plunder Spanish and New World ports and plantations. Though she complained, such a fusion of politics and piracy served her political aims. Voyages such as these were largely private, but were sometimes aided by Crown money and ships, the whole venture often papered over with letters of marque or reprisal. In 1588, aside from a core of Establishment warships, the squadrons that faced the Spanish Armada were largely armed merchantmen, whose commanders such as Drake, Hawkyns and Frobisher were already experienced from years of fighting the Spanish in tropical waters.

Tropical Diseases and Remedies

Long voyages, especially to the latitudes of the tropics, were dogged by disease, particularly malaria, dysentery and scurvy. The New World brought new diseases but also provided some new remedies as well. The mortality rate on tropical voyages was high. One captain rightly singled out scurvy as the 'plague of the sea, and the spoyle of mariners'. As late as 1620, during the fifty-six-day crossing of the *Mayflower* to Massachussets fifty of the 120 pilgrims died of scurvy. No mind that Spanish captains had long been provisioning citric fruits such as tamarinds, lemons, oranges and limes to prevent scurvy, as did a few English captains by the 1590s. Two hundred years later, in the 1790s, the Royal Navy would make provisioning limes and lemons official policy.

Another killer at sea was the bloody flux (dysentery), brought on by filthy conditions, rotten food and foul water. Ships' bilges were cesspools. Drinking water went bad in days. Beer, wine and spirits lasted somewhat longer. A few captains insisted on better sanitation aboard ship, fresh drinking water and wholesome food and, to circulate fresh air, ordered the installation of hammocks (Brazil beds) below decks.

Worse than scurvy and dysentery was the ague (malaria), then thought to be contracted from moist vapours rising from night seas. It was best to wear heavy clothing when on night watch. In Perú, the Quechuan *cinchona* (quinine) bark was found effective. The culprit, the host mosquito *Anopheles vivax*, was not discovered until much later. Once ashore in the tropics, the prudent mariner was warned by one captain to heed poisonous apples and the uncooked root of the casava plant, deadly poisonous. Cooked, manioc was the carbohydrate of the tropics, and safe to eat. Venomous serpents infested jungles, mosquitoes and alligators filled rivers. Survival in the tropics seemed almost accidental.

Trade, Plunder, Profit before Politics

From her accession in the 1550s Queen Elizabeth faced financial, commercial, religious and political problems. Early on, she shored up the pound sterling and, as a result, Continental trade shifted from the Lowlands to London's Royal Exchange. But even with this solid financial ballast, command of the seas and commerce in the Americas was troublesome. Merchant mariners had hoped to trade with Spanish America as they had done for centuries with Spain and Portugal but, denied that, many turned to privateering and piracy to augment commerce. Trade could be plunder, and plunder brought profit. Profit came before politics, and politics before religion.

The end of the period saw a wildly fluctuating economy. There were trade crises, rising prices and lower wages. Plague, famine and years of poor harvests troubled the country from 1604 to 1624. The Thames froze and summer fields flooded. These and other factors drove desperate folk to immigrate to the Americas. Once there, colonists were still desperate to feed themselves, never mind to think of any excess harvest to export. By the mid-seventeenth century the dozen or so Amazon and Orinoco colonies were folding, just as the two or three in North America, after decades of support, were beginning to pay their way. The tropical climate of South America had been found too formidable, and in any case the Portuguese and Spanish were closing in on the fledgling English outposts. The tropical English began to leave South America for the islands of the Caribbean, where they planted sugar cane and tobacco.

In North America, St John's, Newfoundland, the first settlement, continued to grow as an international port for cod fishermen and merchant ships needing provisions for the homebound transatlantic passages to Bristol or the Bay of Biscay. Farther south, the next two attempts by the Virginia Company were at a swampy Jamestown, and a reef-bound Bermuda a few hundred miles off the Atlantic coast. A fourth venture by a group of Brownists and Anglicans set foot on a rocky coast to found Plymouth. All four struggled through years to feed themselves, while to the south the English were settling in the Caribbean islands. By the 1640s there were signs of promise for the English. Virginia sent its first barrels of tobacco back to England in 1614, Barbados also sent back tobacco about that time, and after 1640 exported sugar.

Ralegh's observation made in 1614 and written from the Tower was prescient – trade and command of the sea were one, and essential for empire. In the Americas, the tuns of tobacco and sugar began to pay off decades of expensive support by Crown, City and adventurers. It was tobacco that paid for sending out fresh settlers. By the 1640s the two Americas that had first been viewed as impediments to reaching the riches of the Orient were now viewed, like Ireland, as place to send English dissidents and hungry folk. Traffiques between home country and colony were by mid century beginning to be mutually beneficial. If not the gold, silver and pearls of the Spanish tropics, then settle for turf, twig and hard work farther north.

Pushed by expediency and sailing under English red and white or piratical black flags, England through such indirections was unknowingly moving towards empire. In little over a century Britain's commerce had grown from coastal to global, in both East and West Indies, and in another century would be found around the world. English goods to start were mostly wool, tin, iron and various prosaic manufactures. These were carried to Africa and traded for slaves. These were sold in the Americas to meet a demand from the Spanish colonists for labour. The Spanish paid in hides, dyes and timber, some gold, silver and pearls. But from the 1560s, any English commerce in colonial Spanish waters at best had been to be trade on the wink, conducted under the table, around the corner, in the next bay, anywhere away from eyes of mayors and governors. A single-armed merchantman might well trade one day and plunder the next.

Sotweed, Divine Right

What was the political climate in England and on the Continent in the seventeenth century? Spain's aims did not change, but her power weakened under Philip II. England under James I now had a Scottish king eager to placate Spain, and ruled less adroitly but with a sense that his rights were divinely appointed, not a view shared by Parliament. The Treaty of London, 1604, brought peace in its time, for a time, and while Spain acknowledged a Protestant England, she insisted on retaining Spanish rule in the Americas. James stopped issuing letters of reprisal and of marque to armed merchantmen. With no royal license for private warfare, privateering no longer had legal standing, and sailors turned to other employ-ment. The merchant navy had provided some of England's finest mariners. The sun had set on the likes of Hawkyns, Drake and Cavendish. Gone too by 1620 was the aged knight errant, Ralegh.

Without such seamen the Jacobean Royal Navy was neglected and fell into disrepair. The old ways were lost. The first decades of the seventeenth century found England drifting towards an overthrow of monarchy and the installation of a Comonwealth. When the Commonwealth navy was needed to face the Dutch and French, it was a skeleton of its former self. With rare exception it was com-manded by generals, not admirals. These 'gentleman captains' in velvet breeches had little or no sea time when they found themselves facing tough Dutch fustian and sharp French epées. Dutch oceanic trade and French Catholicism were the main issues. After mid century the Spanish and English were at war once more, but Spain was a shadow of her former self, except in the Americas, where her culture was well-rooted and her forts strong. In the 1620s the English in North America could show only two or three struggling colonies. It was the same of the dozen or so in South America. All were in danger of collapse.

A Perspective Glass

By the 1640s the 'navigations, voyages, and traffiques' promoted more than a half-century earlier by the young Oxford cleric, Richard Hakluyt, had a real promise of fulfillment. He had thought of England's 'other Eden' to be tropical, but what first seemed Paradise, proved to be a paradise lost. Tropical climate and geography were too formidable, the Spanish too strong, the English support too weak for such an endeavour. Where Portugal and Spain's colonial enterprises were directed from Sintra or the Escorial as royal undertakings, England's was supported by City adventurers and merchant mariners. English colonisation was a commercial or religious matter, with only incidental royal backing until near the end of the period. Yet such terms toughened England for her later command of the seas in commerce and empire a century on.

Under the Tudors and Stuarts a nascent overseas trade conducted under the red ensign would grow to the British Empire under the Union Flag. Once the gunsmoke and tropical rains had passed on, the dream of citrus trees, azure seas, white beaches and gold tans remained. In centuries to come, English eyes bleary from mining Tyne coal and manufacturing cheap tin trays would turn to the gloss of Fleet Street travel supplements in hopes of catching at least a few weeks under tropic suns.

6

Appendix A

Chronology

1200s	Monks of St Albans compile tide tables, first English nautical books. Tide tables first printed in England *c.* 1540.
1503	*The Kalendayr of Shippars*, first popular English calendar, printed.
1512	The 1,500-ton carrack *Henry Grâce à Dieu*, familiarly the *Great Harry*, first English warship with gunports, is laid down. Hallowed and launched 1514, rebuilt in 1536 to 1,000 tons with greater firepower. Called first British battleship.
1516–17	Sebastian Cabot and Pert make first English voyage to West Indies, repulsed by Spanish cannon. Martin Luther writes his *Ninety-Five Theses*, 1517, translated to German 1518. Excommunicated by Pope Leo X, 1521.
1518	College of Physicians founded in London.
1526	Paracelsus discovers zinc, key ingredient in casting bronze cannon.
1532	Sugar cane first cultivated in Brazil. Sir John Hawkyns born in Plymouth.
1537	Portuguese mathematician and physician Pedro Nunes publishes navigation books or tracts: *Em Defensam da Carta de Marear, Certas Dúvidas da Navigação* (includes sailing a rhumb line), and *Da Sphera com a Theorica do Sol e da Lua*. Is first to show that a ship following a great circle course actually travels in a loxodrome, or spiral course.
1540	Sir Francis Drake born in Tavistock, Devon.
1543	Nicolaus Copernicus offers mathematical argument for heliocentric universe. Welsh physician and mathematician Robert Recorde publishes *The Grounde of Artes*, 1543, first English book on algebra, popular medical text, *The Urinal of Physick*, 1548, and *The Whetstone of Witte*, 1557, which introduces the equal sign, and, for the English, the plus and minus signs.
1544	Georg Hartmann discovers magnetic dip.
1550s	Tudor household stewards shift accounts from Roman to Arabic numerals.

1554	Sir Walter Ralegh born in East Budleigh, Devon, *c.* 1552–54.
1550–1600	Storms increase 85 per cent from earlier periods, to ten storms and six hurricanes each season, with most from June to November. In September there was one storm a week, in November a storm every two weeks, of which 75 per cent became hurricanes. Bermuda, at 28–36° N, worst place for hurricanes. Best months to avoid storms are January to April.
1552	Edward Wotton publishes *De Differentiis Animalium*, first English book on zoology.
1555–56	English merchant Robert Tomson, sailing in Spanish convoy, provides first extensive description in English of a Gulf Norther, and St Elmo's fire, *cuerpo santo*. First English description of mosquitoes, hookworm and venereal disease (likely gonorrhoea).
1558	Elizabeth Tudor accedes to English throne.
1560–1612	Severe droughts in North America.
1564–65	William Shakespeare born in Stratford-upon-Avon, 1564. Sir John Hawkyns sails on second slaving voyage from the Spanish Main to Hispaniola, is set westward to Jamaica, 1565, makes first English mention of the Caribbean Current, then the Florida Current and Gulf Stream.
1567	William Bourne publishes first English original manual on navigation, *An Almanac and Prognostication for iii Yeres, with Serten Rules of Navigation*.
1569	Flemish cartographer Gerardus Mercator first employs his cylindrical projection of the earth.
1570s	French book published 1623 notes use of the log and line as an English invention first used in 1570s.
1570	*Allerheiligenvloed* strikes Holland, 11–12 November, worst gale in Dutch history. Five-sixths of Holland innundated. After his defeat by the Spanish in 1568, in 1570 Hawkyns builds first race-built galleon, the small 295-ton *Foresight*, and that same year rebuilds to his new design the *Bull* and the *Tiger*, 160-ton galleasses built in 1546. By 1588 sixteen of the Navy's twenty-one front-line ships were race-built.
1572	Italian Raphael Bombelli defines imaginary numbers (numbers that when squared give a negative result).
1574	William Bourne publishes *A Regiment of the Sea*, first original English rutter or sailing manual, written from first-hand experience at sea.
1575	John Oxnam builds 45ft pinnace in Panamanian jungles of Panamá, 20–24 oars, sails, 2 chase cannon, shoal draught less than 6in. First English vessel to sail in Pacific. Two raids on Spanish shipping take largest loot to date in English history.
1577	John Frampton translates a Spanish work as *Joyfull Newes out of*

the New World, first English publication on American vegetables and drugs.

1578   William Bourne publishes *The Art of Shooting in Great Ordnance*, first English book on gunnery and naval tactics. Same year, Bourne publishes *The Treasure for Travellers*, early examination of ocean currents, and in *Very Necessary for all Generalles and Captaines* describes a submarine.

1581   Robert Norman in *The Newe Attractive* writes on magnetic dip.

1583   Sir Humphrey Gilbert claims St John's, Newfoundland, for England. Is first permanent English colony in North America, followed by Jamestown, 1607, Bermuda, 1609, Plymouth, 1620. Danish Thomas Fincke in *Geometria Rotundi* introduces 'tangent' and 'secant' into trigonometry. Flemish Simon Stevin in *De Thiende* introduces decimal fractions.

1584, 1585   Dutchman Lucas Janszoon Wagenaer publishes *Spieghel der Zeewaerdt*, first sea charts reliable enough for sea use, translated to English, 1588.

1585–1604   Anglo-Spanish War.

1586–88   Sir Thomas Cavendish provisions lemons for circumnavigation to prevent scurvy. No cases reported on reaching Strait of Magellan. Though Spanish used lemons thus since 1540s, Cavendish first Englishman to adopt them. Practice made Royal Navy policy 1794. Cavendish's the first intended English circumnavigation. Drake's in 1577–80 decided en route.

1587   Mexican Diego García de Palacio publishes *Instrucción Náutica para Navegar*, first detailed book on ship design and construction published in New World.

1587–89   Most severe droughts in Europe and America in 800 years.

1588   Spanish Armada attacks England. Other unsuccessful attempts in 1590s.

1590   Spanish Crown orders Cuba to build five frigates for the treasue *flota*. Eighteen more frigates ordered built for attack on England. Cuba now important shipbuilding centre. Dutchman Zacharias Janssen and his father invent compound microscope.

1590–1610   Two bitterly cold decades. Consecutively poor harvests in 1591–97, with good yields only 40 per cent of the time.

1593–94   Sir Richard Hawkyns, on voyage for the South Sea in the *Daintie*, rigs a still to distill fresh water from the sea, declares it 'wholesome and nourishing'. First English use, though process known since Aristotle.

1594   From experience gained while sailing with Cavendish, 1591–92, Robert Hues combines theory and practice in *Tractatus de Globis*, a standard work on globes for next 100 years. Captain John Davis publishes *The Seamans Secrets*, best account of navigation to that date, in clear prose. First to define course and traverse and to distinguish three sorts of sailing: horizontal or plane sailing; paradoxal or rhumb line sailing where the compass heading is constant; and great circle sailing. First discussion of parallax error when using cross-staff. Makes first circumpolar chart, still used today, for sailing in high latitudes. *Romeo and Juliet* first performed 1594–95.

1595–96   Captain John Davis invents back-staff and protractor. Word 'trigonometry' first used by Polish mathematician Bartholomaeus Pitiscus in *Trigonometria*, 1595, the year word also first used in English. Ralegh voyages to Guiana, plants English colony, the first such in South America (did not survive). During Hawkyns' and Drake's West Indies Voyage, 1595–96, Hawkyns dies, likely of amoebic dysentery (or malaria), off San Juan, Puerto Rico, in November 1595. Two months later, in January 1596, Drake dies of similar causes off Portobelo, Panamá.

1595–1646   English settle fifteen colonies along Rio Amazonas and Rio Orinoco (all die out).

1596   John Harrington's *The Metamorphosis of Ajax* describes first flush toilet, called the Ajax (the jakes). *The Merchant of Venice*, written 1596–97, has possible reference to Spanish 1,000-ton galleon *San Andrés*, captured in the 1596 Cádiz raid.

1597   John Gerard translates 1554 Dutch work as *The Herball*. Becomes a standard English text on botany. *Romeo and Juliet*, Q1, published. Brazilian *hamacas* (hammocks) requisitioned for fleet by Earl of Essex.

1598   George Wateson, sea captain, Joseph Singer, and G.W. (George Whetstone, soldier and playwright?) publish *Cures of the Diseased*, first English treatise on tropical medicine. Becomes the authority for next 100 years. Gresham College founded. First time navigation taught in an academic curriculum, wedding theory and practice. Spanish King Philip II dies. Hakluyt begins to publish *Principal Navigations*, 1598–1600, sequel to his *Principall Navigations*, 1589.

1599   Edward Wright in *Certaine Errors*, 1599, corrects errors in Mercator's projection. Mercator projection first published in chart of Cumberland's 1589 voyage to Azores. *Julius Caesar* likely written, first performed 1600–01

1600   Dr William Gilbert, *De Magnete*. First truly scientific English treatise on subject by queen's physician. Chilean volcano Huanyaputina erupts. Sediment in upper atmosphere brings on coldest summer since 1400 to entire northern hemisphere. Western North America has coldest summer in 400 years. *Hamlet* first performed 1600–01.

1603   Queen Elizabeth dies. James Stuart, King of Scotland, accedes to English throne. *Hamlet*, Q1, published. Ralegh convicted of treason against the Crown as part of the Main Plot against James, committed to Tower 1603, released on parole 1616.

1604	Treaty of London signed, ending Anglo–Spanish War. French begin colonisation of Guiana. King James convenes committee to produce Authorised Bible, completed 1611. *Othello* first performed 1604–05.
1605	Guy Fawkes and others plot to blow up Parliament. First recorded performances of *Macbeth*.
1606	Giovanni Antonio Magini, born in Padua, compiles highly accurate trigonometric tables (not his contemporary, Giovanni Paolo Maggini, Brescian luthier). First recorded performances of *King Lear*
1607	Winter coldest in 700 years. Just over 100 English colonists land in May to found Jamestown as second permanent English colony in America. Summer driest in 770 years. Galileo invents a thermometer based on expansion of a gas, first used for medical purpose 1612.
1607–25	In 1608 only thirty-eight of the Jamestown colonists still alive. That year, two more voyages brought out more settlers, including the first two women. Summer droughts continue to 1613. Of the 6,000 English who colonised Jamestown between 1607 and 1625, more than 4,800 die of malnutrition, contaminated water, or other ills.
1608	Hans Lippershey demonstrates telescope. John Milton born.
1609	Cornelius Drebbel invents thermostat. *Shakespeares Sonnets* published. Bermuda, then part of the Virginia Company, becomes third permanent English settlement of North America (Chartered 1612), after St John's, Newfoundland, 1583, and Jamestown, 1607.
1610	Galileo Galilei discovers Jupiter's moons with telescope. With the recent shipwreck of the *Sea Venture* at Bermuda in mind, Shakespeare writes *The Tempest*, 1610–11. Jamestown's 'starving time', when in less than a year only sixty of some 500–600 colonists survive.
1611	*The Holy Bible* (King James Version) published. First recorded performance of *The Tempest*.
1613	William Baffin first to record a ship's course not as rhumb of the winds but in degrees of the compass. First to show magnetic variation as deflection of the north end of compass needle. First to use columnar journal at sea. First to record longitude while at sea, a rare feat.
1614	John Napier in *Mirifici Logorithmorum Canonis* first to employ decimal point. Discovers logarithms. Robert Norman publishes *Newe Attractive,* the first published explanation in English of arithmetical navigation. Jamestown exports its first barrels of tobacco.
1616	Henry Briggs shows Napier how to find logarithms by sequential extraction of square roots. William Shakespeare dies in Stratford-upon-Avon.
1617	Society of Apothecaries gets royal charter, making it separate from the Society of Grocers.
1617–50	Cold summers and poor harvests on coasts of the North Atlantic.

1618	Johannes Kepler announces and proves third law of planetary motion, which links a planet's orbital period to the orbit's semi-major axis. Sir Walter Ralegh, the last great Elizabethan mariner, on return from Guiana, is beheaded for treason.
1619	Edmund Gunter in *Canon of Triangles* coins terms 'cosine' and 'cotangent'.
1620	The *Mayflower* carries 102 English colonists to settle Plymouth Plantation in New England. Nearly half die in first winter. Mathematician Francis Bacon notes geological fit of the east and west shores of the Atlantic Ocean. Cornelius Drebbel builds first navigable submarine.
1620–23	Sir Henry Mainwaring writes *Nomenclator Navalis*, first of the sailors word books in English, published 1644. Mainwaring's manuscript is source for Smith's and Boteler's word-books.
1621	Henry Danvers, First Earl of Danby starts physic garden, Oxford University's botanical garden, with medicinal plants and many simples coming from New World.
1622	William Oughtred invents slide rule, allowing for direct multiplication and division, introduces 'x' for multiplication and the proportion sign, '::'. Advances to navigation in *Circles of Proportion*, 1632.
1623	Common logarithms of trigonometric functions first published in Edmund Gunter's *Canon Triangulorum*. Same year, Gunter invents and announces in *De Sectore & Radio* his scale, presented as a Line of Numbers in the form of a slide rule.
1624	Flemish doctor Adriaan van den Spiegel in *De Semitertiana Libri Quator* provides first extensive examination of malaria. On bankruptcy of Virginia Company, Crown appropriates Jamestown as a royal colony.
1625	King James dies, is succeeded by his son Charles I. Thomas Addison's *Arithmeticall Navigation* is the first published solution to navigation problems using logarithmic tables and the first navigational manual devoted solely to arithmetical navigation. Samuel Purchas publishes *Purchas His Pilgrimes*, sequel to Hakluyt's *Principal Navigations*, 1598–1600. Plague in England particularly severe: mid-August toll alone is 4,463 deaths.
1626	Captain John Smith publishes *Accidence*, the first English sailors' wordbook to be published, derived largely from Mainwaring's manuscript. Richard Norwood in *Seamans Practice* is first Englishman to consider ocean currents as a major factor in oceanic navigation.
1630	Richard Delamain's *Grammelogia* gives first description of a slide rule in the form of rotatable disks for use at sea.
1631	Richard Norwood's columnar logbook (distinct from Baffin's journal, 1613) contains entries for date, latitude (observed altitude), course, leagues sailed, wind direction and other observations.

1638	English plan settlement in Amazon, abandon idea 1646.
1639	Girard Desargues introduces concept of infinity to geometry. Casaquiare channel that links rivers Amazonas and Orinoco discovered.
1640	Bayonet invented, in time will supplant the pike. Reticle telescope allows for highly accurate sharpshooting by snipers.
1641	Princess Mary marries Dutchman William, Duke of Orange. Later, in Glorious Revolution, 1688, Parliament narrowly votes them in as joint monarchs.
1642	Charles I flees London, seeks refuge in Oxford. Besieges Nottingham Castle. Start of Civil War. Parliament orders all theatres closed, ending English Renaissance drama. Queen consort Henriette Maria, French-born Catholic wife of Charles I, flees England for Hellevoetsluis, Holland. Christiaan Huygens discovers south polar ice cap on Mars. Dutch mariner Abel Janszoon Tasman discovers New Zealand and Tasmania. Galileo Galilei dies. Irish plan settlement in Amazon, abandon idea 1646.
1643	Earthquake in Santiago, Chile, kills a third of local population. Louis XIV ascends French throne. Evangelista Toricelli invents mercury barometer. Antonie van Leeuwenhoek develops microscope. Isaac Newton born.
1644	Sir Henry Mainwaring publishes *Nomenclator Navalis* from his 1617–23 manuscript. Johan Mauritius van Nassau resigns as governor of Brazil, returns to Netherlands. Milton publishes attack on censorship, *Areopagitica*. Ole Rømer, Danish astronomer, quantifies the speed of light. Quaker pacifist William Penn born, later Crown grants him Province of Pennsylvania to pay off debts owed his father, Admiral Sir William Penn. In 1655 Admiral Penn will fail to seize Hispaniola but will take Jamaica for Commonwealth England. He drew up Navy's first plan of tactics, advocated line-ahead formation and, after Restoration, 1660, fought for Charles II. Parliamentarians, led by Cromwell, win Battle of Marston Moor.
1645	Michael Florent van Langren publishes first map of moon. Sir Robert Dudley, maritime engineer and illegitimate son of Robert Dudley, First Earl of Leicester publishes *Dell'Arcano del Mare* in Italy. It covers navigation, shipbuilding and astronomy and includes first maritime atlas of entire world (using Mercator projection) made by an Englishman.
1646	Blaise Pascal announces law of hydrostatics, that in a perfect fluid, pressure applied anywhere on it is transmitted equally.
1647	First case of yellow fever reported in Barbados. Transmitted there from Africa by a sagouin monkey.
1649	Charles I beheaded. England declared a Commonwealth under Oliver Cromwell.
1651	Parliamentarians defeat Royalists at Battle of Worcester. Civil War ends. Charles II flees to France.

Appendix B

Tropical Climate and Weather

I. Climate

North and South Atlantic Oceans and Caribbean Sea (including Gulf of Mexico)

Tropical climate and weather, unlike those in other parts of the world, have remained much the same through the centuries, including during the Little Ice Age. The tropics, in a 40° to 60° belt around the equator worldwide, were less affected by the cooling climate than the higher latitudes, because the sun's high angle within the tropical belt results in a high degree of insolation as the surface takes in solar radiation. Another factor, considering the expanse of water in the Caribbean, is that albedo (light or radiation reflected from a surface) occurs when radiation is absorbed by the earth's surface, especially strong over water. Tropical oceans are relatively warm (though with some cold currents) and have little diurnal variation (daily range of temperatures).[1]

This appendix takes up aspects of the mariner's climate and weather. It lays out the scientific bases of climate, then considers the resulting weather in the North and South Atlantic, the Caribbean and parts of the Pacific. This appendix should be read together with Chapter Three, 'Western Winds – A Tropical Rutter', the six pilot atlas charts, and the detailed accounts of the voyages found in the author's companion volume, *Tropics Bound* (Stroud, 2010).

An English galleon bound out to and back from the West Indies could expect North Atlantic weather to be ordered by the North Atlantic gyre. Within that gyre two systems mesh: the Azores High pressure system centred at about 38° N, Lat. 28° W Long., located about 800 miles west of Lisbon, and to the north, the Icelandic Low, centred on Iceland at about 65° N, 18° W. The Azores High and the Icelandic Low rotate in opposite directions (clockwise and anticlockwise, respectively) and determine sailing routes both out from Europe and back. To make a North Atlantic passage westward the English captain would best sail south in November (when the northeast Trade Winds are fully developed and the hurricane season is over) to about 15° N, the latitude of the Canaries, or to 28° N, a point some 150 miles north-west of the Cabo Verdes. There he reaches the most reliable northeasterly Trade Winds and the constant westerly current. The north-ern limit of the Trades in winter is about 25° N Lat., and later can be found still farther north. Timing helps.

A part of one of the world's five gyres is the clockwise North Atlantic Circulation, part of the worldwide salty Thermohaline Circulation (THC, from temperature, salt content, hence density gradients). One current of the North Atlantic Circulation is the warm, wind-driven Gulf Stream. Another is the south-erly North Atlantic Current that becomes the Canary Current before it begins to turn somewhat westward at the Canaries, and more reliably so at the Cabo Verdes. This current becomes the North Equatorial Current and flows westward to Cabo São Roque, Brazil. At São Roque, half the current splits into the Guiana, Antilles and Caribbean Currents and flows west and north-westerly along the northern South American coast. The Guiana Current flows west-north-west in a band 200–300m wide, with a current of 1 to 2 knots, strongest about 150 miles offshore. A northerly branch, the Antilles Current, flows to the north of the Leeward Islands and through the Bahamas to the Florida Straits, where it joins the easterly current from the Gulf of Mexico. Off Florida, it then flows north-wards as the Gulf Stream, flowing at a mean rate of 0.5 to 1.5 knots across the North Atlantic to Europe.

The other part of the Equatorial Current turns south at São Roque and enters the anticlockwise South Atlantic gyre. The gyre currentsof the southern ocean include the South Equatorial Current, which becomes the Brazil Current (analo-gous to but weaker than the Gulf Stream), which flows down the eastern South American coast as far as the Río de la Plata. There it forks east towards Africa as the Benguela Current, while the rest continues south to meet the Falkland Current. The Brazil Current flows as far south as 34–37° S Lat., where it turns south-east at about 36° S Lat. to meet the Southern Ocean Current, flowing north-east from Cape Horn.

Ocean Circulation

The kinetic energy in the atmosphere and on the ocean's surface produces cur-rents. Ocean currents are also affected by temperature and differences in salinity (THC) and geography. When an ocean current meets a continental land mass, its current is deflected, and the result is a series of gyres or circular ocean currents. The largest gyres occur in the subtropics and are anticyclonic (clockwise in the northern hemisphere, generated mostly by the northeast trades, anticlockwise in the southern). These gyres are formed by water being pushed by the Trade Winds from the east sides of the great ocean basins to the west. They travel westward but are deflected towards the poles by land masses on the western side. As they travel polewards, the Coriolis force (in which the spinning of the Earth deflects the path of an object in motion) and the drag of the motion deflect the currents eastward by another force, the Ekman Drift or Spiral, in which the ocean water's motion turns at 90° to the right of the wind direction in the Northern Hemisphere (and opposite in the Southern). In the equatorial north latitudes the basic ocean circulation of the subtropical gyres is a westerly current, whereas in the outer subtropical latitudes the current is easterly. There is a cool equator-wards current along the eastern boundary of the ocean basin in the northern hemisphere (and a warm polewards one along the western boundary in the southern).[2]

Four circulation systems function in the tropics: Hadley cell circulation (cells which are the result of meridional circulations at the ITCZ (Intertropical Convergence Zone or Doldrums, a 200–300-mile band of calms, light variable winds and squalls); subtropical anticyclones; the Trade Winds; and upper subtropical westerly and tropical easterly flows. Hadley cells in the tropics occur when warm air rises first in the equatorial zone, then in the upper atmosphere. They next move toward the poles, and sink in the subtropics, to move at the earth's surface as Trade Winds, found globally.

Trade Winds

Why 'Trade Winds'? These winds, warm and moist, take their names from the Anglo-Saxon 'trade' meaning 'path', and follow a predictable course (Spanish, '*alisios*', French, '*alizés*', Italian, '*alisei*', German, '*passat*'). A false etymology equates trade with transoceanic commerce. The Caribbean Sea is dominated by the Trades year round between 12 and 27° N, and is rarely influenced by the ITCZ to the south. The northerly Trade Winds are easterlies. (Direction of winds is always indicated as from their source, though for ocean currents, to where they flow.[3]) The North Atlantic Trades range from the ITCZ north to the Azores, that is, from 2–25° N in winter to 10–30° N in the summer. They average Force 4, or 11–16 knots.[4]

Subtropical anticyclones (generally of high pressure) affect the trade (and other) winds. As the Trade Winds converge and find heat at the ITCZ, low barometric pressure, clouds and rain produce subtropical anticyclones. These subtropical highs produce the winds, and with them, fair weather. Any rain that forms will be on the western side of the cells. The cells on the eastern side produce stable weather. Subsidence produces the few stratocumulus clouds.[5] Trade Winds are regular and steady. In the northern hemisphere troughs of low pressure run south-west to north-east. They move with the easterlies, thus their movement is as an easterly wave.[6] They are a form of low-level circulation with steady easterly winds in the northern hemisphere. Trade Winds are layered as subclouds, clouds and inversion layers. The warmer inversion layer, most intense and frequent in winter, is produced by turbulence, radiation, advection and subsidence.

Doldrums

The Doldrums, now called the ITCZ, lie in the path of the sailor bound west or south from England at about 5° north and south of the equator and are characterised by variable winds or flat calm, a weak north-westerly current, heavy rain, squalls and severe thunderstorms. They are produced by convection that is the result of the warm equatorial ocean, a wet ascending Hadley cell, low barometric pressure and by the northeast and southeast Trade Winds that feed into the area and generate a horizontal wind shear. The position of the ITCZ is a function of the Coriolis effect (from the earth's rotation) that is least near the equator, greatest at the poles. Depending on the season and on solar radiation, the zone can range between about 40° N to 40° S. The band shifts northward during the northern hemisphere's summer.

Central and South American Orography

Land masses also affect climate. Tropical America's orography (Gk., *oros*, mountain) greatly affects Central and South American climate, as the Andes mountains divide the region's climates and weathers between Atlantic and Pacific.[7] The far north of the Central American peninsula is dry. The Atlantic coastal areas are similar to the weather in the Caribbean islands, dominated by the North Atlantic's steady northeasterlies. Because of its leeward position in relation to those easterlies, the Yucatán Peninsula is dry. On the Pacific side of Central America, prevailing northwest winds make the area drier than on the Caribbean or Gulf side.

Tropical South America has three climates and hence a variety of weathers. The first climate is that high in the Andes mountains (Quechua, *anti*, high crest). Between the mountains and the Pacific is the western coastal strip of South America, affected by the cold Humboldt-Perú ocean current. It flows northwards to the equator and brings El Niño and La Niña, discussed below. The second climate is on the continent's east coast, especially in Brazil, characterised by *chapadas* (highland plateaus) or *serras* (mountain ranges). The Atlantic side of north-eastern South America is affected by the seasonal changes in winds in the ITCZ. That coastline also feels the effects of the Equatorial Current, strongly off Guiana and Surinam, less so at Trinidad. North-eastern South America has wet or dry seasons. Year round near the equator, in the Amazon basin, the Guyanas, littoral Venezuela and Amazonian Brazil, the climate is generally always wet, producing swamps and lush vegetation. In contrast, inland Venezuela and large parts of north-eastern Brazil are dry, with droughts common.

Caribbean Maritime Climates

The Caribbean Sea has various climates, though it is within northeast Trade Winds belt and generally enjoys stable weather. Easterly winds average F4 throughout the year, most constant from December to May. Summer and autumn bring heavy rain and thunderstorms followed by light variable winds, and a chance for tropical cyclones. North of the Greater Antilles lies the Gulf of Mexico, whose climate is largely governed by continental North America, and hence its weather. To the south, the Caribbean, especially in hurricane season, can affect the Gulf. The Gulf of Mexico's winds are generally lighter than those in the Caribbean. They are from the east or south-east, except in winter, when northerlies blow strong. In both the Caribbean and the Gulf, tropical cyclones and hurricanes occur from June to mid November, with the worst between August and October. On average there are twelve tropical storms F8 and higher each year in the North Atlantic and the Caribbean. Half of these storms reach hurricane strength. They can be spawned within a swathe as far east as the Cabo Verdes (about 23° W) and west to Venezuela (about 65° W), depending on the season.

Caribbean Winds and Currents

For north-east South America (south-east of Trinidad to 5° N Lat.) the northeast Trade Winds are from November to July, steadiest from January to April, F3–F6. From August to October the ITCZ lies farther north. At that period the winds have swung to the east-south-east and are weaker and less steady. In June and July squalls are common, but gales and tropical storms are rare. Along that coast flows the Guiana Current, spawned by the Equatorial Current, flowing to over 4 knots in April and May, and found between the continental shelf and 300 miles seaward.[8]

The Antilles current flows north-west on the Atlantic side of the string of small islands from the Virgins to Trinidad making up the Lesser Antilles and joins the Gulf Stream north of the Bahamas. Part of it flows west along the Old Bahama Channel[9] to join the Florida Current north of Cuba (Cuba, Jamaica, Hispaniola and Puerto Rico are the islands that constitute the Greater Antilles). Another branch of the North Equatorial Current flows north-west through the Lesser Antilles, through the Caribbean Sea west, then north through the Yucatan Channel, where it flows at a rate of 1–1.5 knots. Once in the Gulf of Mexico, the western part of the current sets into the Gulf, and forms clockwise eddies between Cuba and Florida. These residual currents produce the Florida Current between Florida and Cuba. Along the west coast of Florida a counter-current flows as an eddy northwards at up to 1 knot. The Florida Current sets east and north and flows up to 4.5 knots. Once in the Atlantic it joins the Gulf Stream.

Tides in the Lesser Antilles generally rise westerly into the area for six hours, then flow east as the tide falls back into the Atlantic for the next six hours. The maximum tidal flow is 1 to 1.5 knots. The range is microtidal, with an average 20cm (7.9in) rise and fall. The northerly islands of the Lesser Antilles get a northerly or easterly swell. They have a dry season from February to April (from January to May in Trinidad) and a wet season from July to October. The windward side of these islands is dry, and most rain falls on the downwind side.

If a vessel turns west for Panamá instead of towards the Leewards, those on board find that the Trades are most constant in winter, but light and variable in March and from August to October. They are strongest within 150 miles of the Colombian coast from January to March, in part because of the coastal mountains. It is an area where gales and hurricanes are rare, though squalls are common near land. Current runs from 0.75 to 1.5 knots and sets west or west-north-west, somewhat stronger in winter and spring. Off the Caribbean coast of the narrow Isthmus of Panamá the current swirls in an opposing anticlockwise gyre, making for wind against current in some places.

Such 'square-wave' sea conditions continue up the coast of Central America, where the winds are typically east-north-east F4 and the current is west-north-west at 0.5–1.0 knots. The current sets north-north-east from the Gulf of Honduras to the Yucatán Channel at a rate of 1.5–2 knots. The axis of the strongest current is 35 miles off the Yucatán coast. The humid rainy season from May to December has frequent thunderstorms.

Off the south coast of Cuba a current sets west at 0.5–1.0 knots from west of Jamaica to the Gulf of Mexico, where it increases to 3 knots. There are easterly variable counter-currents of 0.75 knots in the bight of south-west Cuba, just as those found from Cartagena to Panamá. Counter-currents in the set of the current also occur off the western half of Hispaniola, and on the north side of the island the set of current in the Windward Passage, where the current is south-west, 0.75–2 knots.

The closer to the coast, the more the currents are affected by the tides. From the Gulf of Mexico to Florida, north of the Greater Antilles (Cuba, Jamaica, Hispaniola and Puerto Rico) the northeast Trades in the Gulf still dominate, blowing from north-east to east-south-east at an average F4. There is current-wind opposition here too, as the prevailing light easterlies are opposed by a weak easterly flowing current (0.5–1.0 knots).

Weather in the Gulf of Mexico, as noted, is dominated by the North American continental air mass meeting the Gulf's maritime air mass. It thus has an entirely different system of weather from the rest of the Caribbean. Its climate is subtropical, with cyclones and hurricanes in the summer and Northers in the winter. These Northers are cold northwesterly or northerly winds that develop ahead of continental anticyclones, and blow at F8 (a gale) for several days. They begin from a ridge of high pressure that extends from a continental anticyclone south over the Gulf, a mass of thick clouds and produces heavy rain from October and April in particular and most frequently in December and January. On the Mexican coast coastal Northers with heavy squalls are common from September to April. On the north coast of the Gulf, tornadoes to 50 knots occur occasionally over the inland waters between the Mississippi River and Pensacola.

Light easterly Gulf winds and currents (0.5–1.0 knots, driven by the wind) are generally variable. The currents set north through the Yucatán Channel and divide into three streams. One stream sets west and sweeps round the Golfo de Campeche. Another, the central stream, flows west-north-west towards the Mississippi River and then west along the north coast of the Gulf. In the third stream, most of the water turns east to form the Florida Current. The southern end of Florida is at the northern edge of the northeast Trades, which in winter brings light and variable winds that are weaker farther north. Deep troughs from depressions bring strong gale-force winds. Northers develop between November and March, most frequently in December and January. This area is prone to hurricanes, which regularly track across Florida. Gales are rare in summer except those that are part of a hurricane. Squalls are common. The Florida Current that flows swiftly along the west coast of the Florida cape enters the Florida Strait flowing at 1.0–1.5 knots. Its axis lies 25 miles north of La Havana and 46 miles south of Key West. It flows at 2.5 knots, but reaches 6.5 knots at Fowey Rocks, off Key Biscayne.

The Gulf is subject to hurricanes from the south. Of its major storms, hurricanes coming from the Caribbean are the worst. Privateer James Langton in

1593–94, with two ships and a small pinnace, writes that Caribbean hurricanes commonly occur in November and December, when prudence calls for finding a good harbour to ride them out.[10] This was especially so during the exceptionally stormy decade of the 1590s, quite different from the '80s or '70s and earlier. It was certainly so on Drake's final West Indies voyage, 1595–96. Off Panamá (just days before his death) Drake said to a friend that his earlier voyages there in the '60s, '70s and '80s had had favourable weather, but that the winds in the mid-1590s were so variable and the weather so stormy and blustery that it was like nothing he had seen before in those same waters.[11] Climate and weather had changed.

South Atlantic, Cape Horn, Pacific

South Atlantic High, Trade Winds

South Atlantic weather is dominated by the anticlockwise South American High. The southern Trades, blowing from the south-east, are more steady and reliable than the Trades of the North Atlantic. The Doldrums do not extend deep into the South Atlantic. There are no tropical cyclones in the South Atlantic (though storms are notorious at the east and west approaches to the Strait of Magellan and at Cape Horn, and wind and wave are formidable at the Cape of Good Hope). In the northern latitudes of the South Atlantic, the southeast Trades are bordered on the south by variables in the anticyclone band known as the Horse Latitudes (lying about 30–35° north and south of the equator (called 'horse' perhaps because when becalmed, sailors threw the horses overboard to save food and water).[12] The southeast Trades from the ITCZ south to the South Atlantic High are found at 1–30° S Lat. in Febuary, 5° N–25° S Lat. in August, with winds F3–F6. Westerlies predominate south of about 35° S Lat.

Currents

One part of the Equatorial Current turns into the South Atlantic Ocean, the region of the anticlockwise South Atlantic gyre. This gyre, as noted earlier, produces currents from South America to Africa. Along the eastern coast of South America from 20–40° S, from May to August winds are variable, with *abrolhos* (squalls) and heavy evening rains from the east-south-east. Between Cabo Frio and Cabo São Tomé (two capes near Rio de Janeiro) rain squalls from the south and south-west are common from September to November. Farther south, off the Río de la Plata, these south-easterly squalls are called *pamperos* (they come off the *pampas*), following a cold trough moving north-north-east, at F8 with gusts over 70 knots. *Pamperos* are common in winter, and are especially severe if occuring in summer. Some twenty *pamperos*, lasting several days, occur yearly. At the river mouth of the Río de la Plata they produce high seas.[13] The Portuguese mariner Lopez Vaz in 1586 warned of the Río de la Plata, 'one of the greatest rivers in all the world' but 'very often subject to great and sudden storms'.[14]

Westerlies prevail south of the Río de la Plata, at 35° S, as Lows move west to east. The strongest winds come from the north-west, but when a depression passes, these shift to the south-west. Off the South American coast lies the Falkland Current. Gales are frequent south of the Falklands and south of Cape Horn. South of 50° S, the weather moderates, though gales occur, with heavy swells frequent.

Roaring Forties

The weather at the tip of South America has long been the major obstacle to navigators seeking the Pacific from the Atlantic. There are two ways to pass to the Pacific: through the tortuous Strait of Magellan, or around Cape Horn. Each way has difficulties. Westerlies – the Roaring Forties – predominate from 40° S Lat. to the Falkland islands and at 57° S, Cape Horn. Storms with winds F7 and above are caused by cold troughs associated with depressions. Antarctic icebergs are present around Cape Horn. The rare one can be seen as far north as the Río de la Plata. Near Tierra del Fuego the strong winds are katabatic (williwaws, violent squalls that roll down the mountains). Within the Strait of Magellan these are short-lasting but can appear from any direction. Katabatic winds derive from Greek, *katabatikos*, descending. In Greece and in the Mediterranean, katabatic winds are usually dry north winds, once thought brought by Boreas, god of the north wind. In the Strait, these are common west of Cape Froward on the north side of the Strait of Magellan, the cape so named by Thomas Cavendish in 1587 for its rugged wind and rain. The mean temperatures in the Strait are 8°C in summer and 4°C in winter. Ice, precipitation and poor visibility are common.[15]

Vaz comments that the Strait, lying at 52.5° S Lat., has colder temperatures than the comparable latitude in the Arctic. Worse than the cold are the westerly and southerly winds:

> which blow most furiously on that coast, and that oftentimes out of the very mouth of the straits, and so continue for the most part of the year. Also there runneth sometimes such a strong current, that if the wind and it go all one way, the cables cannot hold, neither can the ship withstand the force thereof.

There are no harbours until the sailor is fully 30 leagues (some 100 miles) into the strait. As for a transit from the west, that end of the Strait is a lee shore, with the entire force of the Southern Ocean to drive a galleon onto the rocks.[16]

William Magoths wrote of privateer John Chidley's *Delight* and two other ships and two small pinnaces at the Strait of Magellan intended for the South Sea in summer 1590. Storms had taken their toll. After six weeks in the Strait, Chidley had lost three of his four anchors. Only when his crew petitioned the captain (at that point thirty-eight of the ninety-one original crew had been lost to casualty or sickness) did he turn back for England.[17] The next summer, 1591, Thomas Cavendish, already having sucessfully circumnavigated the globe and made his fortune three years earlier, set out again for the South Sea, but was beaten back 50 leagues north-east by the Strait's extreme storms and constant snow.[18]

If returning from Cape Horn and the Strait of Magellan for Europe, the sailor must first go east to enter the Falkland Current, and then sail east-south-east some 500 miles before turning north. Between October and May, especially from November to February,[19] once he is north of 18° S Lat. and when the winds are easterly or east by south, he need not go offshore so far and can stay closer to the continent. From Rio de Janeiro he should sail south-east to 35° W Long., then if bound for Europe or North America, turn north to cross the equator at about 29° W Long. If bound for the Caribbean, then he should cross the equator farther west.[20] November to February are best for catching the northeast winds along the Brazilian coast. From the north-east of Brazil to Europe the mariner would sail north to pass west then north of the Azores, aiming to use the westerly Trades.

Two other currents warrant mention, both, cold water, both in the eastern Pacific. These are the Humboldt Current, flowing northwards from Antarctica to the equator, and the Japanese Current, which flows from Japan northwards to Alaska, then turns south along the coast of North America.

II. Weather

The one factor any mariner can anticipate but never know sufficiently is weather, a seasonal and regional phenomenon. While climate is long-term and global, weather is a matter of days, weeks and months and seasons, and is regional. No matter how much the experts analyse weather and predict it beyond a few days, the variables make it partly guesswork.

The Caribbean Sea's weather is dominated by the northeast Trades, blowing on average F4. Currents trend westerly, except for the Gulf of Mexico, where they are largely easterly. There are pockets of eddies of wind and current: off Panamá's Caribbean coast, off south-western Cuba, in places in the Gulf. Tides are minimal throughout the entire Caribbean (including the Gulf).

Gulf of Mexico weather is affected from the continent by Northers with gale-force winds (weaker, though, than Northers along the North American coastline). These Northers are intensifications of the northeast Trade Wind augumented by the sea breeze seeking the coast. Cold northwesterly or northerly winds develop ahead of continental anticyclones, and blow at F8 (gale force) for several days. They start from a ridge of high pressure that extends from a continental anticyclone south over the Gulf. With thick clouds and heavy rain, they occur between October and April, most frequently in December and January. Weather in the Gulf is dominated by the continental air mass of North America meeting the maritime air mass of the Gulf. Gulf winds (light easterlies) are generally variable. On the Mexican coast coastal Northers with heavy squalls are common from September to April. On the north coast of the Gulf, tornadoes to 50 knots occur occasionally over the inland waters between the Mississippi River and Pensacola. The Gulf is often within the direct track of hurricanes.

The southern end of Florida is at the northern edge of the northeast Trades. In winter these Trades are light and variable winds, lighter still and and more variable farther north. The Florida Current flows on the west side of the Florida cape, where it enters the Florida Strait, and increases in speed off Key Biscayne when it enters the Gulf Stream. At Florida the western branch of the Antilles sets into the Gulf as the Florida Current, which sets east and north at up to 4.5 knots, with clockwise eddies forming between Cuba and Florida. One eddy occurs along the west coast of Florida as a counter current. It flows north at a speed of up to 1 knot. The best weather in the North Atlantic between Florida and the Azores is in May or June, or after November. Between the Caribbean and Bermuda, winds are fickle or calm but settle into the westerly Trades north of 35° N Lat. and continue until reaching England.

Four Tropical Weathers

In the American Tropics four tropical weathers stand out: *El Niño* and *La Niña*, diurnal winds, Trade Winds and tropical cyclones or storms (including squall lines, gales and hurricanes).

El Niño is affected by the Walker circulation (an east to west circulation along the equator). The Pacific along the South American coast warms rapidly, and when the ocean and the atmosphere coincide, *El Niño*, a southern ocillation (ENSO) forms. Fishermen named its warm southerly surface currents along the Ecuadorian and Peruvian coasts *El Niño* because this weather happens periodically at about Christmas time, at the birth of Christ, *El Niño*, the baby boy. Markedly cold phases are termed *La Niña*, the baby girl. Both reoccur in cycles of four to nine years, usually five. The warmer or cooler water results from oceanic upwelling, Trade Winds, equatorial countercurrents and barometric patterns in the Pacific basin. Upwelling makes the thermocline shallower (to 40m), just as downwelling makes it deeper (to 100–200m). The strength of the Trade Winds greatly affects the location of the thermocline. When winds decrease in an anticyclonic system in the eastern Pacific, as in an *El Niño*, the trans-Pacific water slope collapses, and the warmer water travels eastward as internal oceanic waves known as Kelvin waves. These slow-moving waves take about sixty days to cross the Pacific. When they reach the eastern coast of the Pacific, sea levels rise.[21]

Within these larger patterns (occurring over decades or seasons) there are others found in shorter cycles. Typically, in the tropics, there are diurnal variations from day to night that produce temperature variations. It is these cycles that mainly drive tropical winds along coasts. Solar radiation during the day heats the land, while the water throughout the day remains about the same, and is relatively cooler. A small convectional cell's cooler surface winds at sea blows towards land as a sea breeze. At night, longwave radiation loss cools the land, typically about three hours after sunset until sunrise or later. Winds are off the land. For centuries fishermen have used the outgoing land breeze to head out to sea in the early morning and use the incoming sea breeze in the afternoon to return to port with the day's catch.

Diurnal barometric pressure variation is also characteristic of the tropics. Where mountains come down to the seacoast, there is an anabatic upward flow

(Gk., *anabatikos*, ascending) that produces a diurnal wind.[22] On hot days a warm parcel of air in the lowlands (a valley wind or anabatic flow) rises up the slope of a mountainside. When this occurs the mariner off the coast will often see cumulus near mountain tops and at the top of escarpments. At night, the reverse happens. The temperature in the highlands drops because of longwave radiation loss, and the cooler and denser air now rolls down the slope as katabatic winds.

Clouds

Mariners contemplate clouds as augurs of forthcoming weather, especially storms. Clouds are airborne condensation and form generally at higher latitudes. In the tropics there are fewer stratiform clouds. Most clouds, including cumulonimbus, are found on the upstream side of the ITCZ. Three types of clouds are found in the tropics: amorphous ones with no distinct structure, those with vortex patterns and cloud banks. Rain comes in three types in the tropics: convectional, cyclonic and orographic. Convectional rain occurs when heating produces free convection. Cyclonic rain is found when moist air in a cell of low pressure with high vorticity experiences horizontal convergence. Orographic rain falls when moist air from condensation and clouds has been forced up mountains. All three sorts of rain come from the upward movement of moist air.

Squall Lines

Squall lines are linear (non-revolving) weather systems that grow rapidly, and have a convex leading edge.[23] A single convective cell can last for over an hour, but a line of cells can last as long as several days. Squall lines produce much of the annual rainfall in the Caribbean and South America. Squalls trail an anvil that contains the decaying convective elements. For a squall line to form it needs a moist level at its base, and drier air at the middle levels. The moisture evaporates and cools the middle level, producing downdraughts. These slip underneath the warm moist low-level air, and the convection produces rain. Such action sustains and feeds the squall line. Once the squall passes there is calm as lower-level moisture returns.

Cyclones

Tropical cyclones often move erratically, and can contain damaging winds. Unlike squalls, which are linear, cyclones, as their name implies, rotate. A revolving tropical storm or cyclone begins with a Low that draws moist air into its centre seeded by tropical waves from Africa. If the Coriolis force is strong enough (the farther it is from the equator, the stronger it is), the air will begin to circulate, deflecting to the right. An anticlockwise circulation will begin only at least 7–8° from the equator. Rising air lowers the barometric pressure, draws in more air and accelerates the circulation. Typically, a cyclone forms when the temperature is at least 26°C (79°F) and when there is significant convection. Warm moist air draws in at the bottom, rises, and as water vapour condenses out, it releases heat at the centre of the system. Because the cyclone's core is at a higher temperature than its periphery, it rises and reduces its core pressure. If the air is not warm and moist (as on land) the cyclone will lose its force. When the air parcel reaches upper levels it cools, condenses and can produce thunderstorms. Vertical shear (a large difference in winds at different altitudes) further affects the convection.[24]

Why are these storms found in the North Atlantic and West Indies? In part, they are affected by the Coriolis effect's anticlockwise deflection of circulation to the right (northern hemisphere). This circulation is part of what makes a storm or hurricane. Over a year, the Elizabethan mariner could expect to weather some ten storms and six hurricanes, most occuring from June to November. During the stormy season, there is a 10 per cent chance of a storm along the northern coast of South America at about 10° N and as far east into the Atlantic to include the Cabo Verdes at about 24° W. Along the east coast of Central America there is a 30–40 per cent chance at about 13° N of one hooking north into the Windward Passage and touching Hispaniola and Cuba and the Gulf of Mexico. At about 17° N and east of Antigua and the Lesser Antilles there is a 50–60 per cent chance in certain locations. About the same percentage is found at about 32° N near Bermuda and including the Straits of Florida and extending nearly to the Newfoundland Banks. On average there is one storm a week during the hurricane season's worst month, September. In November 75 per cent of the storms become hurricanes, nearly one storm every two weeks. During hurricane season the worst place to be is near Bermuda, 28–36° N Lat. The best time to avoid these storms is between January and April.

Thunderstorms

Thunderstorms are individual convection cells produced by instabilities in the atmosphere resulting from surface heating (free convection) or orographic (forced convection resulting from land masses). Most of these storms are local, and last only an hour or two, and are caused when warm humid air masses rise and become unstable, as when they rise on late afternoon thermals. Their convection has a cumulus stage, with strong updraughts. In its mature stage the storm is at its most intense, with strong updrafts, though some parts of the cell contain downdraughts and precipitation. Cumulonimbus clouds can rise to 20,000m, and often show the classic anvil shape caused by an upper tropospheric wind shear. The final stage occurs when the cell dissipates, downdraughts prevail and the rain lightens.[25]

Hurricanes

Hurricanes and typhoons (F12–17, 64–138 knots) are violent tropical cyclones.[26] In the Caribbean, the North Atlantic, South Pacific and North-east Pacific these violent cyclones have local names: typhoon (Gk. *tuphōn*, whirlwind; sim. Arabic, deluge, and Mandarin Chinese, great wind); and hurricane (Caribe *Hurican*, the god of evil, the Mayan *Hurakan*, Mayan creator god who 'blew his breath across the chaotic water and brought forth dry land', Port. *furacão*, Sp. *huracan*) with winds characteristically F12 and higher. The number of cyclones per year in the

Caribbean averages ten tropical storms and six hurricanes.[27] They are spawned between 10° and 15° N Lat. when the water is above 27°C in summer. The surface winds are cyclonic, and the systems have nearly circular isobars centred on a core of low pressure. What is the cyclogenesis (origin) of hurricanes and other cyclonic storms? The ITCZ, found between 7° and 15° N Lat., is an ideal spawning ground for the convection that breeds such storms. Once spawned, the cyclone travels west or west–north–west at about 10 knots. At about 20° N it increases to 15 knots. At 25° N Lat. its track often shifts north-east, and the winds increase to 20–25 knots. In tropical waters of the North Atlantic, the storm may have grown to hurricane force (F12 within 75 miles of the centre, a F8 gale within 150 miles, and F6 strong breeze within 200 miles of the hurricane's eye).

Hurricanes have six distinctive characteristics: they have no front; their centre has warmer air than the periphery; they get their energy as the moisture over warm tropical oceans evaporates; their strongest winds are found at the surface; there is a distinct eye at the centre of the vortex; they are generally relatively small (100–300 miles in diameter). Hurricanes are driven by the latent heat of condensation and a humid rising air mass. They form only over large ocean areas where the water temperature is above 27°C (81°F), as at the end of summer in the western part of the Atlantic ocean where there is no upwelling of cold water. They must rotate and contain a vortex, and hence cannot develop below 5° N Lat. since the Coriolis force there is too weak to divert inflowing air.[28] The basic air current in a hurricane has a weak vertical shear, thus allowing for a strong vortex. Hurricanes must have a small low-pressure centre to form, and require low-level convergence and upper-level divergence. When they come ashore they weaken and lose moisture and the deep convection of the warm core.

Hurricanes are their strongest within the vortex and where the winds and the direction of the track are in the same direction and augment each other. In the northern hemisphere the strongest and most dangerous winds are on the right side of the cyclone (when facing forward in the same direction the storm is moving), and the lowest barometric pressure is to the left (Buys Ballot's Law).[29] Besides the high winds, storm surges in the northern hemisphere push waves ahead on that same right side, the Dangerous Quadrant, of the storm.

Navigating a Caribbean Hurricane

For the captain of our galleon, what signals an impending hurrricane, in present terms? Then as now, one sign is experiencing long swells from the direction of the centre of the storm, which can be 1,000 miles away. If the barometer drops 5mb, it is certain that a tropical depression is approaching. If on open water the barometer drops 5mb and the winds are F6, the hurricane's centre will be about 200 miles away, located at 100–125° to the right of the wind direction. That angle decreases to 90° as the storm approaches. If there is a significant change in wind speed and direction, if the wind backs to the north, and if high cirrus clouds are followed by cirrocumulus and altocumulus, a hurricane is imminent.

The captain should check the storm's progress every three hours or so. He should heave to to get accurate fix on wind direction and speed. If at sea, he should if possible stay at least 100 miles from the centre. If at anchor, he should put to sea (but first determine where the centre is and where the storm is heading). The left hand side of storm, where the winds are lower, is the safer navigable semicircle. The right side (right in the northern hemisphere, left in the southern) is the dangerous one, as it adds the storm's forward speed to the circulated wind speed. The worst spot is the leading edge of that dangerous side, where there are high winds and violent, confused seas. If wind is veering (turning clockwise), the vessel is in the dangerous semicircle. If wind direction is steady, then the vessel is in the direct path of the storm. If the vessel is in that dangerous semicircle, the captain must consider if there is time to reach the safe side. If not, he would best sail close-hauled on the starboard tack, and when he can no longer do so, he should heave to. (Close-hauled in a galleon would mean some 5 points or 60° off the wind. If today and under power, the captain should keep the wind 30° off his starboard bow.) If the winds are backing (turning anticlockwise), our galleon is in the safer navigable semicircle. On the left side, sailor can keep the wind abaft the beam to get away. High winds in shoal water can amplify storm surges to over 6m. If the vessel is within the navigable semicircle (the left side), it should make speed with the wind on the starboard quarter away from the storm.

Such measures are age-old and were observed by the Portuguese and Spanish in weathering typhoons in the Indian Ocean in the fifteenth century and by the Spanish and English in facing hurricanes in the Caribbean Sea in the sixteenth and seventeenth centuries.[30]

Notes

1 See Glenn R. McGregor and Simon Nieuwolt. *Tropical Climatology* (2nd edn). (Chichester: John Wiley & Sons, 1998). Abbr. *TC*; and James Clarke, *Atlantic Pilot Atlas, Including the Caribbean & Mediterranean* (4th edn). (London: Adlard Coles Nautical, 2006). Abbr. *AP*. Clarke's atlas and McGregor and Nieuwolt's text have provided many details for this appendix.

2 *TC*, 91–5.

3 *TC*, 65–7, 251–5.

4 Rear Admiral Sir Francis Beaufort, Hydrographer of the Royal Navy from 1829 to 1855, devised a classification of winds, from the calm F1, 0-1 knots, to the hurricane winds, F12, above 65 knots. Sir Francis set this out in 1805 while serving on the HMS *Woolwich*. His classification became the Royal Navy standard in the 1830s, when it was used during Charles Darwin's voyage of HMS *Beagle*, and later by the merchant navy from the 1850s. In 1946 the upper end of the scale was increased to F17 (in excess of 136 knots) to accommodate tropical cyclones or typhoons. A hurricane's effects on land are also additionally measured by the Saffir-Simpson scale, which as well as wind strength, takes into account storm surge, flooding and other elements. See Clarke, *AP*, 76, and Kemp, *Ships and the Sea*, vide hurricane.

5 *TC*, 72–6.

6 *TC*, 80–5.

7 *TC*, 252–5.

8 *AP*, 12. The mile here is the nautical mile, 6,080ft/1,852m, unless noted otherwise.

9 *AP*, 8.

10 *EP*, 236–83.

11 *EP*, 253.

12 *AP*, 34–43.

13 *AP*, 36.

14 *PN*, 10:75–7; 11:227–90.

15 *AP*, 38.

16 *PN*, 10:75–7; 11:227–90.

17 *PN*, 11:381–4.

18 *TB*, 111–16; *PN*, 11:389–416; *PP*, 16:146–78.

19 *AP*, 42.

20 *AP*, 42.

21 *TC*, 101–10.

22 *TC*, 114–15.

23 *TC*, 147–9.

24 *AP*, 6.

25 *TC*, 143–7.

26 *TC*, 151–60.

27 *AP*, 5.

28 *TC*, 153.

29 *TC*, 159. The Baric Wind Law, set forth by Dutch meteorologist Christoph Buys Ballot in 1857, expresses the atmospheric relationship between barometric pressure and wind direction.

30 See K. Adlard Coles, *Heavy Weather Sailing* (Clinton Corners: John de Graff, Inc., 1981 (1967); William J. Kotsch, *Weather for the Mariner* (2nd edn). (Annapolis: Naval Institute Press, 1977); Gary Jobson, *Storm Sailing* (New York: Hearst Marine Books, 1983); D. von Haeften, *How to Cope with Storms* (London: Adlard Coles Nautical, 1997 (trans. of *Sturm Was Tun*); Alan Watts, *The Weather Handbook* (2nd edn). (London: Adlard Coles Nautical, 2004 (1994, 1999); William P. Crawford, *Mariner's Weather* (New York: W.W. Norton & Company, Inc., 1992 (1978); Nathaniel Bowditch, *Marine Weather* (New York: Arco Publishing, Inc., 1979).

Appendix C

Glossary

Select list of works consulted for word usage in the Tudor, Stuart and early Commonwealth periods:

Sir Henry Mainwaring, *Nomenclator Navalis*, or *Seaman's Dictionary*. Ms. 1620–23. London: 1644; Capt John Smith, *An Accidence or the Path-way to Experience*. London: Jonas Man and Benjamin Fisher, 1626. Rpt. and ed. Philip L. Barbour, in *The Complete Works of Captain John Smith*. 3 vols. Institute of Early American History and Culture, Williamsburg, Va., Chapel Hill: University of North Carolina Press, 1986; Smith, *A Sea Grammar, with the Plaine Exposition of Smiths Accidence for Young Sea-men, Enlarged*. London: John Haviland, 1627. Rpt. and ed. Barbour, vol. 3: 39–121, rpt. *A Sea Grammar*, ed. Kermit Goell. London: Michael Joseph, 1970; W.H. Smyth, *The Sailor's Word-Book*, London, 1867 (facs. rpt. London: Conway Maritime Press, 1996, rev. edn. as *The Sailor's Lexicon* (New York: Hearst Books, Sterling Publishing, 2005); Richard Henry Dana, *The Seaman's Friend*, Boston, 1879 (facs. rpt. Mineola, N.Y.: Dover Publications, Inc., 1997); H. Paasch, *Vom Kiel zum Flaggenknopf*, Antwerp, 1885 (trans. facs. rpt. as *From Keel to Truck*, New York: Lyons & Burford, Publishers, 1997). Also *The Oxford English Dictionary*, ed. J.A. Simpson and E.S.C. Weiner (Oxford: Clarendon Press, 2002); *The Oxford Companion to Ships & the Sea*, ed. Peter Kemp (London: Oxford University Press, 1976).

barque (bark). Generally a small ship with a square stern, without headsails, three masts square-rigged, on the fore- and main masts, and fore-and-aft sail on her mizzen.

beakhead. Orig. a brass piece at the head of a galley, shaped as a beak, used to ram. Later, part of ship before the forecastle or knee of the head, supported by the main knee. In Tudor ships, it broke up head seas and kept the forecastle dry. Later use shortened it to 'head' or 'heads', the latrine.

BM (Builder's Measurement). Cargo capacity (volume) of a ship in tons (orig. tuns, or casks), calculated on length and beam. Matthew Baker, Royal Master Shipwright (and son of James Baker, Henry VIII's Master Shipwright), in 1582

established a formula for determining the cargo capacity of a ship to super-
sede the wine measurement of capacity found in *Fragments of Ancient English
Shipwrightry*. Baker's Formula for BM or capacity pre-1570 was K x B x D ÷ 94
or 97, and after 1570 amended to 100 for merchantmen and after 1603 for warships. The datum points were the keel length from the start of the stem curve
to the inside edge of the stern post, the breadth taken from the length of the
main frame deck beam plus the thickness of the side planking, and the depth,
from under the main deck beam to the lower edge of the keel. The formula
was reconsidered and modified in 1628, and remained until 1849, with the
advent of iron vessels. (See Nelson, *Tudor Navy*, 87–100)

bowsprit, boltsprit. Large spar projecting forward of the stem on which are
secured the forestays. The foresails carried on the bowsprit counter the forces
of the after sails, thus driving the vessel forward instead of heading into the
wind. To increase sail area, Tudor vessels often carried various spritsails underneath the bowsprit.

busse. Small three-masted merchant vessel of the North Sea and Baltic, with a large
square sail on the fore and main masts, and a lateen on the mizzen. Bluff-bowed,
related to the hulk. Without the foremast, known as the North Sea Dogger.

butt-joined. Timbers, as planking, joined end to end (as opposed to a scarf point,
where the wood is cut on an angle and overlapped).

caravela, caravela redonda. Gk. '*karabos*' (horned beetle, small ship). Developed by
Portuguese in fifteenthh century, generally with three masts carrying lateen
sails and sometimes a square on the foremast. No beakhead or sterncastle.
Originally had two masts, was lateen-rigged (*caravela latina*), then modified
for oceanic sailing as the caravela rotunda or redonda, with three masts with
squares on the two forward masts and a lateen on the mizzen. Length 75–100ft.
Used by Columbus, Dias, Magellan. Derived from the late medieval carvel, a
Mediterranean vessel, same as the caravela latina.

carvel-planked. Hull planking that is flush, smooth, as opposed to clinker-built
or lapstrake, in which the planking overlaps.

carrack. Large European trading vessel, to 1,000 tons, some to about 1,500 tons,
fourteenth to seventeenth centuries. In the north, clinker-built, and in early
sixteenth century, with three or four masts. These carried both squares and
lateen sails, thus similar to the caravela rotunda, but the hull was larger, beamier,
stronger, with high fore and sterncastles. The mainstay of the Portuguese and
Spanish merchant fleets to the East Indies and Americas, and by the Hansa in
Scandinavia and Northern Europe. Superseded in the mid-sixteenth century
by the galleon, especially by race-built galleons after 1570.

carrera de Indias. The trading enterprises of the Spanish to their colonies, from the
sixteenth century, following the earlier Portuguese Careira da Índia enterprises.

clinker-built. Small-boat building technique in which the planking overlaps
(US, lapstrake).

crank. A tender ship, from construction or stowage of cargo or insufficient ballast,
so she heels excessively, is incapable of carrying sail and subject to capsizing.

Typical in ships of deep draught and narrow beam. Such were the *Mary Rose* and the *Vasa*.

deadwood. Timbers, generally oak, on the upper side of the keel, particularly at both ends, placed to some height, equal in depth to two-thirds of the depth of the keel, and not exceeding the breadth of the keel.

decks. Floors running the length of a ship, as the orlop, main and upper decks. In race-built galleons the upper and main decks were cut down aft of the mizzen to accommodate the upper and lower gun rooms. A partial deck included the non-continuous forecastle and sterncastle deck. The uncovered middle of the upper deck was called the waist. The quarterdeck was located above the after end of the halfdeck. That halfdeck was built over the upperdeck, which along with the orlop and main decks ran the length of the ship.

draught (draft). Depth of water that a ship draws (depth needed to float vessel).

fluyt **(flute).** Dutch merchant vessel from Vlieland. Short, flat-bottomed, round stern, narrow deck, no poop deck. Three masted, with sqauares. Between 120 and 500 tons, 8 to 20 cannon.

frigate, *fragata*. Originally a large Spanish pinnace with sails and oars, used as a tender and small warship. Later a three-masted Dutch vessel, small, fast, of shallow draught. Generally a three-masted fully-rigged vessel, both merchant and naval, the latter armed with 24 to 60 cannon on a single gundeck (5th or 6th rate, hence not in the line of battle). Superior sailing qualities.

furring. To increase stability, extra planking was fitted inside the hull near the lower wale to lower the centre of gravity and to increase buoyancy. Mainwaring, 1644: 'There are two kinds of furring, the one is after a ship is built, to lay on another plank upon the side of her (which is called plank upon plank). The other, which is more eminent, and more properly flurring, is to rip off the first planks and to put other timbers upon the first, and so to put on the planks upon these timbers. The occasion of it is to make a ship bear a better wale, for when a ship is too narrow, and the bearing [freeboard] either not laid out enough, or too low, then they must make her broader, and lay out her bearing higher.'

futtocks. Foot-hooks, or corner braces of timber that serve as ribs or frames from near the keel to the top timbers.

galiot (galliot, galleot). Orig. a small galley (16–20 oars), with a single mast and sail. English vessel with a mainmast with a square topsail and lateen mizzen.

galleass. A mix of a rowed galley and a sailed galleon. Relatively broad-beamed and deep draught. Lateen rigged on two or three masts. A poor compromise, as it could not carry sufficient sail or manoeuvre well. Type of merchant vessel in Mediterranean in sixteenth and seventeenth centuries, to 150ft length, 25ft beam. Tried in England in 1530–40s, soon discarded.

galleon, *galeón*. Evolved from the great ship and carrack, armed with cannon on upper and main decks. Most successful were built according to Sir John Hawkyns' redesigned galleon in the 1570s. It was race-built, with lower hamper, deeper draught, flatter sails. Lower top hamper reduced to make half deck, quarterdeck, poop, and a low forecastle. High waisted, had tumblehome, beakhead. Design adopted by Spain about the time of the Armada, 1588. Originally a warship, later supplanting the carrack as a merchant vessel.

galley. Oared fighting ship of the Mediterranean, from 3000 BC. to eighteenth century. Single to multiple banks of oars. One or two masts with squares (later lateens) allowed for sailing before the wind while passage making. Weapon was a spur on the bow used to ram at speeds of up to 9 knots. In sixteenth and seventeenth centuries, cannon fixed on bow as bow chasers. Fast, manoeuvrable, but unstable, suitable only in calm waters.

gallizebra. In northern Europe, a frigate.

great ships. Highly charged carracks with gunports on main deck, common 1530–40. High fore- and sterncastles, low waists, crank.

Hansa, Hanseatic League. Trading confederation of north German towns dating from 1240, especially in Lübeck and Hamburg. The hansa were the trading guildhalls established in foreign cities.

hermaphrodite rig. Where the sailplan mixes squares with fore-and-aft sails, as in a brig, schooner or barquentine, the foremast rigged as a brig, and mainmast as a schooner.

hog, hogged. When the deck's ends at the bow and stern droop lower than amidships, straining her keel and bottom to curve upward. Opposite of sagging.

hulk. Originally a large transport or merchant ship especially in the Mediterranean (to 400 tons) in thirteenth and fourteenth centuries. Later in sixteenth century compared to or synomous with the carrack. Shell-built around a transom-type framework. Single-masted, with one square sail, in-line rudder. Ancestor of the busse.

jangada. Fishing boat from north-east Brazil. Traditionally six wooden logs, lashed together, with two seats, one to support the mast, the other, the sailor. Employs a lateen sail, centreboard and steering oar.

keel. Lowest timber on a ship. Its backbone.

keelson. An internal keel, laid immediately over the keel for additional strength and support.

lapstrake. See entry above, clinker-built.

lateen sail, lateen rigged. Latin, fore-and-aft triangular Mediterranean sail, bent on a long yard whose forward end is bowsed down to the deck. Rides obliquely on mast, has high peak. Probably ancient Arab origin. Mast generally raked forward, as on the Italian leudo, on the Egyptian felucca, and the Arab dhow.

leak, as 'proved leak'. AS 'leccinc'. A chink, hole, in the deck, sides, bottom, that allows water to leak into and potentially sink the the ship.

mizzen mast, sail. The aftermost mast, sail on a vessel.

nau, nao. General Portuguese and Spanish names for a ship, thirteenth to sixteenth centuries. Three or four masts, square-rigged on fore and main masts, lateen on mizzen. One such, the carrack, for ocean passages. Typically had flat stern, high fore- and sterncastles. Used in Portuguese exploration and trade to Far East and Americas, and similarly by Spanish.

orlop. Originally, all the continuous decks on a vessel, later the lowest deck. Platform laid over the beams below the turn of the bilge. In warships, where cables stowed, anchors weighed, powder kept. In merchant vessels, the floors of the cargo holds.

pay. Fr. *poix*, pitch. As verb, to pour hot pitch and tar into a seam after caulking, to keep the oakum dry. Also to pay a mast, yard, bottom. To pay off is to fall off, drop off to leeward, and also to dismiss officers and crew from active to ordinary service. As noun, to the pirate, 'pay' was plunder.

pinnace. Small vessel from sixteenth century with oars and sail, two or three masts rigged with squares and some fore-and-aft sails. Carvel-built. Initially 20–80 tons, later to 180 tons. Advice boats, often called frigates, armed with 9–20 guns. Seaworthy, ran the galleys off the seas.

pitch. Tar and resin heated and poured to cover oakum in a vessel's seams. Motion of hobby-horsing as ship first lifts her bows then her stern to the waves.

plain sailing. Plane, as flat. Spherical navigation transferred to small flat segments by the pilot.

race-built. Fr. *razer*, cut, scrape away. John Hawkyns' modified design of the 1570s made to highly-charged galleons, cutting down the high bow and stern hampers, deepening the draught, narrowing the beam, flattening the sails, to increase speed and ability to go to windward. Later adopted by the Spanish.

ribs. Frames, timbers that rise from the keel to form the shape of the hull.

shrouds. Standing rigging giving lateral support to the masts (stays provide fore-and-aft support).

stays. Support the mast fore and aft. In anchoring, the position of the ship in relation to the anchor and cable. When a vessel is head to wind, and when she does not pay off, she is 'in stays', or if she falls back on the original tack, she 'missed stays'.

stem, stempost. Foremost vetical timber that forms the bow of a vessel, joined to the keel.

swimming line. Elizabethan term for waterline.

tons burden. Cubic capacity of a ship's hull, calculated from builder's measurement (BM) of a vessel's length, beam, depth.

trunnels. Tree nails, made from tree roots, to join wood.

tumblehome. Inward curve of a ship's side to her gunwales.

tun, ton, tonnage, *tonelada, tonel*. At sea, always a measure of volume, not weight. Originally, a tun, or wine cask. Tonnage was how many casks a ship could carry. Superseded in latter sixteenth century by Matthew Baker's measurements of a ship's length, breadth, and depth to determine cargo capacity. Warships measure displacement tonnage.

whole moulding. Traditional ship construction, where the main frame determines shape of other frames.

Bibliography

Abbreviations

(Full entries given in Sources)

AN   Waters, David W. *The Art of Navigation in England in Elizabethan and Early Stuart Times.*

AP   Clarke, James. *Atlantic Pilot Atlas, Including the Caribbean & Mediterranean.*

DE   *Documents Concerning English Voyages to the Spanish Main 1569–1580,* ed. Irene A. Wright.

DG   *The Discovery of the Large, Rich, and Beautiful Empire of Guiana by Sir W. Ralegh,* ed. Robert H. Schomburgk.

DV   Andrews, Kenneth R. *Drake's Voyages: A Re-Assessment of Their Place in Elizabethan Maritime Expansion.*

DW   *Sir Francis Drake's West Indian Voyage 1585–86,* ed. Mary Frear Keeler.

EP   *English Privateering Voyages to the West Indies 1588–1595,* ed. Kenneth R. Andrews.

ES   Quinn, D.B. and A.N. Ryan. *England's Sea Empire, 1550–1642.*

FE   *Further English Voyages to Spanish America 1583–1594,* ed. Irene A. Wright.

HP   Williamson, James A. *Hawkins of Plymouth.*

JH   Williamson, James A. *Sir John Hawkins: The Time and the Man.*

LI   Fagan, Brian. *The Little Ice Age: How Climate Made History, 1300–1850.*

LV   *The Last Voyage of Drake and Hawkins,* ed. Kenneth R. Andrews.

PN   *Principal Navigations Voyages Traffiques & Discoveries 1598–1600,* ed. Richard Hakluyt. Rpt. 1903–05.

PP   *Hakluytus Posthumus, or Purchas His Pilgrimes 1625,* ed. Samuel Purchas. Rpt. 1905–07.

SD   *Spanish Documents Concerning English Voyages to the Caribbean 1527–1568,* ed. Irene A. Wright.

TB   James Seay Dean. *Tropics Bound.*

TC   McGregor, Glenn R. and Simon Nieuwolt. *Tropical Climatology.*

Primary Sources

Boteler, Nathaniel (Boeteler, Butler). *Six Dialogues about Sea Services. Between an High Admiral and a Captain at Sea*. Ms. 1634. London: Moses Pitt, 1685. Rpt. and ed. W.G. Perrin, *Boteler's Dialogues*. London: Navy Records Society, 1929.

Documents Concerning English Voyages to the Spanish Main 1569–1580 I: Spanish Documents Selected from the Archives of the Indies at Seville ... English Accounts 'Sir Francis Drake Revived'; and Others, Reprinted, ed. Irene A. Wright. Hakluyt Society, Ser. 2, No 71. London: Hakluyt Society, 1932.

English Privateering Voyages to the West Indies 1588–1595, ed. Kenneth R. Andrews. Hakluyt Society, Ser. 2, No 111. Cambridge: Cambridge University Press, 1959.

English and Irish Settlement in the River Amazon 1550–1646, ed. Joyce Lorimer. Hakluyt Society. Second Series, No. 171. London: Hakluyt Society, 1989.

Fighting Instructions, 1530–1816, ed. Sir Julian S. Corbett. 1905. Rpt. Annapolis: United States Naval Institute Press, 1971, and London: Conway Maritime Press, Ltd, 1971.

Further English Voyages to Spanish America 1583–1594, ed. Irene A. Wright. Hakluyt Society, Ser. 2, No. 99. London: Hakluyt Society, 1951, issued for 1949.

Hakluytus Posthumus or Purchas his Pilgrimes, Contayning a History of the World in Sea Voyages and Lande Travells by Englishmen and Others, by Samuel Purchas ... 1625, ed. Rev. Samuel Purchas. Rpt. 20 vols, Hakluyt Society, Extra Ser., Nos 12–33. Glasgow: James MacLehose & Sons, 1905–07.

The Last Voyage of Drake & Hawkins, ed. Kenneth R. Andrews. Hakluyt Society, Ser. 2, No 142. Cambridge: Cambridge University Press, 1972.

Mainwaring, Sir Henry. *Nomenclator Navalis*, or *Seaman's Dictionary*. Ms. 1620–23. Pub. London: 1644.

———. 'Of the Beginnings, Practices, and Supression of Pirates', otherwise, the 'Discourse of Pirates'. Ms. 1617–18. Rpt. in *The Life and Works of Sir Henry Mainwaring*, ed. G. E. Mainwaring and W. G. Perrin. 2 vols. Publications of the Navy Records Society, vols 54, 56. London: Navy Records Society, 1920, 1922.

The Naval Tracts of Sir William Monson, ed. Michael Oppenheim. Navy Records Society, vols 22 (1902), 23 (1902), 43 (1913), 45 (1914), 47(1914). London: Navy Records Society, 1902–14.

Papers Relating to the Navy During the Spanish War, 1585–1587, ed. Sir Julian Corbett. London: Navy Records Society, 1898. Rpt. 1987.

Principal Navigations Voyages Traffiques & Discoveries ... 1598–1600, ed. Richard Hakluyt. Rpt. 12 vols, Hakluyt Society, Extra Ser. 1–12. Glasgow: James MacLehose and Sons, 1903–05. Facs. rpt. of 1903–05 edn. New York: Augustus M. Kelley Publishers, 1969.

Ralegh, Sir Walter. *The Letters of Sir Walter Ralegh*, ed. Agnes Latham and Joyce Youings. Exeter: Exeter University Press, 1999.

Sir Francis Drake's West Indian Voyage 1585–86, ed. Mary Frear Keeler. Hakluyt Society, Ser. 2, No 148. London: Hakluyt Society, 1981.

'Sir Walter Ralegh's Journal of his Second Voyage to Guiana', in *The Discovery of the Large, Rich, and Beautiful Empire of Guiana ... by Sir W. Ralegh, knt*, ed. Robert H. Schomburgk. Hakluyt Society. Ser. 1, No 3. London: Hakluyt Society, 1848.

Smith, Captain John. *An Accidence or the Path-way to Experience*. London: Jonas Man and Benjamin Fisher, 1626. Rpt. and ed. Philip L. Barbour, *The Complete Works of Captain John Smith*. 3 vols. Institute of Early American History and Culture, Williamsburg, Va., Chapel Hill: Univ. of North Carolina Press, 1986.

————. *A Sea Grammar, with the Plaine Exposition of Smiths Accidence for Young Sea-men, Enlarged*. London: John Haviland, 1627. Rpt. and ed. Barbour, vol. 3: 39–121. Barbour abbr. as Smith.

Spanish Documents Concerning English Voyages to the Caribbean 1527–1568, Selected from the Archives of the Indies at Seville, ed. Irene A. Wright. Hakluyt Society, Ser. 2, No 62. London: Hakluyt Society, 1929.

Secondary Sources

Andrews, Kenneth R. *Drake's Voyages: A Re-Assessment of Their Place in Elizabethan Maritime Expansion*. London: Weidenfeld and Nicholson, 1967.

————. 'The Elizabethan Seaman'. In *The Mariner's Mirror*, vol. 68 (1982) 245–62.

————. *Trade, Plunder and Settlement, Maritime Enterprise and the Genesis of the British Empire, 1480–1630*. Cambridge: Cambridge University Press, 1984.

Arents, George. *Books, Manuscripts and Drawings Relating to Tobacco*. Washington: Library of Congress, Government Printing Office, 1938; www.tobacco.org.; www.historian.org.

Barron, Jeremy Hugh. 'Sailors' scurvy before and after James Lind – a reassessment', *Nutritional Reviews*, International Life Sciences Institute, 2009, vol. 67, no 6, pp. 315–32.

Bartlett, Merrill L. *Assault from the Sea: Essays on the History of Amphibious Warfare*. Annapolis: Naval Institute Press, 1983.

Bell, Dion R. *Lecture Notes on Tropical Medicine*. 4th edn. Oxford: Blackwell Science Ltd, 1995.

Biddlecombe, Sir George. *Naval Tactics and Trials of Sailing*. London: Charles Wilson, 1850.

Black, J.B. *The Reign of Elizabeth, 1558–1603*. 2nd edn. Oxford History of England. Oxford: Clarendon Press, 1969.

Bowditch, Nathaniel. *The American Practical Navigator*. 1802. Bethesda: Defense Mapping Agency Hydrographic/Topographic Center, 1995.

————. *Marine Weather*. New York: Arco Publishing, Inc., 1979.

Cartwright, Frederick F. and Michael Biddiss, *Disease & History*. Stroud: Sutton Publishing Ltd, 2000.

Casson, Lionel. *The Ancient Mariners*, 2nd edn. Princeton: Princeton University Press, 1991.

————. *Ships and Seamanship in the Ancient World*. Baltimore: Johns Hopkins University Press, 1995.

Childs, David. *The Warship Mary Rose: The Life and Times of King Henry VIII's Flagship*. London: Chatham Publishing, 2007.

Clarke, James. *Atlantic Pilot Atlas, Including the Caribbean & Mediterranean*, 4th edn. London: Adlard Coles Nautical, 2006.

Clerk, John of Eldin. *An Essay on Naval Tactics, Systematical and Historical*. 1782. Edinburgh: Adam Black 1827.

Clucas, Stephen. 'Thomas Harriot's A briefe and true report: Knowledge-making and the Roanoke Voyage'. In *European Visions: American Voices*, ed. Kim Sloan. London: British Museum, 2003. See also www.britishmuseum.org/pdf/1-Clucas-Hariots brief and true report.

Coles, K. Adlard. *Heavy Weather Sailing*. 1967. Clinton Corners: John de Graff, Inc., 1981.

Corbett, Sir Julian S. *Drake and the Tudor Navy: With a History of the Rise of England as a Maritime Power*, 2 vols. London: Longmans, Green, and Co. 1898; rpt. London: Temple Smith, 1988.

Crawford, William P. *Mariner's Weather*. 1978. New York: W.W. Norton & Company, Inc. 1992.

Davies, Godfrey. *The Early Stuarts, 1603–1660*. 2nd edn. Oxford History of England. Oxford: Clarendon Press, 1959.

de Cordova, Luis Cabrera. *Felipe Segundo Rey de España*. Libro 8, Cap. 10, pp. 513–5. Madrid, 1619. U.S. Library of Congress Rare Books Reading Room, www.loc.gov/rr/rare book/catalogue/drake, article by Hans P. Kraus, with English trans.

Dean, James Seay. 'Bearding the Spaniard: Captain John Oxnam in the Pacific'. In *The Northern Mariner/le Marin du Nord*, vol. 19, no 4 (Oct. 2009): 379–92.

————. *Tropics Bound: Elizabeth's Seadogs on the Spanish Main*. Stroud: The History Press, 2010.

Desowitz, Robert S. *Who Gave Pinta to the Santa Maria? Torrid Diseases in a Temperate World*. New York: W.W. Norton & Company, 1997.

Dunlap, G.D. and H.H. Scufeldt. *Dutton's Navigation and Piloting*. Annapolis: Naval Institute Press, 1972.

Duro, Cesáreo Fernández. *Armada Española desde la Union de los Reinos de Castilla y de Aragón*. Madrid: El Progreso Editorial, 1894.

Earle, Peter. *Sailors: English Merchant Seamen, 1650–1775*. London: Methuen, 1998.

Fagan, Brian. *The Little Ice Age: How Climate Made History, 1300–1850*. New York: Basic Books, Perseus Books Group, 2000.

Fissel, Mark Charles. 'English Amphibious Warfare, 1587–1656: Galleons, Galleys, Longboats and Cots'. In *Amphibious Warfare 1000–1700: Commerce, State Formation and European Expansion*, D.J.B. Trim and Mark Fissel, eds. Leiden: Brill, 2006, 217–61.

Friel, Ian. 'The Three-Masted Ship and Atlantic Voyages'. In *Raleigh in Exeter 1985: Privateering and Colonisation in the Reign of Elizabeth I*, ed. Joyce Youings. Exeter Studies in History No. 10. Exeter: Exeter University Press, 1985.

Glete, Jan, ed. *Naval History 1000–1680.* Aldershot: Ashgate, 2005.

Gough, Barry. *Juan de Fuca's Strait: Voyages in the Waterway of Forgotten Dreams.* Madeira Park: Harbour Publishing, 2012.

Greenhill, Basil. *The Evolution of the Sailing Ship 1250–1580.* London: Conway Maritime Press, 1995.

Guerrant, Richard L., D.H. Walker, and P.F. Weller. *Tropical Infectious Diseases,* 2 vols. Philadelphia: Churchill Livingstone, 1999.

Harriot, Thomas. 'Articon'. MS now lost. Parts in his *A Briefe and True Report of the New Found Land of Virginia,* London: [s.n.], 1588.

Hughes, Wayne P., Jr., *Fleet Tactics: Theory and Practice.* Annapolis: Naval Institute Press, 1986.

Jamieson, Alan G. *Lords of the Sea: A History of the Barbary Corsairs.* London: Redaktion Books, 2012.

Jobson, Gary. *Storm Sailing.* New York: Hearst Marine Books, 1983.

Keevil, J.J. *Medicine and the Navy, 1200–1900.* Vol. 1, 1200–1649. Edinburgh and London: E. & S. Livingstone, Ltd, 1957.

Kelsey, Harry. *Sir Francis Drake, The Queen's Pirate.* New Haven: Yale University Press, 1998.

———. *Sir John Hawkins: Queen Elizabeth's Slave Trader.* New Haven: Yale University Press, 2003.

Kiple, Kenneth F., ed. *The Cambridge Historical Dictionary of Disease.* Cambridge: Cambridge University Press, 2003.

———. *Plague, Pox & Pestilence.* Phoenix Illustrated. Weidenfeld & Nicholson Ltd, 1999.

Knighton, C.S. and David Loades, eds. *Elizabethan Naval Administration.* Farnham, Surrey: Ashgate for Navy Records Society, 2013.

Kotsch, William J. *Weather for the Mariner,* 2nd edn. Annapolis: Naval Institute Press, 1977.

Lacey, Robert. *Sir Walter Ralegh.* London: Phoenix Press, 1973.

Lenman, Bruce. *England's Colonial Wars, 1550–1688.* Harrow: Pearson Educational Ltd, Longman, 2001. Ch. 8, 'The clash of European states and the rise of the imperial factor in the Caribbean and North America', 255–93.

Lewis, Michael. *The Hawkins Dynasty, Three Generations of a Tudor Family.* London: George Allen and Unwin Ltd, 1969.

Loades, David. *England's Maritime Empire: Seapower, Commerce and Policy, 1490–1690.* Harrow: Longman, 2000.

Mackie, J.D. *The Earlier Tudors, 1485–1558.* Oxford History of England. Oxford: Clarendon Press, 1972.

Mahan, Alfred Thayer. *Naval Strategy Compared and Contrasted with the Principles and Practice of Military Operations on Land. Lectures Given Between 1887 and 1911.* Boston: Little, Brown, and Company, 1911.

Marcus, Leah, Janet Mueller and Mary Beth Rose, eds. *Elizabeth I: Collected Works.* Chicago: University of Chicago Press, 2000.

McGregor, Glenn R. and Simon Nieuwolt. *Tropical Climatology.* 2nd edn. Chichester: John Wiley & Sons, 1998.

Milton, Giles. *Big Chief Elizabeth*. London: Hodder and Stoughton, 2000.

———. *White Gold: The Extraordinary Story of Thomas Pellow and North Africa's One Million European Slaves*. London: Hodder & Stoughton, 2004.

Meide, Chuck. 'The Development and Design of Bronze Ordnance, Sixteenth through Nineteenth Centuries,' paper (35 pp.) delivered Williamsburg, Va.: College of William and Mary, Nov. 2002.

Monson, Sir William. *Naval Tracts*. In *The Naval Tracts of Sir William Monson*, Michael Oppenheim ed. Navy Records Society, vols 22 (1902), 23 (1902), 43 (1913), 45 (1914), 47 (1914). London, 1902–14.

Morrison, John S. *The Age of the Galley*. London: Conway Maritime Press, 2004.

Mudie, Colin and Rosemary Mudie. *The History of the Sailing Ship*. New York: Arco Publishing, 1975.

———. *The Sailing Ship, a Voyage Through the Ages*. London: Marshall Cavendish, 1984.

Mudie, Colin. *Sailing Ships, Designs and Re-creations of Great Sailing Ships from Ancient Greece to the Present Day*. London: Adlard Coles Nautical, 2000.

———. *Ships and Seamanship in the Ancient World*. Baltimore: Johns Hopkins Press, 1995.

Naish, F.C. Prideaux. 'The Mystery of the Tonnage and Dimensions of the *Pelican-Golden Hind*. In *Mariner's Mirror*, 34 (Jan. 1948): 42–5.

Nedwitt, Malyn. 'Portuguese Amphibious Warfare in the East in the Sixteenth Century (1500–1520)'. In *Amphibious Warfare 1000–1700: Commerce, State Formation and European Expansion*, ed. D.J.B. Trim and Mark Charles Fissel. Leiden: Brill, 2006.

Nelson, Arthur. *The Tudor Navy: The Ships, Men and Organisation 1485–1603*. London: Conway Maritime Press, 2001.

Oliveira, Fernão. *A Arte da Guerra do Mar (The Art of War at Sea)*. 1555. Rpt. as *Arte da Guerra do Mar: Estratégia e Guerra Naval no Tempo dos Descobrimentos*. Lisboa: Edições 70, 2008.

Oxford Companion to Ships & the Sea, ed. Peter Kemp. London: Oxford University Press, 1976.

Oxford Dictionary of Quotations, ed. Elizabeth Knowles. London: Oxford University Press, 1999.

Oxford English Dictionary, ed. J.A. Simpson and E.S.C. Weiner. Oxford: Clarendon Press, 2002.

Parker, Geoffrey. 'The Dreadnought Revolution of Tudor England'. In *The Mariner's Mirror*, vol. 82, 269–300. Rpt. Glete, 49–80.

Parry, J.H. *The Age of Reconaisssance*. London: Weidenfeld and Nicholson, Ltd, 1968.

Phillips, Carla Rahn. *Six Galleons for the King of Spain: Imperial Defense in the Early Seventeenth Century*. Baltimore: Johns Hopkins University Press, 1986.

Quinn, D. B. 'Sailors and the sea'. In *Shakespeare in His Own Age*, ed. Allardyce Nicoll. Cambridge: Cambridge University Press, 1964: 21–36.

———. *Raleigh and the British Empire*. London: Hodder and Stoughton Ltd, 1947.

————. and A.N. Ryan. *England's Sea Empire, 1550–1642*. London: George Allen & Unwin, 1983.

Ralegh, Sir Walter. *The Letters of Sir Walter Ralegh*, ed. Agnes Latham and Joyce Youings. Exeter: Exeter University Press, 1999.

Robison, S.S. *A History of Naval Tactics from 1530 to 1930*. Annapolis: Naval Institute Press, 1942.

Rodger, N.A.M. *The Safeguard of the Sea, A Naval History of Britain, 660–1649*. 1997. New York: W.W. Norton & Company, 1998.

Rodgers, W.L. *Naval Warfare under Oars, 4th to 16th Centuries*. Annapolis: Naval Institute Press, 1939.

Rubin, Vera, ed. *Cannabis and Culture*. The Hague: Mouton & Co., 1975.

Scammell, G.V. 'European seamanship in the great age of discovery'. In *The Mariner's Mirror* 68 (1982): 357–76.

————. 'Manning the English merchant service in the sixteenth century'. In *The Mariner's Mirror* 56 (1970): 131–54.

Southey, Thomas. *Chronological History of the West Indies*, 3 vols. London: Longmans, 1827.

Strickland, G. Thomas. *Hunter's Tropical Medicine*, 8th edn. Philadelphia: W.B. Saunders Company, 2000.

Thompson, I.A.A. 'Spanish Armada Guns'. In *Mariner's Mirror*, vol. 81 (1995), 148–55. Rpt. Glete, 183–99.

Trim, D.J.B. and Mark Fissel, eds. *Amphibious Warfare 1000–1700: Commerce, State Formation and European expansion*. Leiden: Brill, 2006.

Tucker, Spencer. *Arming the Fleet: U.S. Navy Ordnance in the Muzzle-Loading Era*. Annapolis: Naval Institute Press, 1989.

Tunstall, Brian. *Naval Warfare in the Age of Sail: The Evolution of Fighting Tactics 1650–1815*. London: Conway Maritime Press, 1990 and Annapolis: Naval Institute Press, 1990.

von Haeften, D. *How to Cope with Storms (Sturm was tun)*. London: Adlard Coles Nautical, 1997.

Waters, D.W. *The Art of Navigation in England in Elizabethan and Early Stuart Times*, 2nd edn. Greenwich: National Maritime Museum, 1978.

————. 'The Elizabethan Navy and the Armada Campaign'. In *Mariner's Mirror*, vol. 35 (1949), 95.

Watts, Alan. *The Weather Handbook*, 2nd edn. London: Adlard Coles Nautical, 2004.

Wear, Andrew. *Knowledge & Practice in English Medicine, 1550–1680*. Cambridge: Cambridge University Press, 2000.

Wernham, R.B. *After the Armada: Elizabethan England and the Struggle for Western Europe 1588–1595*. London: Oxford University Press, 1984.

————. 'English amphibious warfare, 1587–1656: galleons, galleys, longboats, and cots'. In Trim and Fissel, 200–13.

————. *The Return of the Armadas: The Last Years of the Elizabethan War Against Spain 1595–1603*. London: Oxford University Press, 1994.

Williamson, James A. *Hawkins of Plymouth*. 2nd edn. 1949. London: Adam &
    Charles Black, 1969.
————. *Sir John Hawkins, The Time and the Man*. Oxford: Clarendon Press, 1927.
Youings, Joyce. 'Did Raleigh's England Need Colonies?' In *Raleigh in Exeter 1985:
    Privateering and Colonisation in the Reign of Elizabeth I*, ed. Joyce Youings. Exeter
    Studies in History, No. 10. Exeter: Exeter University Press, 1985.

About the Author

James Seay Dean, emeritus professor, University of Wisconsin-Parkside, has been Director of International Studies, Professor of English and Humanities and Adjunct Professor of Modern Languages (Portuguese) and Music, as well as having long taught maritime history and literature. He gained a doctorate at the Shakespeare Institute, University of Birmingham. In America he has been awarded a Senior Fulbright Fellowship to Brazil (where he started a graduate programme in American literature, and was associate principal contrabass in the Orquestra Sinfónica de Minas Gerais). He has been awarded numerous National Endowment for the Humanities grants and research fellowships: in England at Harris Manchester College, Oxford; at Exeter and East Anglia universities; and in America at Mystic Seaport (Williams College), and at Wisconsin, Vanderbilt, Chicago, Illinois and Brown universities.

He has served on the editorial board of *The American Neptune,* advised for the Canadian *Northern Mariner/Le Marin du Nord,* published numerous articles in other nautical, literary, and historical journals, as well as in popular boating magazines in England, Canada and the United States. He is author of *Sailing a Square-Rigger* (1995), and two volumes published by The History Press: *Tropics Bound: Elizabethan Seadogs on the Spanish Main* (2010), and now *Tropic Suns: Seadogs Aboard an English Galleon,* written as companion volumes. Dean has also authored two other books, one on an Elizabethan writer, and one one music. He has lectured on Caribbean history and crewed on the *Corwith Cramer* (Woods Hole, Massachusetts), a 140ft brigantine engaged in oceanographic research. For twelve years he was honorary sailing master and lecturer on barquentines in the Atlantic, Mediterranean and Caribbean.

He has made several transatlantic passages under sail, most lately as first mate and navigator on a 43ft sloop from the Caribbean to England. In the same capacity, he has sailed the Canadian Maritimes, from England to Gibraltar, in the Adriatic and in the Mediterranean from Gibraltar to Turkey. As captain of a 37ft cutter, he has sailed the Pacific coast of Canada. For six years he explored the Norfolk Broads in 1930s engineless gaff-rigged sloops, and for many years single-handed America's Great Lakes in his own yacht, a small 40-year-old Westerly sloop, presently moored in a creek off the Chesapeake Bay.

Index

Ships' names and most foreign names of plants and some diseases are italicised. Captain (not capitalised) means sea captain, master generally ship's master; if capitalised, these generally refer to status ashore. All naval ranks, whatever the nationality, are given English style. Place names generally follow modern usage.